THE FUTURE OF THE MUSIC BUSINESS

HOW TO SUCCEED WITH THE NEW DIGITAL TECHNOLOGIES

A Guide for Artists and Entrepreneurs

BY STEVE GORDON

Backbeat
Books
San Francisco

Published by Backbeat Books
600 Harrison Street, San Francisco, CA 94107
www.backbeatbooks.com
email: books@musicplayer.com

An imprint of CMP Information
Publishers of *Guitar Player*, *Bass Player*, *Keyboard*, and *EQ* magazines

CMP
United Business Media

Distributed to the book trade in the US and Canada by
Publishers Group West, 1700 Fourth Street, Berkeley, CA 94710

Distributed to the music trade in the US and Canada by
Hal Leonard Publishing, P.O. Box 13819, Milwaukee, WI 53213

Cover design by Patrick Devine
Composition by Michael Baughan
Front cover photos: Powell Burns (upper)
          Comstock Images © Getty Images (lower)

Library of Congress Cataloging-in-Publication Data

Gordon, Steve.
The future of the music business : how to succeed with the new digital technologies /
by Steve Gordon.
       p. cm.
Includes index.
ISBN 0-87930-844-3 (alk. paper)
1. Music trade—Vocational guidance. 2. Sound—Recording and reproducing—
Digital techniques. I. Title.
 ML3790.G67 2005
 780'.68—dc22

                                        2005007155

Printed in the United States of America

05 06 07 08 09   5 4 3 2 1

For Harry and Stella

Contents

Part I: The Rules

An overview of the rules applicable to the music business and the *new* rules evolving in today's digital environment.

Part II: Crisis & Solutions—The Music Industry in Transition

A look at the recording industry's tumultuous past few years: the decline in CD sales, the struggles to harness the power of the Internet, and the battle between the record labels and file sharers. Plus proposed solutions for the industry's woes and an analysis of the most recent legal cases and legislative initiatives.

Part III: How to Succeed in the *New* Music Business
Strategies for using the unprecedented power of the Internet to promote your music, and profiles of successful artists and record labels working in the digital marketplace.

Part IV: New Business Models—Stories of Ambition, Independence, Imagination, and Success

Inspirational interviews with independent artists and music-industry entrepreneurs whose business models aim high without huge start-up costs. Plus the future of peer-to-peer file sharing and a new business model based on the convergence of music and fashion.

Foreword

On November 14, 1971, I opened for Jethro Tull at the Albany Palace Theatre. It was an incredible evening for a young singer-songwriter opening his first big show. The sound of 3,000-odd people chanting, "You suck, we want Tull" brought me back to reality and taught me the humbling lessons of being the opening act. Once again, I'm in the unenviable position of being the opening act. Fortunately, this time I can't hear the chanting!

Steve Gordon and I shared a common experience: he was an attorney at Sony Music at the same time I managed one of their artists. We have both witnessed the cosmic change that our industry has seen since the mid 1990s, and while some like to complain that the labels stuck their heads in the sand and tried to ignore the coming digital music landslide, those closer to the action knew it was more of a mixed bag.

Sony Music Nashville broke new ground when they released an "interactive" press kit for Mary Chapin Carpenter's *Stones in the Road* album in 1994. The kit was released on discs for both Mac and Windows and allowed a user to click on a bio, a discography, some photos, and other features. No one was thinking about the Internet, but PC-related interactive products were the rage. Would we like to create a screensaver? Some CD-ROM specials for an enhanced CD? We participated in a Microsoft interactive sampler with other artists. But few in the industry were preparing for the onslaught just around the corner.

RIAA President and CEO Jay Berman, on behalf of his members, was looking down the road, and, along with members of AFTRA, the AFofM, and other artists' groups, went to Congress in 1995 to obtain the first performance right in U.S. history for performers and sound-recording copyright owners. On behalf of the industry, Berman warned that a performance right was essential to the protection of copyright, as digital services would soon be capable of making available perfect copies to consumers. Clearly some in the industry were looking toward the future and how digital music would transform things.

Internally, record companies were trying to gauge what this would mean for their businesses. Promotion departments, for example, were excited by the cost savings of no longer having to mail promo copies to radio stations, that they could deliver new music via satellite or some other digital means for all stations to use at a specified time. Other departments were similarly studying how they could benefit from digital music distribution.

We are now looking back at the revolution in technology that has dramatically transformed our industry. Steve Gordon, who worked at one of the major labels and then transitioned into private practice during this tumultuous time, was perfectly positioned to see the impact of this technology shift on the industry's business practices. He tackles some very tough issues and reflects on the conflicting perspectives that have fashioned the debate over peer-to-peer, webcasting, and other new technologies.

Gordon has done a very fine job of explaining the statutory licensing regime put in place by Congress when they created the Digital Performance Right in Sound Recordings Act of 1995 and the Digital Millennium Copyright Act of 1998.

The book also helps artists take advantage of the new technologies by detailing the steps for building Web sites, online music stores, Internet music broadcasts, blogs, and more. The interviews with artists and entrepreneurs offer fascinating insights into new business models that did not even exist a few years ago. Gordon shows that the future of the music business is indeed full of new opportunities for those who have the imagination and energy to take advantage of them.

—John Simson

The Executive Director of SoundExchange, former singer-songwriter John Simson has managed artists such as Mary Chapin Carpenter and Matraca Berg, and has practiced entertainment law for more than 20 years. He received an Emmy nomination for his music supervision of the PBS American Roots Music *series. John is an adjunct professor of entertainment law at American University's Washington College of Law and was recently elected president of the Washington, D.C., chapter of the Recording Academy.*

Introduction

New technologies are revolutionizing the music industry. While peer-to-peer file-sharing and CD burning are blamed for eroding CD sales and harming the major record companies, the Internet is also creating new opportunities for independent artists and entrepreneurs to create, promote, and distribute music. New technologies such as low-cost, high-quality digital recording equipment have dramatically reduced the cost of producing musical recordings. At the same time, new technologies have created the opportunity of reaching a worldwide audience for recorded music without the packaging, manufacturing, and physical distribution required to sell CDs.

When I was working as a lawyer at Sony Music, a senior VP in the legal department organized a trip to visit to the Pitman plant in New Jersey. It was 1999. The factory was huge—at least several square blocks. When we entered the building it looked like the Kennedy Space Center. Men and women were walking around in what looked like astronaut uniforms complete with plastic masks and white gloves. They were tending to big machines cranking out thousands upon thousands of shiny little discs—CDs with labels carrying the names of Sony Music's biggest artists at that time, including Celine Dion, Mariah Carey, Bruce Springsteen, and Pearl Jam. The plant must have cost tens of millions of dollars. And to think, Sony operated factories like this all over the world. There still are factories like this all over the world pouring out more shiny discs, but fewer people are buying them. There were and still are warehouses and trucks, and trains and ships to hold and deliver those discs. And there were and still are, but not as many, sales agents throughout the world to persuade the big retail chains and superstores to buy those shiny discs. But sales of CDs are down approximately 20% since I visited Pitman. A lot of the chains and superstores are more interested in selling video games than audio CDs. Times have changed.

Today, for a few hundred dollars you can create a Web site including your music that can reach potentially everybody in the world, replacing all those factories, all those trucks, and all those people. It's breathtaking and amazing, and it presents opportunities to artists and entrepreneurs that never existed in the music business before.

This book will focus on the opportunities that the new technologies provide, and the new business models that are developing to take advantage of them. Our focus is how new artists, independent labels, and entrepreneurs can take advantage of the new digital technologies to make music and succeed financially in the new music business. The book also presents a comprehensive discussion of new laws and business practices that apply to online music distribution.

The genesis of this book was a party at ASCAP celebrating the great Jerry Herman, the composer and lyricist of *Hello Dolly*. During the party I was chatting with a book editor about my idea about a book on the future of the music business. She was very encouraging and asked me to develop a proposal. I did, but the publisher took too long to green-light the proposal. So I called my friend and literary agent, Andrew Stewart. He got me a deal practically within the time it takes to sing one of Jerry's songs. But what better origin for a book about the future of the business than a party celebrating a brilliant chapter from its past.

Part I of the book, titled The Rules, summarizes the laws and business practices applicable to the traditional music business, and then sets forth the rules that specifically apply to the new digital music industry.

Part II provides a history of the record companies' battles with the Internet and the reasons for the crisis now befalling it. This part also offers solutions for the major labels—so they can survive and continue to discover, nurture, and promote new music. The key is embracing the new technologies instead of trying to destroy them. The last chapter in this part of the book sets forth the latest legal developments.

Part III focuses on how *you* as an artist or an entrepreneur can take advantage of the new technologies to succeed in the new music business.

Part IV provides inspirational stories of and interviews with those courageous entrepreneurs and artists who are using the Internet to make their dreams become reality.

Finally the CD-ROM accompanying this book includes:

- A two-hour seminar on the future of the music business recorded in fall 2004 at CUNY Graduate Center, featuring voices from the record labels, the P2P world, a leading music industry journalist, and a student/artist entrepreneur who is creating his own online record company.
- Interviews with leading academics and music industry professionals.
- A comprehensive list of active links to resources that the reader can use to build a great Web site, create an online music store, construct a weblog for fans, partner with online digital music services, and much more.

Most importantly, the CD-ROM includes a link to Web pages updating the book. Hardly a day passes without news of a new business model or a new technology that will affect the music industry. At the time this book went to press the hot item was wireless transmission of music on the next generation of cell phones. By the time the book is published, the hot thing could very well be something else. That is one reason why I will keep the book updated online. The other reason is that this is also a book about the law. In response to the new technologies, the law is also changing rapidly. New court decisions such as the Supreme Court's decision in the *MGM vs. Grokster* case or legislative initiatives such as the Induce Act, which may become law, could reshape the music industry. In these Web pages I will report on and provide analysis of every new important legal development that relates to the subject matter of the book, including new legislation, cases, and forms of agreements affecting the music business. These updates will continue until the next edition of *The Future of the Music Business*.

DISCLAIMER

The information in this book has been prepared for informational purposes only and does not constitute legal advice. This book should be used as a guide to understanding the law, not as a substitute for the advice of qualified counsel. You should consult an attorney before making any significant legal decisions.

The accompanying CD-ROM contains links to other resources on the Internet including legal resources. Such links are intended to help the individual readers identify and locate resources that may be of interest and are not intended to state or imply that the author or publisher sponsors, is affiliated with, or is associated with such links.

CD-ROM Menu

I. Link to Web Pages Updating This Book

II. Seminar on the Future of the Music Business, 10/26/04
The CUNY Graduate Center
Ariel Taitz, Esq., V.P. Legal and Business Affairs, Atlantic Records
Eric de Fontenay, Editor, Musicdish.com and Mi2N.com
Alphonzo Terrell, President, CU Records at Columbia University

III. Select Interviews from the Author's Internet Radio Show
(on MyRealBroadcast.com and DigitalMusicNews.com)
- Professor Lawrence Lessig, Stanford Law School, author of *Free Culture: How Big Media Uses Technology and the Law to Lock Down Culture and Control Creativity* (Penguin 2004)
- Jay Frank, Head of Label Relations for Launch, The Music Destination on YAHOO!
- John Simson, Executive Director, SoundExchange
- Eric Garland, CEO, and Joe Fleisher, Senior VP, Big Champagne
- Professor Siva Vaidhyanathan, New York University, author of *The Anarchist In the Library* (Basic Books 2004).
- Jay Gilbert, Senior Director for Universal Music Enterprises and UMe Digital
- Tim Mitchell, VP of Business and Product Development, Independent Online Distribution Alliance (IODA)
- Brian Camelio, Founder and President of ArtistShare
- Stan Soocher, Associate Professor, University of Colorado; Editor, *Entertainment Law & Finance*
- Eric Kline, radio host and author of *Inside the Music Business*

IV. List of Active Links to Digital and Traditional Music Business Resources. This list presents thumbnail descriptions and active links to over 200 Web sites that complement the contents of this book.
A. "Legal Resources" complements Part I of the book (The Rules) by presenting Web sites that offer legal information and advice.
B. "News Sources" complements Part II (Crisis & Solutions: The Music Industry in

Transition) by presenting Web sites, most of them free, that you can use to stay on top of new developments in the music business.

C. "Web Sites and Web Services" complements Part III (How to Succeed in the *New Music Business*) by presenting Web sites that help artists, record companies and music industry professionals take advantage of new technologies. These Web sites will help you:

- Design your Web site
- Register your domain name
- Host your Web site
- Download, stream, webcast and podcast your music
- Create your online music store
- Monetize your music for P2P
- Partner with online music stores featuring indie and major artists
- Construct blogs and chat rooms
- Market and promote your music online

D. "New Business Models" complements Part IV (New Business Models) by providing lists of Web sites of businesses only made possible due to new technologies, including:

- Online record companies
- Online record stores
- Online financing
- Subscription and download services featuring indies and unsigned bands
- Subscription and download services featuring major labels
- P2P services: authorized and unauthorized
- Webcasting and satellite radio
- Ringtones and wireless platforms
- Online services designed to market and promote indie artists

This section of the CD-ROM includes two additional groups of resources:

E. Traditional music industry resources such as industry trade groups, unions, performing rights organizations, major and leading independent record companies and music publishers, and databases containing contact info for artists, managers and agents.

F. Activist Web sites and organizations.

While every attempt is made to ensure that this CD-ROM will operate in most systems, we cannot guarantee that it will operate in all systems. If you have trouble using this CD-ROM please notify us at cdrom@myrealbroadcast.com. Please include the barcode number on the back cover of this book in your e-mail. We will provide you with a link or password to a site where you can access all the content on the CD-ROM, plus updates.

Chapter 1
Music Law & Business Primer

T his chapter is intended to provide an overview of the laws pertaining to the traditional music business. It is not intended to cover all the ground of music-business books that detail the traditional arrangements between record companies and artists, or music publishers and songwriters. At the end of the chapter is a list of very good books in which you can find additional information about the matters outlined here. The CD-ROM accompanying this book contains active links to online legal resources. The chapter deals with music rights in the United States only. While many of the principles discussed below apply in other countries as well, there may be significant differences, and resolution of foreign issues is outside the scope of this chapter.

Copyright

Copyright is the basis of virtually every music business transaction. Without copyright there would be no protection for musical compositions and recorded music. Without copyright they would have no financial value.

What Is Copyright? Copyright is a form of protection provided by the laws of the United States, that is, the Copyright Act (Title 17 of the U.S. Code), to the authors of "original works of authorship," including literary, dramatic, musical, artistic, and certain other intellectual works.

What Kind of Work Does Copyright Protect? Copyright protects original works of authorship fixed in any tangible medium of expression, rather than mere ideas. Works of authorship include the following categories:

(1) Literary works;
(2) **Musical works, including any accompanying words;**
(3) Dramatic works, including any accompanying music;

(4) Pantomimes and choreographic works;
(5) Pictorial, graphic, and sculptural works;
(6) Motion pictures and other audiovisual works;
(7) **Sound recordings**; and
(8) Architectural works.
Section 102 (emphasis added).

Musical works are musical compositions including songs, as well as longer works such as a symphony or a movie score. Sound recordings are defined in the Copyright Act as "works that result from the fixation of a series of musical, spoken, or other sounds . . . regardless of the nature of the material objects, such as disks, tapes, or other phonorecords, in which they are embodied." The Act further defines "phonorecords" as "material objects in which sounds, other than those accompanying a motion picture or other audiovisual work, are fixed by any method now known or later developed. . . ." The difference is that "sound recordings" refers to works that are subject to copyright, and "phonorecords" are physical embodiments of such works. In music business parlance, though, the word "master" is used to refer to the copyright in a sound recording.

What Are the Rights That Copyright Protects? Section 106 of the 1976 Copyright Act generally gives the owner of copyright the exclusive right to do and to authorize others to do any of the following:

(1) To reproduce the copyrighted work in copies or phonorecords;
(2) To prepare derivative works based upon the copyrighted work;
(3) To distribute copies or phonorecords of the copyrighted work to the public by sale or other transfer of ownership, or by rental, lease, or lending;
(4) In the case of literary, musical, dramatic, and choreographic works, pantomimes, and motion pictures and other audiovisual works, to perform the copyrighted work publicly;
(5) In the case of literary, musical, dramatic, and choreographic works, pantomimes, and pictorial, graphic, or sculptural works, including the individual images of a motion picture or other audiovisual work, to display the copyrighted work publicly; and
(6) In the case of sound recordings, to perform the copyrighted work publicly by means of a digital audio transmission.

The origins of copyright law go back to the protection of books by the Statute of Queen Anne adopted by the British Parliament in 1710. The law provided protection for publishers against those who would make physical copies and sell them without permission. The United States continued this tradition by including a provision in our Constitution that specifically protects "works of authorship." The copyright law was eventually expanded to protect other works, including songs, and then with the invention of the phonograph record, to sound recordings. The rights of copyright owners were also expanded to include all the additional rights set forth above. The history of copyright is laid out in various sources[1] Our focus, of course, is the present and the future.

Why Is Copyright Important in the Music Business? The Copyright Act specifically protects songs ("musical works") and masters ("sound recordings") by spelling out the precise rights reserved to the copyright owner. For example without (3) above, anyone could record your song and sell copies without paying you. Without (1), anyone could take your record and make copies without your permission and without paying you. Without (4), anyone could publicly perform your song, on the radio, for instance, and not pay you. Copyright is the house in which the music business lives, and without it the business would be homeless and broke.

Note that the public performance right in (6) applies to sound recordings, but only by means of digital distribution, not traditional "analog" methods of performance such as radio. We will discuss this critical distinction in Chapter 2, and in more detail in Chapters 3 and 4.

The Rules for Songs

Introduction. Now that we know what copyright is, the rights it protects, and the kind of works to which it applies, we're ready to discuss how copyright law applies to the music business.

First, it's important to distinguish between rights in a song and rights in a master, that is, a sound recording embodying a musical composition. When we hear a song on the radio, two separate and distinct intellectual properties are involved that need to be identified. The first is the song or music composition—the words and music composed by the songwriter(s) or composer(s). There is also another copyright: the sound recording—the physical embodiment of sounds resulting from the recorded performance of that musical composition. Therefore, a CD is like a copyright sandwich: the songs embodied in the CD are protected by copyright as musical works, and the masters are protected by the copyright protection applicable to sound recordings.

---

1. *For instance, Professor Lawrence Lessig discusses the interesting history of the Statute of Queen Anne in the chapter titled "Property" in his book* Free Culture *(Penguin 2004). You can buy this book, but Professor Lessig has also made the book available for anyone to read for free at* www.free-culture.cc/freeculture.pdf *under a "Creative Commons" license. We discuss Creative Commons in Chapter 16.*

Music Publishers. Rights in a song are generally controlled by the songwriters or their representatives, the music publishers. Major music publishing companies include EMI Music, Warner/Chappell, Sony/ATV, Universal Music, BMG, and Famous Music. These are major corporations that have worldwide operations and generate hundreds of millions of dollars each year. But there are thousands of other publishers throughout the world, ranging in size from big companies to one-person operations. The relationships between songwriters and music publishers vary, but historically the standard deal provides that the songwriters assign the copyrights in songs that they write during the term of the agreement to the publisher, and the writer and publisher share fees that are received from most uses on a 50-50 basis. The publisher's 50% is generally referred to as the "publisher's share." The other 50% is known as the "writer's share."[2] The publisher earns its 50% by undertaking certain crucial functions, including negotiating and issuing licenses for use of the songs, collecting the money, registering copyrights in songs (see the discussion on registration below) and other administrative chores. The publisher is also supposed to promote the writer's songs and interest others in using them, such as recording artists, record labels and producers, TV and movie music supervisors, etc.

A popular song can earn money in a remarkable number of ways. The majority of revenue comes from sales of records embodying the song (these are called mechanical royalties, or "mechanicals") and public performance on radio, TV, and now the Internet. Other sources of revenue include the "synchronization" of the song in movies, TV programs, documentaries, video games, and TV commercials. Sales of printed music, including "sheet music" (printed music of single songs), used to be a principal source of income but has largely been supplanted by other uses.[3] The publisher's primary responsibility, though, is to assure that all these uses are properly licensed and paid for.

Subsequent sections of this chapter discuss mechanical, synchronization, and public performance licenses in further detail.

Since publishers generally negotiate rights on behalf of the writer, if, for example, you were to seek a license to use Bob Dylan's "Blowin' in the Wind" in your movie you would contact his publisher, Special Rider Music, rather than Dylan's manager, agent, or lawyer. If the writer has passed away, instead of contacting his estate, you would communicate with the publisher. For instance, you would contact Warner/Chappell Music instead of the estate of Cole Porter for a license to use "Night and Day." If there is more than one

---

2. *Today it is common for the writer and the publishing company to co-own the copyright and split the publisher's share while the writer keeps the writer's share. This arrangement is referred to as a co-publishing deal.*

3. *Unlike mechanicals, synch fees and public performance royalties, the writer's share for print income is generally 20% of retail for sheet music and 10% to 12.5% for printed collections of songs ("portfolios").*

writer, or if a song contains a sample, you can expect that there will be more than one music publisher. The following databases are good sources of information for ownership of songs: www.ASCAP.com, www.BMI.com, and www.SESAC.com.

Master recording rights, on the other hand, are generally controlled by record companies. When Norah Jones does another album for Blue Note, Blue Note Records, not Norah, will control the copyright in the master. Generally the deal between an artist and a record company requires the artist to agree that the record label acquire ownership in the copyright in any recording made under the agreement. Sometimes, if the artist is sufficiently powerful, he or she can negotiate that the record company does not own the copyright in the masters but merely has an exclusive license to sell those masters, and that the copyright in the sound recordings will revert to the artist after the termination of the recording agreement and after the label "recoups" costs. (See section on recoupment below.) Generally, however, the record company will retain the copyright in the masters even after the recording agreement has terminated and the artist no longer records for the label.

So using a recorded performance of a song for any purpose generally requires clearing two owners: the label, which owns the copyright in the sound recording, and the music publisher, which controls the rights in the song.

Mechanical, Synchronization and Public-Performance Rights. As we discussed, the three most lucrative sources of revenue from songs are mechanicals, synchronization, and public performance. The following conversation discusses each in more depth.

Mechanical Rights. The right to reproduce and distribute to the public a copyrighted musical composition on audio "phonorecords" such as CDs, tapes, and vinyl is referred to as the "mechanical" right. This terminology dates back to the days of the player piano, when a mechanical object—a perforated cylinder—was inserted into a piano, and the music was literally "mechanically" reproduced. Phonorecords, as we will discuss in subsequent chapters, also include MP3s and other means by which recordings of music are distributed on the Internet.

Compulsory License for Mechanicals. Licenses to exploit mechanical rights are called mechanical licenses. The Copyright Act contains compulsory licensing provisions governing the making and distribution of phonorecords of musical compositions including songs, although "dramatic works" such as operas are excluded from the compulsory license (see the section on Dramatic Works below). Section 115 of the act provides that once phonorecords of a nondramatic musical work have been publicly distributed in the United States with the copyright owner's consent, anyone else may obtain a "compulsory" license to make and distribute phonorecords of the work without securing the owner's consent. For instance, once the Beatles recorded and released the record containing the song "Yesterday" by Lennon and McCartney, anyone else could rerecord "Yesterday" without having to obtain consent.

Anyone may use the compulsory licensing provisions of the Copyright Act to rerecord a previously released song by following the procedures established by the act. Those procedures require giving notice to the owner and paying a statutory royalty for each phonorecord manufactured and distributed. This is called a statutory, or "compulsory," license because the copyright owner cannot deny permission. On the other hand, it assures that copyright owners will be paid for the use of their work. For the period from January 1, 2004, to December 31, 2005, the statutory mechanical royalty rate was 8.5 cents for songs five minutes or less. For songs or other nondramatic musical works that exceed five minutes, the rate is 1.65 cents per minute or fraction thereof over five minutes. For example: 5:01 to 6:00 = \$0.099 ($6 \times \$0.0165$ = 9.9 cents); 6:01 to 7:00 = \$.1155 ($7 \times \$0.0165$ = 11.55 cents); 7:01 to 8:00 = \$.132 ($8 \times \$0.0165$ = 13.32 cents). On January 1, 2006, the rate will be raised to 9.1 cents for songs five minutes or less and 1.75 cents per minute or fraction thereof over five minutes. These rates are set, pursuant to the Copyright Act, by a Copyright Arbitration Panel (CARP) administered by the Copyright Office. As we discuss in Chapter 3, these rates also apply to digital downloads of songs.

Harry Fox Agency. Publishers may, and usually do, issue voluntary mechanical licenses at the rates set forth above rather than depending on the compulsory rate provisions of the act. For this purpose most publishers utilize the Harry Fox Agency to handle mechanical licensing on their behalf. In 1927, the National Music Publishers' Association, an organization representing music publishers, established HFA to act as an information source, clearinghouse, and monitoring service for licensing musical copyrights. The Fox Agency acts as licensing agent for more than 27,000 music publishers, who in turn represent the interests of more than 160,000 songwriters. Although the rate is the same whether the licensee obtains a license directly from the owner or from the Fox Agency, the license issued by the Fox Agency is far simpler to comply with. For example, Fox requires quarterly accounting instead of monthly accounting required under the Copyright Act. Also the Copyright Act requires filing with the copyright owner a detailed annual statement of account certified by a public accountant. Dealing with the Fox Agency is much easier, and many music publishers depend on Fox to handle mechanical licenses. If you are planning to release your own original recording of someone else's song and your arrangement of the song hasn't substantially altered it, the quickest and most efficient action is usually to contact Harry Fox.

Uses Not Covered by Compulsory Mechanical License. Now that we know what the compulsory license for mechanicals is, and how to secure such a license, and how much it costs, let's be clear about what it does not cover. The compulsory license is available only for musical works that have previously been authorized for release to the public. It does not extend to recordings of songs, such as private demos, that have never been released to the public. Also, you cannot secure a compulsory mechanical license for the use of music in audiovisual works such as television programs or motion pictures (see discussion of "Synchronization Rights" in the next section). The technical reason for this is that the mechanical compulsory license only gives you the right to make and distribute "phonorecords" of a previously recorded song, and "phonorecords" do not include audiovisual works such as TV programs and movies. It also makes sense that the law limits the compulsory license to "phonorecords" because it would be unfair to the copyright owner of a song to be paid the same amount for different uses that may be radically unlike in terms of their financial character. For instance, think of the use of "New York, New York" by Fred Ebb and John Kander over the credits in the next Steven Spielberg blockbuster, compared to the use of the same song in an indie documentary film. It would be unreasonable to make the owner of that song accept the same compensation for both uses.

The compulsory mechanical license was intended to permit "covers," that is, new recordings of songs that are faithful to the original music. The compulsory license includes the privilege of making a musical arrangement of the work "to the extent necessary to conform it to the style or manner of interpretation of the performance involved." However, Section 115 of the act also provides that the arrangement "shall not change the basic melody or fundamental character of the work, and shall not be subject to protection as a derivative work . . . except with the express consent of the copyright owner." For instance, you cannot change the lyrics. If you do, you will need the consent of the copyright owner.

Synchronization Rights. The right to record a musical composition in synchronized relationship to the frames or pictures in an audiovisual production, such as a motion picture, television program, television commercial, video production, or Web site, is called the synchronization (or "synch") right. There is no compulsory license for this right; it is subject to the licensor and licensee negotiating an agreement. The Harry Fox Agency used to negotiate synch licenses for some of its publisher members but discontinued this services in June 2002. So you must generally secure synchronization rights by contacting the publisher. You can search for publisher information using the database of the Fox Agency, www.songfile.com, as well as the Web sites of the performing-rights organizations discussed below.

The fees for synch licenses can vary wildly depending on a variety of circumstances, including the popularity of the song and the nature of the audiovisual work. For instance, it will cost a great deal more to use an American standard such as "They Can't Take That Away from Me" by the Gershwins in a major motion picture than a song by an obscure garage band in a low-budget indie movie. We will revisit clearing music for TV programs and movies in more detail in Chapter 6, Music-Licensing Fundamentals.

A television producer is generally required by the television service on which the program will air (including a TV network, pay cable service, or basic cable) to acquire "synch" rights for any copyrighted music that is included in the program. The television service, as we discuss below, generally handles the license of "public performance" rights.

Public Performance Rights. Section 106(4) of the Copyright Act gives the copyright owners of songs, but not sound recordings (or, as they are referred to in the music business, masters), the exclusive right to "perform the copyrighted work publicly." The Act first recognized the right of public performance in musical compositions approximately 100 years ago. Today, this is the most lucrative source of income for many songwriters. What does "perform publicly" mean? The Copyright Act defines it as follows:

> To perform or display a work "publicly" means—
>
> (1) to perform or display it at a place open to the public or at any place where a substantial number of persons outside of a normal circle of a family and its social acquaintances is gathered; or
>
> (2) to transmit or otherwise communicate a performance or display of the work to a place specified by clause (1) or to the public, by means of any device or process, whether the members of the public capable of receiving the performance or display receive it in the same place or in separate places and at the same time or at different times.

In the case of songs, public performances defined in subparagraph (1) include concerts and live performances (e.g., Bruce Springsteen performing at the Meadowlands or your gig at CBGB), a jukebox playing in a bar, background music at a bowling alley, or music playing at any other public venue. But public performances go well beyond performances at physical venues. Playing music on the radio and television also constitutes public performance because these are "transmissions" to the public under subparagraph 2. Also, as we discuss in Chapters 2 and in more detail in Chapter 3—transmitting music on the Internet is also a public performance, and consequently a new and important source of income for songwriters.

ASCAP, BMI, and SESAC. Since copyright owners of songs enjoy exclusive public performance rights, those who wish to perform songs publicly need permission, that is, a "public-performance license." Typical licensees include radio and TV stations (and now music Web sites, webcasters and other digital music services), as well as venues such as nightclubs, hotels, amusement parks, and arenas.[4] There are literally tens of thousands of such users in the U.S., so it would be virtually impossible for individual songwriters or publishers to license all of them. In fact, performances of copyrighted music even 100 years ago were so numerous, geographically diverse, and transitory that it was virtually impossible for each songwriter or his music publisher to monitor them all. In 1914 a group of prominent songwriters—including Irving Berlin, Jerome Kern, and John Philip Sousa—and music publishers came together to create ASCAP (American Society of Composers, Authors, and Publishers), the first American performing-rights organization (also known as a PRO), in order to license users, collect public performance royalties, and pay those royalties to the publishers and songwriters. In 1939 the broadcast community helped establish a competitor to ASCAP called BMI (Broadcast Music, Inc.). A third, much smaller PRO, SESAC (which used to stand for "Society of European Stage Authors and Composers") subsequently emerged. SESAC originally represented contemporary classical music but now represents and licenses all kinds of music.

The primary purpose of ASCAP, BMI, and SESAC is to assure that music creators are fairly compensated for the public performance of their works. These organizations represent public performance rights on behalf of their writers and publisher members. Each PRO grants "blanket licenses" to users. A blanket license includes the right to publicly perform all the songs represented by the PRO. The PROs collect license fees from each such license, and after deducting expenses, distributes the income to their writers and publisher members. Although they compete with each other, together these three PROs license the performing rights in virtually all the previously recorded music in the United States, and, through their reciprocal relations with foreign PROs, virtually all the previously recorded music in the world. PROs throughout the world include:

Australia: APRA	Austria: AKM
Belgium: SABAM	Brazil: SBACEM
Brazil: SICAM	Brazil: UBC
Canada: SOCAN	China: MCSC
England: PRS	France: SACEM
Germany: GEMA	Greece: AEPI
India: IPRS	Ireland: IMRO
Israel: ACUM	Italy: SIAE
Japan: JASRAC	Mexico: SACM
Poland: ZAIKS	Russia: RAO
South Africa: SAMRO	Spain: SGAE

Active links to these PROs are supplied in the Resources section of the CD-ROM included in this book.

---

4. PROs do not license movie theatres in the U.S. This is the result of antitrust claims brought decades ago having to do with certain publishers being owned by the same companies that also owned movie theatres. Movie producers therefore must and do secure public performance rights directly from composers for new music or music publishers for pre-existing songs.

PROs represent a very important source of income for writers and publishers. For instance, ASCAP has over the last three years distributed nearly $1.7 billion in royalties. BMI paid its members $573 million for the 2004 fiscal year alone.

The fees charged by the PROs to acquire blanket licenses are usually based on a small percentage of income. There is a mutual benefit to blanket licensing for the PROs and their licensees. The PROs collect money from users of music on a continuing basis for their members. The licensees acquire comfort that they can play any song without fear of copyright infringement. It would be virtually impossible, for example, for a radio station to negotiate a license for every song it plays with each songwriter or publisher.

PROs pay their songwriter and publisher members based on assigning value to each performance of their songs, which is determined by various factors such as the amount of license fees collected in a medium (television, cable, radio, etc.), the type of performance (visual vocal, background music, theme song, jingle, etc.), and the economic significance of the licensee (for example, how much a particular TV or radio station pays the PRO). Allocations for each song are made through various methods including sampling, review of playlists and logs, and other methods that are intended to capture the actual use of music as accurately as possible.

Each PRO pays 50% of income to its publisher members and 50% to the writers *directly*. This is important because the publishers cannot deduct any administration fees from the writer's share. They also cannot deduct any advances they may have paid the writers. This practice started with ASCAP, which, as we discussed, was created with the collaboration of some of the most successful songwriters of all time.

We will explore the licenses that the PROs use for digital media, including webcasting and streaming over the Internet, in subsequent chapters. For more about the PROs' membership requirements, formulas for paying royalties, and the services that they provide to young songwriters, such as showcases and networking opportunities, check out ASCAP.com, BMI.com, and SESAC.com.

Dramatic Works. PROs do not grant public performance licenses for "dramatic works." Dramatic works refer to productions which use music to directly advance the plot such as an opera, musical comedy, or ballet. Public performance rights for music in dramatic works are called "grand rights." The producer of a dramatic work must negotiate such rights directly with the publisher or composer.

The Rules for Masters

Overview. The Copyright Act protects sound recordings produced on and after February 15, 1972. Sound recordings first fixed before February 15, 1972, may nonetheless enjoy protection under the common law or antipiracy statutes of the various states.[5] The owners of sound-recording copyrights enjoy all the same rights as those who own musical compositions except, as we will discuss, public-performance rights. Generally if an artist is signed to a label, the record company will own the master pursuant to contract.

Master-Use Licenses. A master-use license is permission to use a pre-existing recording of music for audiovisual projects such as a movie or in a new record such as an audio compilation. For instance, a movie producer who wishes to use a recording of music in his film will need to negotiate a master-use license with the copyright owner of the master—usually a record company. Similar to synch licenses, there is no compulsory rate for master-use licenses. Note that record companies usually do not own the song embodied in their masters. Thus, in order to use Frank Sinatra's recording of Kander and Ebb's "New York, New York" in a film or a TV show, the producer would need a synch license from the music publisher of the song as well as a master-use license from the record company that owns the Sinatra recording.

Public-Performance Rights. The Copyright Act does not recognize a public-performance right in sound recordings (except, as we will discuss in Chapters 2 and 3, for digital-audio transmission), Therefore, a license is not needed to publicly perform a recording of music (in contrast to any copyrighted music embodied in the recording). For example, Yankee Stadium needs a public performance license to play the song embodied in the Sinatra recording of "New York, New York" after Yankees ball games, but does not need a license from the record company that owns the recording. Also, radio stations need a public-performance license to broadcast copyrighted songs. Radio stations (except for digital stations) do not need a public performance license to play recorded music.

Record Companies. Record companies make and sell records. But first they must acquire the rights in the performances on a recording. Unlike a song, which is created by one person or one band or is a simple collaboration between a lyricist and a composer, a master is a collaborative enterprise usually involving multiple parties including the artist, the producer, and the background singers and musicians. Therefore, the performances embodied on a master are a result of various creative contributions. Yet the record company generally will usually be the only copyright owner of the master. This is generally accomplished as follows: The record company acquires rights in the artist's performance under

---

5. *State anti-piracy laws generally mirror the federal laws. Most states have unauthorized duplication statutes that make it illegal to copy, reproduce, and distribute sound recordings without authorization. Those statutes apply to songs recorded before February 15, 1972, the date that sound recordings were added.*

the recording contract with the artist (see discussion below). For backup musicians who are members of the AFofM (American Federation of Musicians) and the backup vocalists who are members of AFTRA (American Federation of Television and Radio Artists), a transfer of rights is included in the standard union contract to which the record companies are signatories. Record producers also make many creative contributions to the recording. Producers help select the songs, the arranger, and the side musicians, and they supervise the recording session as well as the mixing and mastering process. The record company will generally insist that the artist enter into an agreement with the producer under which the producer transfers all his or her rights to the record company.

Recording Agreements. A detailed analysis of recording agreements is beyond the scope of this book. However, we can outline basic terms of the standard deal. These terms have been offered by the major labels and most independent labels for decades, and they have served as the foundation on which the recording industry has done business.

Exclusivity. A standard record contract requires the artist to record music exclusively for the record company. This means that only the record company has the right to distribute records and music videos containing the artist's performances produced during the term of the agreement. The artist of course may perform live concerts without permission. Generally the exclusivity clause, no matter how broadly drafted, will not be enforced in such a manner as to prevent the artist from performing on a television program, although technically a TV show usually entails a recording. For instance, Sony Music produced a TV series featuring performances of new and some established recording artists. The show was called *Sessions at West 54th* and aired initially on PBS. Many artists performed on the show who were not signed to Sony. Those artists did not secure the consent of their record companies to perform on *Sessions*. But when Sony wanted to include their performance in a "best of" CD, it needed to secure the permission of the record companies for each artist who was not signed to Sony.

Duration and Options. Perhaps the most important provision in the record contract is its duration. Generally the record companies require the artist to deliver one or two albums followed by a series of "options" under which the record company can require the artist to deliver additional albums. A typical record deal may have five option periods or more and may require two albums during each option period. The record company can terminate the contract at any time. The artist cannot. The result of this structure is that the record company can drop the artist even before the first album is released, or they can require an artist to record multiple albums over a number of years that may encompass an artist's entire career. Approximately a decade ago George Michael wanted to terminate his relationship with Columbia Records. But his recording contract required him to record more albums at Columbia's option. Michael brought a lawsuit in England to get out of his contract. He alleged, among other things, that Columbia's option for additional albums should be unenforceable because it made him a virtual slave of the record company. He also argued that since every major record company has these options for additional records, he had no real choice and no real bargaining power. He lost the case. The English court found that he entered the contract voluntarily and that he could not prove collusion between the major labels. From the record companies' point of view, the rationale for options is that the label makes a very substantial financial investment in an artist's career, and they want to be around to share in the artist's success.

Advances and Royalties. The record company may provide a "budget" from which the artist pays for the production of an album and retains any money not used during the course of production. Or the record company may pay for the costs of production directly and pay an "advance" to the artist on top of production expenses. As we discuss in the next section, in either scenario, all these payments are "recoupable" from the artist's royalties.

The normal recording royalty for new artists and artists with niche audiences like jazz musicians ranges from 10% to 15% of the suggested retail price of a record. Ten percent of a $15 CD is $1.50, but there are all sorts of deductions such as packaging (25% to 35% of retail) and producer fees (which range from 3% to 5% and are deducted directly from the artist's royalty) that significantly reduce that $1.50. These deductions vary from label to label, but generally the normal royalty is in the range of 75 cents to $1 after all the deductions are subtracted from royalties.

Recoupment. All the money that a label spends to produce an album, whether they pay the artist to make the album or pay for costs themselves, are treated as "recoupable advances." In addition, at least 50% of independent promotion and video costs are generally treated as advances, as well as any money that the label pays directly to the artist. Under the standard record contract the artist is supposed to repay all these advances to the label. This repayment happens through "recoupment." Suppose that recording costs, and the artist's share of promotion and video expenses add up to a million dollars. In record company parlance, the artist recoups at his royalty rate. If the artist's royalty is $1, the album must sell one million units before the artist has repaid the record company. Some artists' advocates claim this is unfair, because if the record company has sold a million units at a wholesale price of, for instance, $7 a unit, the record company has pocketed $7 million. In other words the record company has already made enough money to pay itself back for all its costs and make a profit. But the record companies argue that very few albums ever sell 1 million units, and they usually barely break even or lose money on most releases. In other words, they need the surpluses from the hits to subsidize all the losers.

In any event, this is the way the game has been played. The result is that very successful artists who sell millions of units recoup and make substantial royalties. The record companies also reward such artists with huge advances. There are relatively very few artists, however, who ever reach this level of success.

Controlled Composition Clauses. Controlled Compositions are songs written or co-written by the artist or the producer of the track in which the song is embodied. Typically, the recording company will pay 75% of the minimum statutory rate (see above for the current "stat" rate). Also they usually impose a "cap" of ten songs per album. So if the artist writes 12 songs he will only be paid for ten at 75% of stat. In addition, even if the artist only wrote two songs, if the company has to pay another writer or writers for ten songs the artist gets zilch. Many in the songwriting community have complained about this practice for years, claiming there is no justification for it except that all the major labels do it and so artists have little choice than to accept it. It is true that if an artist becomes a huge success he or she may be able to negotiate the Controlled Composition clause out of their contract as well as increase their recording royalty. Generally all artists, even stars, grant the label a free promotional synch license for use of Controlled Compositions in music videos.

Limitations on Rights to the Master. While the record company usually owns the master, this does not mean that it has unlimited rights to use the master. The labels' rights are limited by the contract with the artist. For example, the artist will usually convey the right to the record company to license masters for use in movies and television programs. However, the artist will usually retain consent over the use of masters to endorse a product or service.

Registration: Why and How

Why Register? Copyright registration is a legal formality intended to make a public record of the basic facts of a particular copyright. Registration is not a precondition of copyright protection. A copyright comes into existence when the work is created. Even though registration is not a requirement to secure a copyright, the Copyright Act provides several very important inducements to encourage registration. Among these advantages are:

- Registration establishes a public record of the copyright claim.
- Before an infringement suit may be filed in court, registration is necessary for works of U.S. origin.
- If made before or within five years of publication, registration will establish prima facie evidence in court of the validity of the copyright and of the facts stated in the certificate.

- If registration is made within three months after publication of the work or prior to an infringement of the work, statutory damages and attorneys' fees will be available to the copyright owner in court actions. Otherwise, only an award of actual damages and profits is available to the copyright owner.
- Registration allows the owner of the copyright to record the registration with the U.S. Customs Service for protection against the importation of infringing copies.

The fourth factor above is absolutely crucial. Statutory damages can be awarded up to $150,000 in cases of "willful" infringement, that is, where someone intentionally violated your copyright. For instance, you would be entitled to an award of up to that amount if someone intentionally took the hook of your song to create a new tune, or if they made copies of your record without your permission and sold them in the street, to retail stores, or on the Internet. If you do not comply with the registration requirements, you will have to prove "actual" damages, and proving this can often be very difficult or even impossible. In addition, the award of attorneys' fees can be an extremely important incentive to any lawyer, let alone a highly experienced copyright attorney who is skilled in litigation. So if you don't register your work, you can have a great case and never find a good lawyer because even if he wins the case for you, there may not be enough money to compensate him for his time. So you should definitely register each song and master you produce. The Copyright Office has made that procedure extremely easy and very inexpensive. The steps and the prices are laid out below.

In case you have not heard this or read it in a book, note that the only way to secure the benefits of copyright registration is to register with the U.S. Copyright Office. These benefits cannot be obtained by sending a copy of your song or master to yourself (even by certified or registered mail) or sending your song or master to any other organization, union, or group.

How to register. To register a work, including a song or a master, you need to submit a completed application form, a nonrefundable filing fee of $30, and a nonreturnable copy of the work. More details are provided below—but you can get all the details from the Web site of the U.S. Copyright Office (www.copyright.gov). Here are answers to some of the most important questions:

Where can I get application forms? You can download the forms from the above referenced Web site. In addition, you can call the form "hotline" at (202) 707-9100. If you download the form from the Web site, keep in mind that applications must be printed out on a single sheet of paper. If your computer can't do this, simply make a two-sided copy. At the time this book was written you could not file online. But the Copyright Office was hoping to make online registration available some time in 2005.

May I register more than one work on the same application? First, you can use Form SR to make one registration for both the sound recording and the underlying song. In addition, you may register a group of songs and masters in one application if they are "unpublished." The Copyright Act defines "publication" as follows:

> [T]he distribution of copies or phonorecords of a work to the public by sale or other transfer of ownership, or by rental, lease, or lending. The offering to distribute copies or phonorecords to a group of persons for purposes of further distribution, public performance, or public display constitutes publication. A public performance or display of a work does not of itself constitute publication.

You also have to comply with these additional requirements:

> Under the following conditions, a work may be registered in unpublished form as a "collection," with one application form and one fee:
>
> • The elements of the collection are assembled in an orderly form;
> • The combined elements bear a single title identifying the collection as a whole;
> • The copyright claimant in all the elements and in the collection as a whole is the same; and
> • All the elements are by the same author, or, if they are by different authors, at least one of the authors has contributed copyrightable authorship to each element.

How do I register songs? Musical works include both original compositions and original arrangements or other new versions of earlier compositions to which new copyrightable authorship has been added. Form PA is the appropriate form for registration, whether it is accompanied by the deposit of a "copy" (lead sheet or sheet music) or a "phonorecord" (disk or tape).

How do I register masters? Form SR is for registration of "sound recordings." If you are signed to a label, they will usually register the masters for you. If you are unsigned, note that if the master contains your songs, you can register both at the same time. As stated above, Form SR may be used to register both a musical work and a sound recording fixed in a phonorecord, provided that the same person or organization owns the copyrights in both works.

Can you register the copyright in your Web site? Yes, the original authorship appearing on a Web site may be protected by copyright. This includes original writings, artwork, photographs, music, and sound. Procedures for registering the contents of a Web site may be found in Circular 66, Copyright Registration for Online Works.

The U.S. Copyright Office's Web site (*www.copyright.gov*) is an invaluable source of information not only on registration but also how copyright law protects songs and masters.

Duration of Copyright

The term "public domain" refers to the status of a work having no copyright protection, and therefore belonging to the "public." When a work is in or has "fallen" into the public domain it means it is available for unrestricted use by anyone. Permission and/or payment are not required for use. Once a work falls into the public domain (has become "PD"), it can never be recaptured by the owner (except for certain foreign-originated works eligible for restoration of copyright under section 104A of the Copyright Act).

Copyright protection does not last forever. Many musical compositions, such as most of the great classic repertoire, are now PD. Generally a work goes into the public domain after a period of time. This section outlines what that period is.

Works Originally Created on or after January 1, 1978. A work that has been created (fixed in tangible form for the first time) on or after January 1, 1978, is automatically protected from the moment of its creation and is ordinarily given a term enduring for the author's life plus an additional 70 years after the author's death. In the case of "a joint work prepared by two or more authors" the term lasts for 70 years after the last surviving author's death. For works "made for hire," also sometimes referred to as a "corporate copyright," the duration of copyright will be 95 years from publication or 120 years from creation, whichever is shorter. A work made for hire generally refers to a work made by an employee of a corporation, such as a staff writer at a company that creates commercial jingles. A work for hire may also refer to a person who is "commissioned" to do a job under certain circumstances. For whether masters are works for hire under standard recording agreements, see the section below, Works for Hire in Recording Contracts.

The term of copyright used to be life plus 50, and for a corporate copyright the term was 75 years from publication or 100 years from creation, whichever was shorter. The duration of copyright was extended under the Sonny Bono Term Extension Act, signed into law on October 27, 1998. The act is named after its sponsor, the pop star and former husband of Cher who became a Republican congressman before his untimely demise in a skiing accident. The act is also sometimes referred to as the Mickey Mouse protection act, as it was heavily supported by Disney and other corporations that make a great deal of money by licensing their copyrights.

Many have criticized the extension. It is interesting to consider that originally copyright protection only endured 14 years. Professor Lawrence Lessig, the principal attorney representing a party challenging the constitutionality of the law, has argued that the law was designed to protect big corporations who use the copyright law to control culture and extract profits at the expense of those who would use previous works to contribute to society. On the other hand, your songs and masters are protected for a longer period than ever before. You should protect them by taking the steps to register them set forth above.

Works Originally Created before January 1, 1978, But Not Published or Registered by That Date. These works have been automatically brought under the statute and are now given federal copyright protection. The duration of copyright in these works will generally be computed in the same way as for works created on or after January 1, 1978; the life-plus-70 or 95/120-year terms will apply to them as well. The law provides that in no case will the term of copyright for works in this category expire before December 31, 2002, and for works published on or before December 31, 2002, the term of copyright will not expire before December 31, 2047. For the definition of "publication" see the section above on registration, and for further information see the U.S. Copyright Office Web site, Circular 1, *Copyright Basics*, section "Publication."

Works Originally Created and Published or Registered before January 1, 1978. For works published or registered before 1978, copyright was secured either on the date a work was published with a copyright notice or on the date of registration if the work was registered in unpublished form. In either case, the copyright endures for a first term of 28 years from the date it was secured. During the last (28th) year of the first term, the copyright is eligible for renewal. The Copyright Act of 1976 extended the renewal term from 28 to 47 years for copyrights that were subsisting on January 1, 1978, making these works eligible for a total term of protection of 75 years. Public Law 105-298, enacted on October 27, 1998, further extended the renewal term of copyrights still subsisting on that date by an additional 20 years, providing for a renewal term of 67 years and a total term of protection of 95 years.

Works for Hire in Recording Contracts. Standard recording agreements, including those offered by the major labels—that is, EMI, Sony BMG, Warner, and Universal—as well most important indie labels, stipulate that any recordings of music made by the artist during the term of the agreement are "works for hire," or if for any reason they are not deemed to be works for hire, the artist assigns the copyrights in the master recordings made under the agreement to the record label. Despite this standard clause, does the artist retain any rights in his masters?

The Copyright Act of 1976, which went into effect in 1978, makes a crucial distinction between a work for hire and work created by an artist or author that is not a work for hire. The act provides for only two legal categories of work for hire:

A "work made for hire" is—
(1) A work prepared by an employee within the scope of his or her employment; or
(2) A work specially ordered or commissioned for use as a contribution to a collective work, as a part of a motion picture or other audiovisual work, as a translation, as a supplementary work, as a compilation, as an instructional text, as a test, as answer material for a test, or as an atlas, if the parties expressly agree in a written instrument signed by them that the work shall be considered a work made for hire.

Note that a master or phonorecord is not included in the list of works listed in (2). Therefore unless an artist is deemed to be "an employee," the work-for-hire language in the standard recording agreement may not be enforceable.

The importance of this distinction is that if a work is not deemed to be a "work for hire," even if the artist assigned the copyright in the master to the record company, the grant can be "recaptured" by the artist at any time during a period of five years beginning at the end of 35 years from the date of execution of the grant. Notices of intent to terminate can be filed ten years before that. Therefore, if the artist entered into a standard recording agreement in 1978, he or she could file a notice to the record companies in 2003, and such notices have already been sent. It is yet to be determined whether the work-for-hire language in the standard record company agreements are valid. Therefore, it is conceivable that the record companies could eventually lose the right to distribute tens of thousands of records or more. A more comprehensive analysis of this issue is beyond the scope of this book, but an artist who has entered into a record contract in 1978 or thereafter should consult with competent counsel.

Fair Use

Fair use is a complete defense to copyright infringement. Under Section 107 of the Copyright Act, the defense applies where a work is used "for purposes such as criticism, comment, news reporting, teaching . . . scholarship or research. . . ." In evaluating whether the fair use defense is available, courts must evaluate (1) the purpose and character of the use, including whether such use is of a commercial nature or is for nonprofit educational purposes; (2) the nature of the work; (3) the amount and substantiality of the portion used in relation to the copyrighted work as a whole; and (4) the effect of the use upon the potential market for or value of the copyrighted work.

In the context of the music business, fair use arises frequently in the context of parody. In order to constitute fair use, a parody of a song must be targeted at the original work and not merely borrow its style. In the Two Live Crew case, the Supreme Court of the United States determined that that band's parody of "Pretty Woman" was a fair use because it poked fun at the original even though it used some of the lyrics and melody of the original song. *Campbell vs. Acuff-Rose Music, Inc.*, 510 U.S. 569 (1994).

In addition to fair use, the doctrine of "de minimis" use has provided wiggle room to many creators, especially in the area of digital sampling of music. See Chapter 16 for a conversation about the de minimis rule and a recent court case that puts that doctrine in jeopardy together with those who sample music.

Additional Resources

There are many books about copyright law and its application to the traditional music business. The following is a list of some of the best of them; each offers more information on the topics outlined above.

> Moses Avalon, *Confessions of a Record Producer: How To Survive the Scams and Shams of the Music Business*, 2nd Edition (Backbeat Books, 2002).
>
> Jeffrey Brabec and Todd Brabec, *Music Money and Success: The Insider's Guide to Making Money in the Music Business*, 4th Edition (Schirmer, 2004).
>
> *Entertainment Industry Contracts: Negotiating & Drafting Guide* (Vol. 4 Music), Donald Farber, Editor (Matthew Bender Publishing Co., 1992).
>
> Al Kohn and Bob Kohn, *Kohn on Music Licensing*, 3rd Edition (Aspen Law and Business, 2002).
>
> M. William Krasilovsky and Sidney Shemel, *This Business of Music*, 9th Edition (Billboard Books, 2003).
>
> Lawrence Lessig, *Free Culture, How Big Media Uses Technology and the Law to Lock Down Culture and Control Creativity* (Penguin Press, 2004).
>
> Melville B. and David Nimmer, *Nimmer on Copyright* (Matthew Bender, 2004). This ten-volume work is the leading treatise on copyright law.
>
> Donald S. Passman, *All You Need to Know About the Music Business*, 5th Edition (Simon & Schuster, 2003).
>
> Alan H. Siegel, *Breaking into the Music Business* (Simon & Schuster, 1990).
>
> Peter M. Thall, *What They'll Never Tell You About the Music Business: The Myths, the Secrets, The Lies (& a Few Truths)* (Billboard Books, 2002).

The CD-ROM accompanying this book contains active links to online legal resources.

Chapter 2
Overview of Digital Music Law

T his chapter is intended to provide a snapshot of digital music law. Succeeding chapters will explore the new rules in detail as they apply to webcasting, downloading, and interactive streaming. We start with summaries of the relevant statutes that in addition to the Copyright Act provide the basic rules for transmission of music on the Internet. Then we define those delivery methods, followed by an outline of how the rules apply to each.

Statutes

Home Audio Recording Act. The Audio Home Recording Act of 1992 (AHRA) was the first piece of major legislation affecting digital music.

The Act imposes a levy on "digital audio recording device(s)" (such as a digital tape recorder) and "digital audio recording medium(s)" (for example, blank digital audiotapes) to compensate copyright owners and artists for lost sales because of copying. The payments are made to the U.S. Copyright office, which then distributes the royalties to copyright owners and creators including labels, artists, music publishers, and songwriters. The income generated by the levy has been negligible because the AHRA does not apply to new generations of technology, including personal computers and MP3 players. But the Act does provide a model, which we will discuss in Chapter 9, for a possible solution to the woes that currently ail the music business.

In addition to paying the levy, digital audio recording devices that are covered by the AHRA must include a system that prohibits "serial" copying. The most common system in use is the Serial Copy Management System (SCMS), which permits first-generation digital-to-digital copies of prerecorded music but prohibits serial copies of those copies. In exchange for complying with the Act, the copyright owners waive the right to claim copyright infringement against both the manufacturers of covered devices and consumers who use those devices to make copies of copyrighted music for their own personal use.

Private Copying. Many people rip their CDs—that is, copy and save the songs as computer files—and copy those files to their MP3 players for portable listening. But is this legal? The AHRA states in relevant part: "No action may be brought . . . alleging infringement of copyright based on . . . the noncommercial use by a consumer of such a device or medium [i.e., a device or medium subject to the act] for making musical recordings." The statute therefore exempts personal copying for noncommercial purposes—on devices and blank media covered by the act. But a computer is not subject to AHRA. Neither are MP3 players. The Ninth Circuit did state in *RIAA v. Diamond Multimedia* (the "Rio" case) 180 F.3d 1072 (9th Cir. 1999) that using a computer to make a copy of recorded music for private, noncommercial use was "entirely consistent with the purposes of the act." But this statement was "dicta," that is, it was not central to the ruling in the case, and is generally treated by other courts as extraneous material that they need not be bound by. Other than the Rio case, there is no direct law on this point. Yet the practice of ripping a CD to a computer and copying the file to an MP3 player for personal use has not been challenged. According to some experts, it is an issue that the record labels and music publishers don't want to fight over because they are afraid they would lose or that they would incur the wrath of both consumers and the electronics business.

The Digital Performance Right in Sound Recordings Act. The Digital Performance Right in Sound Recordings Act of 1995 (DPRSRA) created a new right for owners of sound recordings. Under the DPRSRA, owners of copyrights in sound recordings were given exclusive "public performance" rights for the purposes of "digital audio transmissions." This means that an online music service cannot play any prerecorded music still protected by copyright without a license. As we pointed out in Public Performance Rights section in the previous chapter, the labels do not have a right to prohibit or license the public performance of sound recordings on traditional (analog) radio. They tried repeatedly to acquire such a right but failed at least in part because the broadcast community has consistently rallied against it. But the labels were able to convince Congress to give them a public performance right for digital transmission. They argued convincingly that digital transmissions can be reproduced without loss of quality, which could lead to massive copying, which could lead to a massive decline in sales of recorded music.

The Digital Millennium Copyright Act. The Digital Millennium Copyright Act (DMCA) of 1998 provided for a statutory license that grants certain digital music providers called "webcasters" the automatic right to use sound recordings in their *noninteractive* streamed programming, sometimes referred to as "Internet radio."[1] This means that notwithstanding the new digital public performance right in sound recordings under the DPRSRA, certain digital music services are entitled to use prerecorded music without the labels' specific permission, provided they comply with certain eligibility requirements and pay fees mandated pursuant to the act.

Webcasters are entitled to a statutory license under DMCA only if they comply with certain fairly stringent "eligibility" requirements. For instance, a webcaster may not play in any three-hour period more than three songs from a particular album, including no more than two consecutively, or four songs by a particular artist or from a boxed set, including no more than three consecutively. (We will set out other important eligibility criteria in the next chapter.) Webcasters who stream content that does not meet the criteria of the statutory license have to negotiate a separate license with the sound recording copyright owners of the tracks they want to use.

A nonprofit entity, SoundExchange, was established to oversee the administration, collection, and payment of the royalties to sound-recording copyright owners and to the artists, who share the income from this statute on a 50–50 basis.

Note that there was no need to create a new public-performance right for songs, as the law was already clear that their public performance through any means of transmission, be it analog or digital, was protected. The same PROs (ASCAP, BMI, and SESAC) that offer public performance licenses to radio and TV stations also offer blanket public performance licenses to Internet-based music services. We will outline how this works in the context of webcasting, downloading, and interactive streaming below and in more detail in the succeeding chapters.

Delivery Methods

Webcasting. Webcasting, as discussed above, generally refers to the noninteractive streaming of audio on the Internet ("Internet radio"). We have explained how eligible webcasters are entitled to a statutory license for use of masters. A synch license for songs is not necessary for audio webcasting. A public-performance license, which is available from the PROs, is necessary for performing the songs.

Downloading. Downloading is generally defined as transferring a file from one computer to another. When we talk about downloading music files we usually mean making a permanent copy of prerecorded music with unlimited portability, meaning that after you download a recording of a song on your computer you can hear it for the life of your computer and transfer it to any other compatible device such as an MP3 player. In regard to masters, there is no compulsory license for downloads. You need the permission of the

---

1. *A statutory license is a license provided by the law, as opposed to one that is voluntarily granted by individual copyright owners. Another example is the compulsory mechanical license which we discussed in Chapter 1*

owners of the copyrights in the masters. The copyrights of the masters of unsigned artists are generally owned by the artists themselves. But the copyrights of artists signed to labels are usually controlled by the labels. In regard to songs, a "statutory" license does apply. Under Section 115 of the Copyright Act, downloads of records embodying songs are referred to as digital phonorecord deliveries, or DPDs. These downloads are subject to the same rates applying to traditional copying of musical compositions on CDs or cassettes (currently the greater of 8.5 cents, or 1.65 cents per minute of playing time or fraction thereof).

Interactive Streaming. Interactive streaming refers to real-time delivery of music, like traditional radio—except that the listener has the ability to choose to hear any particular song on demand and to create playlists. The playlists remain on your computer until you stop paying the service and they disappear. This is sometimes referred to as "tethered downloads." These are part of the dynamic of the early subscription models such as MusicNet and continue today as part of the menu at MusicNet and services such as Rhapsody and the new Napster. As is the case for downloading, there is no compulsory license for interactive streaming of masters. You need the permission of the owners of the copyrights in the masters.

In regard to the songs, there is also no compulsory license. You need the specific permission of the music publishers. Digital services such as Rhapsody that offer interactive streaming must secure permission to use the songs with Harry Fox, plus those publishers that choose not to be represented by Fox. We will discuss this in more detail in Chapter 4.

Interactive streaming is also a "public performance" requiring permission from the PROs, that is, ASCAP, BMI, or SESAC.

Application of the Rules to Webcasting, Interactive Streaming, and Downloading

Here is an outline of how the rules discussed above apply to

- Webcasting or Internet radio
- Interactive streaming
- Downloading

Let's discuss clearing songs for each category, and then masters:

Songs

1. Webcasting or Internet radio. You need a public-performance license unless you own the songs or they are in the public domain. The public-performance rights are available from ASCAP, BMI, or SESAC.

2. Interactive streaming. You need a public-performance license unless you own the songs or they are in the public domain. In addition, you need a license to copy each song because interactive streaming requires making at least one copy of each song on the provider's service before it can be streamed to subscribers. Such a license must be negotiated with the music publishers or their representative, Harry Fox. There is a currently a blanket license in place between Fox and the Recording Industry Association of America for interactive streaming, but you can take advantage of it only if you are a member of the RIAA.

3. Downloading. You are entitled to a compulsory license under which you must pay the statutory rate: 8.5 cents per song or 1.65 cents per minute for songs longer than five minutes. This license is available from Harry Fox. ASCAP and BMI have announced that "it can be said" that audio downloads should not require payment for the public performance right. In any event, none of the PROs are actively pursuing licenses for downloading. (See further discussion of this issue in Chapter 4.)

Masters

1. Webcasting or Internet radio. Eligible webcasters are entitled to a compulsory license under the DMCA for use of masters. The license is administered by a not-for-profit called SoundExchange. The rates vary according to whether your service is commercial or noncommercial, and other criteria. Eligibility and rates are discussed in depth in the next chapter.

2. Interactive Streaming. You need permission from the owners of the recordings—usually the record companies.

3. Downloading. You need permission from the owners of the recordings—usually the record companies.

Chapter 3
Webcasting

According to a recent study by Arbitron, more than 100 million Americans have listened to or seen Internet audio or video broadcasts, and the number of webcast users has doubled over the last three years. Under the Digital Millennium Copyright Act, eligible webcasters may use any recorded music they wish in exchange for paying rates established in accordance with the law. This chapter tells you who is eligible and what the rates are.

What Is Webcasting?

Webcasting, sometimes referred to as "Internet radio," generally refers to the noninteractive streaming of audio on the Internet. The content can originate from various sources, including live or prerecorded talk, live musical performance and sporting events, and prerecorded music. There are basically two types of webcasts: Internet-only services, and radio stations that simultaneously broadcast and stream the same transmission in digital form on the Web.

Internet-only webcasting services such as Yahoo's Launchcast or Radio@AOL often feature many different channels of highly themed genres of music programming. Independent webcasters may often only program one or two channels consisting of their favorite music. Small labels sometimes webcast streams of their artists' records. Higher bandwidth results in better sound quality and allows for a greater number of simultaneous listeners. Bandwidth, which is the number of "bits" of information transmitted per second, is usually the single largest expense in a webcaster's budget. For webcasters who transmit music, music-clearance costs are usually the second greatest expense. Individuals who webcast usually offer their music streams for free. Some try to get sponsorship or advertising to offset expenses, or even return a profit.

Broadcast radio stations who choose to stream online, that is, webcast their signal, will usually use the same methods of raising revenue that they do in their analog world. For instance National Public Radio (NPR), which offers its broadcast on the Web, supports this operation the same way it supports its radio component—by corporate, government, and listener contributions. Commercial radio stations that also webcast may seek additional advertising money from advertisers for the additional exposure that the Internet provides. Keep in mind that once a radio station's signal goes online, it becomes available to the world—not just the relatively narrow geographical confines of a standard radio signal.

Why Is Webcasting Important?

One of the most exciting things that webcasting offers in terms of music is the enormous variety of programming it can provide. Broadcast radio is profoundly constricted, compared with the Internet, by the limited broadcast spectrum. The number of channels available on standard AM/FM radio is limited in most locations to a couple of dozen choices. Those choices are further limited by the domination of commercial radio by a handful of corporate conglomerates such as Infinity Radio and Clear Channel. A great deal of mainstream commercial radio sounds like one long commercial "interrupted" by shouting shock jocks and conservative talk-show hosts. Webcasting makes it possible for a potentially unlimited number of independent voices to be heard. The Internet can also provide each webcaster a virtually unlimited number of channels.

Internet radio, as opposed to traditional broadcast radio, also offers listeners an unlimited number of musical choices. Tens of thousands of Internet radio stations are available on the Web. For a sample of the variety, check 365Live (www.365Live.com) or Launch Music (*www.launch.yahoo.com*). The music is as diverse as the not-for-profit and commercial operators running the stations. Live365, for instance, has thousands of independent operators each programming their favorite form of music, whether classical, rock, hip-hop, jazz, dance, Latin, folk, world, etc. Launch, on the other hand, has one programming department whose job it is to see that every music taste is represented.

The day before this manuscript was delivered, the Sunday magazine of the *New York Times* ran a story called "Easy Listening: A California Radio Station Leverages Its Tastemaker Status Nationally by Going Online."[1] The article pointed out that KCRW.com is trying to make "new media and old media" allies rather than enemies by building an online listener base throughout the country. KCRW, a member-supported, noncommercial station based in Santa Monica, has long been known for the diversity of music that it plays and for giving time to artists that cut across a wide swath of genres, from singer-songwriters to club favorites and indie rock. The station claims that it was the first to play Norah Jones and the first in the U.S. to play Dido and Coldplay. The article reports that as commercial radio has become increasingly "timid, canned, and predictable," there is an opportunity for a station like KCRW to leverage its tastemaker status by going online. The article further

---

1. By Rob Walker, January 23, 2005.

points out that "while satellite radio[2] is providing one alternative, it's built on the idea of restricting your tastes one genre at a time. So stations like KCRW (along with Philadelphia's WXPN and its syndicated *World Café* show and a few others, like WFUV in the Bronx) are now crucial to idiosyncratic bands like Brazilian Girls and the small record labels that promote them and the music consumers who want to be surprised."

As the story about KCRW.com illustrates, another important thing about Internet radio is that it is not limited by geography the way standard radio is. Even the strongest radio signal can only travel a few hundred miles. Webcasters, on the other hand, can reach the entire world. A listener can hear the same webcast in Texas or Tunisia or anywhere else in the world with an Internet or satellite connection. Many experts agree that as high-speed Internet access continues to permeate society, the potential growth for Internet radio and webcasting is practically unlimited. According to a June 2004 study by the General Accounting Office (GAO), the audit, evaluation, and investigative arm of Congress: "The popularity of webcasting is growing, with the number of listeners tripling over the past three years."

Statutes

The recording labels have always wanted to get the radio stations to pay them to play their records. The Recording Industry Association of America (RIAA) is the trade group that represents the U.S. recording industry.[3] According to the RIAA Web site:

> The lack of a broad sound-recording performance right that applies to U.S. terrestrial broadcasts is an historical accident. In almost every other country broadcasters pay for their use of the sound recordings upon which their business is based. For decades, the U.S. recording industry fought unsuccessfully to change this anomaly while broadcasters built very profitable businesses on the creative works of artists and record companies. The broadcasters were simply too strong on Capitol Hill.

As the RIAA points out, the broadcast industry has succeeded in preventing the labels from amending the copyright law to create an exclusive right of public performance for sound recordings. Normal radio stations therefore still do not pay record companies to play music. On the other hand, radio play has long been recognized as promoting record

---

2. *See discussion on XM and Sirius in section titled DMCA below, and section on Satellite Radio in Chapter 13.*

3. *Its members include the major record labels, Universal, EMI, Warner and Sony BMG and many of the indies. Collectively, its members create, manufacture and/or distribute approximately 90% of all legitimate sound recordings produced and sold in the United States.*

sales. So much so, in fact, that record companies have been accused of paying stations and DJs to play their records. This is known as "payola" and is prohibited by federal law.

Nevertheless, in 1995, the labels succeeded in getting Congress to establish a sound-recording performance right for digital transmissions by enacting the Digital Performance Right in Sound Recordings Act. The RIAA's take on it is:

> [W]ith the birth of digital transmission technology, Congress understood the importance of establishing a sound recording performance right for digital transmissions, and did so in 1995 with the Digital Performance Right in Sound Recordings Act ("DPRSRA"). In doing so, Congress "grandfathered" the old world of terrestrial broadcasting, but required everyone (including broadcasters) operating in the new world of digital transmissions to pay their fair share for using copyrighted sound recordings in their business.

The labels successfully argued that, unlike analog signals, listeners could copy digital transmissions of music and make a recording of the same quality as a CD. Such copying could therefore compete with CD sales, so the owners of sound recordings should be compensated. By giving the labels an exclusive right of public performance, they could charge webcasters a license fee to play their records.

The DMCA. In 1998, Congress enacted the Digital Millennium Copyright Act (DMCA), under which eligible services may secure a statutory license for the use of sound recordings instead of having to negotiate with individual artists and labels. This statutory license, incorporated into Sec. 114 of the U.S. Copyright Act, covers public performances by four classes of digital music services:

- Eligible nonsubscription services (i.e., noninteractive webcasters and simulcasters that charge no fees).
- Preexisting subscription services (i.e., residential subscription services providing music over digital cable or satellite television).
- New subscription services (i.e., noninteractive webcasters and simulcasters that charge a fee).
- Preexisting satellite digital audio radio services (i.e., XM and SIRIUS satellite radio services).

The last category of satellite radio, which specifically includes XM and Sirius, are not technically "webcasts" because these services are delivered through satellites directly to devices that play the transmissions, not through the Internet. However, it makes sense that satellite radio is covered by the DMCA's compulsory license provisions because satellite radio is noninteractive and delivered by digital transmission. Both Sirius and

XM provide subscribers with dozens of commercial-free music channels as well as other programming. At the time of delivery of this manuscript Sirius had approximately 1 million subscribers and XM had about 3 million. In Chapter 13 we will explore satellite radio in more detail, including how independent artists may take advantage of this new technology. At the end of that chapter we'll interview Lee Abrams, XM's Senior VP and Chief Programming Officer.

The Conditions a Webcaster Has To Meet in Order To Qualify for the Statutory License. The DMCA established conditions that a webcaster must satisfy in order to be eligible for a statutory license. The most important one is that eligible transmissions must be "non-interactive," i.e., not on-demand or personalized programming. A listener cannot be allowed to select particular songs or create playlists. This excludes a huge portion of music on the Internet, including the peer-to-peer (P2P) model. When it comes to interactive models of distributing music, the record companies can deny permission for any reason and can charge whatever they want to those they choose not to deal with.

A number of other conditions are set forth in the DMCA, including the following, which is referred to as the "sound recording performance complement." A webcaster may not play in any three-hour period:

- More than three songs from a particular album, including no more than two consecutively, or
- Four songs by a particular artist or from a boxed set, including no more than three consecutively.

The point of this condition is to prevent listeners from being tempted to record a digital transmission of, for example, a Sinatra album, or an hour of Elton John music.

Other important eligibility criteria are:

Obligation to identify song, artist, and album. When performing a sound recording, a webcaster must identify the track, album, and featured artist.

Prior announcements not permitted. Advance song or artist playlists may not be published.

Archived programming. Archived programs—those that are posted on a Web site for listeners to hear repeatedly on-demand—may not be less than five hours in duration and may reside on a Web site for no more than a total of two weeks.

Looped programming. Looped or continuous programs—those that are performed continuously, automatically starting over when finished—may not be less than three hours in duration.

Certain other conditions apply. For the full list see the RIAA's section on webcasting at *www.riaa.com*.

The most important obligation that a webcaster has under DMCA's statutory license is to pay the required fees. The section below discusses the agency that collects those fees and what it does with the money. We then turn our attention to what the rates are and how they were established.

SoundExchange

Originally a division of the RIAA, SoundExchange is now an independent, nonprofit performance-rights entity jointly controlled by artists and sound-recording copyright owners through an 18-member board of directors with nine artist representatives and nine copyright owner representatives. The U.S. Copyright Office has designated Sound-Exchange to collect and pay out fees derived from the statutory license for digital transmission of masters provided under the DMCA.

SoundExchange is authorized to deduct reasonable administrative fees and thereafter pay the recording copyright owners, generally the record companies, 50%, and the artists the other 50%. The "featured artist" receives 45% of the total artist share. This money is paid directly to these artists, not the record companies. Nonfeatured artists receive 5%; 2.5% is paid to AFTRA on behalf of nonfeatured vocalists, and 2.5% is paid to the AFof M on behalf of background musicians. Inquiries about royalties that may be due to nonfeatured musicians or nonfeatured vocalists can be directed to the AFofM and AFTRA Intellectual Property Rights Distribution Fund, which is a joint project of both unions, at www.raroyalties.org.

It is significant that the law requires SoundExchange to pay the artists directly. If the payments were made to the record companies on the artists' behalf, the labels could deduct such payments from the amount that the artists owe them for "unrecouped" production and marketing costs. Since most artists are unrecouped—that is, have not sold enough records to repay the record companies for production and marketing expenses—if the law did not require payment directly to the artists, they might never receive any of the money paid by SoundExchange.

All royalties collected by SoundExchange are accompanied by extensive electronic play logs submitted by the licensee, the service offering the digital transmission to consumers. These logs are "matched" to a database of unique sound-recording information, which are in turn referenced to an owner of the sound recording and featured artist. This allows SoundExchange to accurately match unique performances with record companies and artists, and pay exactly what has been earned. According to its Web site, SoundExchange has matched "millions" of digital performances from play logs submitted by the subscription services.

SoundExchange made its first payments in 2001. After a slow beginning, Sound-Exchange has begun to rapidly increase its annual payment to artists and labels. SoundExchange paid out $17.5 million for the first nine months of 2004. In 2005 it expects to collect and allocate $35 million. The recent payments include royalties earned on XM and Sirius satellite radio transmissions, adding to revenue streams already in place from services like Music Choice, Muzak, and DMX. Barry M. Massarsky, a music industry economist and a consultant for SoundExchange, predicted that total revenue from satellite radio alone would increase by six to ten times over the next five years.

The following conversation explains how the fees that are payable to SoundExchange were established and what those rates are.

Webcasting Rates

Controversial History. The DMCA did not actually stipulate the fees. Instead Congress provided that the rates should represent what they would have been if negotiated in the marketplace between a willing buyer and a willing seller. The DMCA additionally stipulates that if the webcasters and the copyright owners (usually record companies) cannot agree on the royalty rates for the license, the rates are to be established by the office of the Librarian of Congress, which would be required to convene a copyright arbitration royalty panel (CARP) composed of three independent arbitrators. Ultimately that is exactly what happened. During the initial negotiations, the record companies asked for more than many webcasters wanted to pay, and in 2001, the U.S. Copyright Office did establish a CARP to resolve the issue.

This particular CARP (one of many that the Copyright Office has empowered, each ruling on a different issue in a different industry) held hearings for six months, reviewed testimony and evidence from copyright owners and webcasters, and delivered a report to the Librarian of Congress in February 2002 with recommended rates and terms. The CARP based their recommended rates on a special deal that was negotiated between Yahoo and the RIAA on behalf of the record companies. That deal was a good basis for fashioning rates, the CARP claimed, because the parties had comparable bargaining power. Critics suggested that Yahoo had an interest in accepting higher rates in order to dissuade less-well-financed competitors from entering the business.[4]

The Librarian of Congress's Revisions of the CARP. Perhaps in response to some of this criticism, in June 2002 the Librarian of Congress rejected some of the terms and rates recommended by the CARP and issued its own regulations and rates. The most significant

---

4. *In fact, Mark Cuban, owner of the Dallas Mavericks and founder of Broadcast.com, which Yahoo purchased, was reported as having said the Yahoo/RIAA deal was made to "shut out small Webcasters and decrease competition." "Yahoo's Role In Webcasting Fees Attacked" by Ken Liebeskind (*Media Daily News, 7/5/02*).

difference between the CARP's determination and the Librarian's decision was that the Librarian abandoned the CARP's two-tiered rate structure of $0.0014 (14/100 of 1 cent) per performance for "Internet-only" transmissions and $0.0007 (7/100 of one cent) for each Internet retransmission of a performance in an AM/FM radio broadcast. Instead, the Librarian decided that the lower rate of $0.0007 should apply to both types of transmission (or 7 cents for every 100 listeners to a given song).

The Librarian also abandoned the CARP's two-tiered rate structure of $0.0002 (2/100 of one cent) for noncommercial broadcasters (excluding stations not affiliated with the Corporation for Public Broadcasting, or CPB, which made a special deal with copyright owners) who simulcast their AM or FM stations on the Internet, and $0.0005 for noncommercial stations that transmit archived programming. The Librarian determined that the rate of $0.0002 should apply to both types of transmissions. Also, the fee that webcasters must pay for the making of temporary or "ephemeral" recordings, needed to facilitate the transmission of performances of sound recordings, was reduced from 9% of performance fees to 8.8%.

The Librarian established Sept. 1, 2002, as the effective date of the rates. In addition, webcasters and Internet radio stations using the statutory licenses were to pay royalties for all their activities under the licenses since Oct. 28, 1998.

Unhappiness with the Librarian's Rates. Many webcasters were still unhappy with the Librarian's rates even though they were more favorable than the CARP's recommendations. The webcasters argued that the rates adopted by the Librarian of Congress were still much too high. According to the GAO report cited earlier, the small webcasters argued that "they would have to close their operations because they could not pay the rates set by the Librarian and that these rates would put an end to the promise of webcasting." Many of them preferred a percentage-of-revenue model similar to that required by the performing-rights societies. To give some idea of the costs involved, assume that 20,000 people "tuned in" to listen to a commercial webcaster transmit 50 songs each day. That would amount to $700 (20,000 × 50 × .0007) per day and about $250,000 per year. In addition, there would be the extra charge of 8.8% for a license to make "ephemeral" recordings. More than 200 Internet-based stations reportedly shut down because they could not afford to pay the new rates.

The small webcasters also claimed that the record companies were trying to stamp out a new form of delivering music that would offer the consumer many more choices. Ultimately, the webcasters contended, the labels are just hurting themselves, as there are so few places on traditional radio (or TV for that matter) that play any new music. The webcasters pointed out that Internet radio promotes sales of records by listing the name of each track, album, and artist (required by the DMCA), and that many offered links to online retailers like Amazon.com where consumers can purchase records.

At the same time, the record companies argued that the rates were too low, did not reflect the true market value of the music and that royalties are simply another cost of doing business, like buying bandwidth, and webcasters that could not afford to pay them should not be operating.

Small Webcasters Settlement Act. In response to these concerns, Congress passed the Small Webcasting Settlement Act of 2002 (SWSA). The SWSA did not set new rates. Instead it designated SoundExchange to negotiate new rates with the copyright owners and the small webcasters, and further stipulated that negotiated rates were to be based on a percentage of revenues or expenses, were to include a minimum fee, and were to apply in lieu of rates set by the Librarian of Congress. In December 2002, the U.S. Copyright Office published the resulting agreement.

Small Webcaster Rate. The rates are as follows:

> 2004 and 2005: The greater of 10% of the first $250,000 in gross revenues and 12% of any gross revenues in excess of $250,000 during the applicable year, or 7% of the webcaster's expenses during the applicable year.

Minimum annual fees are:

> For transmissions made in any part of calendar years 2003 and 2004: $2,000 for eligible small webcasters that had gross revenues during the prior year of not more than $50,000 and expect gross revenues of not more than $50,000 during the applicable year; or $5,000 for eligible small webcasters that had gross revenues during the prior year of more than $50,000 or expect gross revenues to exceed $50,000 during the applicable year.

To be eligible for this rate, a webcaster's gross revenues for 2004 cannot have exceeded $1.25 million and for 2005, the webcaster cannot "expect" to have gross revenues in excess of such amount.

Dozens of small webcasters have signed up for the rates, but among a certain group there is continuing unhappiness. The Webcaster Alliance, an association of approximately 400 small webcasters, filed a complaint in 2003 in the U.S. District Court for the Northern District of California alleging anticompetitive conduct against the RIAA. The crux of the complaint is that the new rates eliminate the commercial viability of most small commercial webcasters by imposing unreasonably high minimum fees. In April 2004 the district court granted the RIAA's motion to dismiss. *Webcaster Alliance Inc. v. Recording Industry Association of America Inc.*, C 03-3948 WHA. The plaintiffs are appealing the ruling.

Current Rates for Commercial Webcasters/Broadcast Simulcasters

For commercial webcasters who cannot qualify for the small webcaster rate, the following rates, which were announced in the Federal Register on Feb. 6, 2004, apply:

Monthly Royalty Fees—Licensees select between options (1) and (2)

1) Per Performance Option: $0.000762 per performance, except that 4% of performances shall bear no royalty.
2) Aggregate Tuning Hour Option:
   - Non-Music Programming: $0.000762 per aggregate tuning hour for programming reasonably classified as news, talk, sports, or business programming.
   - Broadcast Simulcasts: $0.0088 per aggregate tuning hour for broadcast simulcast programming not reasonably classified as news, talk, sports, or business programming.
   - Other Programming: $0.0117 for programming other than broadcast simulcast programming and programming reasonably classified as news, talk, sports, or business programming.

The minimum annual fee is $500 per channel, but no more than $2,500 regardless of which royalty option is selected.

For purposes of these rates, the term "performance" means each instance in which any portion of a nonpublic-domain musical recording is transmitted to a listener. The term "aggregate tuning hour" means the total hours of programming that the service has transmitted during a month to all listeners in the U.S. from all channels and stations, less actual running time of sound. The SoundExchange Web site gives the following example of how the rates work: If a service transmitted one hour of programming to ten simultaneous listeners, the service's aggregate tuning hours would equal ten. As an additional example, if one listener listened to a service for ten hours (and none of the recordings transmitted during that time was directly licensed), the service's aggregate tuning hours would equal ten.

Small webcasters have the option of paying these commercial rates rather than the small webcaster rate.

Rates for Noncommercial Webcasters/Broadcast Simulcasters

A "noncommercial webcaster" includes nonprofit (that is, tax-exempt organizations) and governmental entities. The rate for these webcasters are the same rates as set forth by the Librarian of Congress for noncommercial broadcasters. Those rates are $0.0002 (.02 cents) per performance, plus an additional 8.8% for any temporary or "ephemeral" phonorecords that are made, with an annual minimum fee of $500. Those rates cover a simulcast of the station's over-the-air signal, plus up to two Internet-only side channels.

Transmissions on additional side channels are subject to a per-performance rate of $0.0007 (.07 cents), plus an additional 8.8% for any ephemeral phonorecords.

Noncommercial Educational Entities

A "noncommercial educational entity" (NEE) is a noncommercial webcaster that is operated by or affiliated with an officially accredited school, college or university. NEEs have the option of paying the minimum annual fees set forth below or the rates adopted by the Librarian of Congress for non-CPB, noncommercial broadcasters.

Beginning in 2004, NEEs with more than 146,000 aggregate tuning hours of transmissions in any month (i.e., more than 200 average simultaneous listeners for the month) must pay for the excess transmissions at the rate of either $0.0002176 (.02176 cents) per performance or $0.00251 (.251 cents) per aggregate tuning hour ($0.0002 [.02 cents] per aggregate tuning hour for news/talk/sports). NEEs that transmit more than three channels (or broadcast station groups that transmit more than two side channels with up to three simulcast channels covered by one minimum payment) pay for the excess programming at commercial rates.

Minimum Annual Fees

Year	Minimum Annual Fee
2004	$500, or $250 at schools with fewer than 10,000 students.
2005	$500, or $250 at schools with fewer than 10,000 students.

Other Rates

There are also new rates just for business-establishment services that must operate under a broadcast-style model whereby all files are stored on central servers that transmit non-interactive audio programs to individual business establishments for real-time performance. In additional there are rates that apply to new and pre-existing subscription services (eg, Music Choice, Muzak, and DMX Music). Rates pertaining to these webcasters can be found at SoundExchange.com.

Confidential Rates

There are certain rates that continue to be confidential. The terms are not open to public scrutiny. These include deals with the satellite radio services, that is, XM and Sirius, and noncommercial webcasters such as NPR stations and public stations that are qualified to receive funding from the CPB. Some webcasters complain that these rates should be made public and that the reason they are not may be that they contain rates that are more favorable than the rates being offered to other webcasters.

Public Performance Rights

Any performance of songs by broadcast *or by digital transmission*, including a webcast, requires a public performance. As noted in Chapter 1, Section 106(4) of the Copyright Act gives the copyright owner of a song, the exclusive right to "perform the copyrighted work publicly." The act states that "to perform a work 'publicly' means" to perform a work at a physical place open to the public, *and*

> [T]o **transmit** or otherwise communicate a performance or display of the work ... **to the public, by means of any device or process**, whether the members of the public capable of receiving the performance or display receive it in the same place or in separate places and at the same time or at different times.
>
> Section 101. Emphasis added.

Playing music on standard broadcast radio, for instance, is a public performance because radio "transmits" songs to the public. Similarly, playing songs on the Internet or on satellite radio is also a transmission to the public. Therefore, any webcaster who wishes to transmit copyrighted songs must secure a public performance license. A webcaster can obtain public performance licenses to play virtually any song ever recorded by securing a blanket license from the three PROs, i.e., ASCAP, BMI, or SESAC.

ASCAP, BMI, and SESAC Licenses and Royalty Rates. ASCAP offers two different types of license for Internet services. One is called "Internet Sites & Services." The other is called "Interactive Sites & Services." The first of these applies to webcasting because it is designed for Internet sites and services whose Internet transmissions do not enable users to select individual songs. (We'll discuss the other ASCAP Internet licenses in the next chapter.) ASCAP's repertory, the largest in the world, contains more than 7.5 million copyrighted musical works of every style and genre, in addition to works in the repertories of over 60 affiliated foreign performing-rights organizations.

The ASCAP Internet Sites & Services license provides three different rate schedules. The licensee may choose any one of the three schedules. The first is 1.615% of a Web site's revenues. The second and third schedules are alternatives designed to give some flexibility depending on how much music is used. For instance, under the second schedule the percentage of revenues is 2.42%, but the amount against which this percentage is multiplied is adjusted to reflect income derived directly from the use of music on the site. The minimum annual fee is $264.

BMI's "Web Site Music Performance Agreement" applies to webcasting as well as interactive streaming of music (see next chapter). This agreement is based on a percentage of revenues and offers two choices at the licensee's option: 1.75% of gross revenues[5] or 2.5% of revenues derived from music sections of the site. The gross revenue calculation can be used if webcasting music is a primary feature on your Web site. The second option allows you to reduce the revenues subject to fee by factoring the traffic to pages with music in relation to your total Web site traffic. You can choose the most economical calculation for your particular Web site upon submitting your first quarterly revenue report, and you can change the calculation under which you file up to four times in a calendar year, depending on which is best suited to your business. If your business model changes and you decide to add more music to your site, you can switch calculations and save money. Under the terms of the license agreement you are required to submit separate quarterly financial reports as well as quarterly music-use reports.

BMI's minimum-payment schedules in 2004 were $274 for gross revenues up to $12,000, $396 for gross revenues exceeding $12,000, or $528 for gross revenues in excess of $18,501. The minimums will go up a few dollars in 2005 in conformity with the U.S. consumer price index.

BMI makes licensing for the Internet easy by allowing you to secure a license online through their Web site (see the Digital Licensing Center at BMI.com). You can even automatically calculate the amount you will have to pay. Today BMI serves nearly 3,700 different Web sites and digital music offerings, offering blanket licenses permitting use of all 4.5 million songs in the BMI repertoire. If your Web site's primary function is to promote the offline business that your company is in, or generates little or no directly attributable revenue, BMI offers a "Corporate Image" license which includes a rate based on traffic. BMI also offer a special Web site license for bonafide nonprofit 501(C)(3) organizations.

SESAC's license charges 0.00802 (less than 1%) multiplied by the average number of "page requests" (individual requests or hits for "HTML" Web pages) per month, and multiplied by 1.3 for pages with Web sites with advertising. The minimum license for any six-month period is $84 or $164 per year. SESAC also has a maximum license fee of $1,646 for each six-month period for Web sites with no advertising, and a $2,139 for each six month period for Web sites with advertising.

---

5. *Gross revenues include revenues generated from advertising, sponsorship, subscriptions, donations, commissions from third party transactions such as CD sales, the fair market value of goods and services received in lieu of cash consideration (trade and barter), and proprietary software.*

Rates for Sound Recording vs. Public Performance Royalties. Some small commercial webcasters complain that the minimum fee required for a DMCA license costs approximately twice as much as the minimum required by ASCAP, BMI, and SESAC combined. The percentage of income (10%) is approximately double that charged in aggregate by the PROs. The labels argue that they pour a lot of money to produce the masters that are subject to the DMCA and deserve compensation that reflects that contribution.

Live365 Licenses. We mentioned at the outset of this chapter that Live365.com has thousands of independent operators, each programming its favorite form of music, whether classical, rock, hip-hop, jazz, dance, Latin, folk, or world, etc. This company will help you start a webcast and maintain it for you on their network. They will also handle public-performance licensing for their webcaster clients unless you wish to launch your webcast directly from your Web site (rather than linking to your station page on Live365 and launching your player from its Web site), or if the webcaster wants to earn revenue from his station or Web site (for example, by selling audio ads or soliciting donations). However, in that case Live365 has made special arrangements with SESAC, BMI, and ASCAP to offer discounted versions of their standard Internet licenses to Live365 broadcasters. See the Live365 Web site for more information.

We discuss Live365 again in Chapter 19, which includes an interview with Rags Gupta, Live365's Chief Operating Officer.

Special Deals for Commercial Radio Broadcasters who Webcast. In October 2004 ASCAP and the Radio Music License Committee (RMLC), representing most of the nearly 12,000 commercial radio stations in the U.S., announced a new agreement totaling in excess of $1.7 billion. This is the largest single licensing deal in the history of American radio. The settlement, which was approved by Federal District Court Judge William C. Conner on October 15, 2004, provides stations with the right to perform ASCAP music over the air *and* as part of a simultaneous stream of their over-the-air signals on their Internet Web sites. It also provides fee certainty to both the radio industry and ASCAP's members.

The agreement finalizes license fees for the period 2001–2003 and establishes new ASCAP licenses for the period 2004–2009. The negotiated settlement replaces revenue-based license fees with a set payment schedule for the stations that will provide significant guaranteed income to ASCAP composers, songwriters, and music publishers. Both sides will also benefit from a simplified and streamlined administration process.

In July 2003 BMI reached a similar deal with RMLC. That agreement also included a separate fee for the right for RMLC radio stations to simultaneously stream their over-the-air signals on their Internet Web sites. "The new licenses offer an increase in our royalties and a predictable revenue stream from 2001 through 2006 totaling more than $1 billion," said then–BMI President and CEO Frances W. Preston.

Interview with John Simson, Executive Director of SoundExchange

You can learn more about the rules pertaining to webcasting by listening to my interview with John Simson, the Executive Director of SoundExchange, that's included in the CD-ROM accompanying this book.

Chapter 4
Downloading and Interactive Streaming

his chapter deals with the rules for licensing songs and masters for digital music ser-vices that offer interactive streaming and/or downloads.[1] Some of these rules derive from the Copyright Act and the recent statutes dealing with digital music that we discussed in Chapter 2. Others have emerged from agreements among the copyright owners themselves. Changes in digital transmission of music are happening at breakneck speed. The rules that are in place now may change to accommodate emerging technologies such as podcasting (see Chapter 13), and new rules may have to be created to accommodate means of delivering music that don't even exist at this moment but may be hugely popular a year or two from now. This chapter is meant to provide the best possible roadmap for licensing music for digital uses now. As the rules and business practices change, I will report on them in the Web pages available to you by clicking on the link provided in the CD-ROM accompanying this book.

It is much easier for those that already control sound recordings, as record companies do, to launch digital music stores than it is for those who do not own masters. Except for restrictions in its agreements with the artists, a label can pretty much use its masters for any commercial purpose without having to pay upfront to clear the rights. Those brave souls who do not own their own masters must negotiate individual licenses with the la-bels. Except for noninteractive webcasting, as we discussed in the last chapter, there is no compulsory license or statutory rate for the use of prerecorded music. The situation is pretty much the same for songs, except there is a compulsory license for downloading musical compositions, as we discuss below.

In 2001 the five major record companies (now four, as Sony and BMG have merged) that collectively controlled approximately 80% of recorded music launched their own digital music services. MusicNet (a joint venture between Time Warner, BMG, and EMI)

---

1. For definitions of downloading and interactive streaming, see Chapter 2.

and Pressplay (a joint venture between Universal and Sony Music)—were subscription-based services offering interactive streaming and tethered downloads (i.e., playlists that disappear once the subscriber stops paying). Since that time a lot has changed. Universal and Sony sold their interest in Pressplay to Roxio, a company that prospered from selling software that allowed people to rip CDs and burn copies on blank discs. (Roxio also bought the rights in the name "Napster" and renamed the service, although the new Napster has nothing to do with the original P2P service.) New digital music services were launched, including Rhapsody, Musicmatch, iTunes, Sony Connect, and Microsoft's MSN Music. Some of the new services such as iTunes sell only downloads, while others such as Musicmatch offer a variety of downloads, portable interactive streaming, and Internet radio. Although these services are still basically in their infancy, some are optimistic about their chances for success. Apple iTunes, for instance, has sold over 200 million tracks since opening its digital music store in April 2003. In January 2005 the International Federation of the Phonographic Industry (IFPI) issued a report that the market for digital music on the Internet boomed in 2004 and that the global recording industry collected significant revenues from the segment. The report stated that there are now more than 230 online sites where consumers can buy music legally, up from 50 a year ago. The IFPI, which represents more than 1,450 record companies across the globe, said digital music revenues in 2004 were approximately $330 million (euro 253 million), up sixfold from the previous year. "Digital music is now in the mainstream," the report glowed.[2]

Acquiring Rights in Masters for Downloading and Interactive Streaming

Record Companies. The deals for acquiring rights from record companies to sell their masters on the Internet vary in accordance with the quantity and quality of the records being provided. For instance, payment of substantial advances and a high royalty can be expected for the catalog of an important label. On the other hand, many indie labels as well as unsigned artists will usually be happy to license their music for no money upfront.

The digital music service will seek the broadest possible rights to enable it to deliver music in a variety of ways or to experiment with different delivery models to see which will catch on with users. However, the content provider may wish to strictly limit the manner in which its masters may be used. For instance, Apple Records still refuses to allow anyone to sell downloads of individual tracks by the Beatles.

---

2. In an editorial published in Billboard magazine (January 22, 2005) titled "Digital Music On a Roll," John Kennedy, Chairman/CEO of IFPI, wrote "In the last year the industry saw its first significant revenue from digital music. Such third-party analysts as Jupiter Media suggest sales ... rising to $680 million in 2005. Major players in the record industry believe digital sales could rise to as much as 25% of their total sales in five years' time."

Another important deal point will be deductions from royalties. Services will try to deduct transaction costs such as credit card processing fees, content storage and bandwidth, bad debts, fees paid to distribution agents or other service providers, and performance royalties. The content provider will try to reduce these deductions by, for instance, insisting that all costs be prorated in proportion to the amount of content subject to the license divided by the total amount of content on the service.

The content provider may also demand that downloads and streams be offered at certain minimum prices because the provider has an interest in preventing displacement of record sales at traditional outlets. The provider may also insist on additional fees to cover artists' royalties and mechanicals.

Licensing Issues. Even the labels, which generally own the recordings they distribute, must carefully review their agreements with each artist to confirm whether they have the rights necessary to commercially exploit recordings online.

Whether the labels have the rights to digitally distribute their own masters is a crucial issue not only to the labels but to the future of authorized digital delivery of music. The "legal" services such as iTunes and Musicmatch have to compete with unauthorized free P2P services that offer potentially every song ever recorded.

The authorized services eliminate the fear of lawsuits and provide quality control. Unauthorized services are subject to "spoofing," the practice of uploading files that seem like songs but are actually only fragments or noise. Labels have been known to hire companies to launch these phony files. Even certain artists have engaged in the practice. For instance, in 2003 Madonna released a new album, *American Life*, and simultaneously distributed decoy files on peer-to-peer networks, greeting listeners with an admonition from Madonna herself angrily demanding, "What the fuck do you think you're doing?" To fool downloaders the file names included Madonna's name and song titles. (Madonna's effort inspired hackers, eager to prove their technological superiority, to deface the singer's Web site and post downloadable, real versions of previously unreleased Madonna songs.)

Authorized services are free of spoofing because the digital services and the content providers control what is offered on the service. But it is important to have all the songs that listeners want to hear if they are to effectively compete with the free services.

In order to clear their masters for digital distribution the labels have to check each recording agreement and every modification to make sure the artist conveyed the necessary rights. The standard recording agreement provides that the label has the sole and exclusive right to sell or license an artist's recordings made during the term of the contract. But many recording contracts predate the Internet. It is unlikely that any contracts written more than ten years ago specifically refer to "digital" transmission or the Internet at all. Such contracts would include not only catalog artists such as Frank Sinatra and Miles Davis, but active artists such as Dylan and Springsteen. However, the music business has had to contend for many years with new distribution formats. As "new technologies" such as audio cassettes came into vogue, the labels revised their agreements to include the right to distribute and manufacture "records by any method and by any means or format now or hereafter known." This broad grant of rights can be reasonably interpreted as giving the label the right to sell recordings through digital transmission including the Internet as well as on cassettes and CDs. Of course, more recent agreements will specifically grant Internet and digital rights to the label. However, each agreement for each artist, and all the modifications of such agreements, must be evaluated separately to assure that the label has the necessary rights. A third-party digital music service should require the record company to warrant and represent that it owns and controls these rights, and indemnify the service against any claims.

Royalty Issues. At the core of any recording agreement is the understanding that the artist receives compensation for the label's commercial use of his or her recordings. If no means of calculating compensation for a particular method of distribution is included in a recording agreement, the artist has a strong argument that he or she did not intend to transfer such rights. A standard artist's contact will always include specific royalty provisions for sales of records "through normal retail channels" (i.e., record stores, record clubs, television ads, etc.). Recent agreements, as we pointed out, will have specific royalty provisions dealing with digital distribution. (For reasons presented in the next section, these provisions should be carefully scrutinized by the artist's attorney.) But many older agreements will include a "catch-all" royalty provision providing that for any sale of a record not specifically enumerated in the agreement, the label shall pay the artist a certain percentage of net receipts (usually 50%). This provision in conjunction with a broad grant of rights could be reasonably construed to give the label the right to digitally download and/or stream music on demand.

The Artist's Share. In the mid '90s the Internet started to get the attention of the music business. Many labels started to revise their basic form agreements to specifically deal with digital delivery of music. Major labels employ very bright lawyers who are focused on getting the best deal for the company. One of the things some these bright lawyers came up with when digital transmission started to catch on was to change the 50–50 split for licensing income from digital sources. Instead of the standard 50%, certain labels changed their basic form agreement to make the artist's share equal his royalty for normal retail sales. That royalty is considerably less than 50%. Most deals for new artists are from 10% to 15%. In addition, the smart lawyers at some of the record companies incorporated every conceivable deduction applicable to CDs, including the standard packaging deduction, although digital exploitation of masters generally does not include packaging. Sophisticated music attorneys took these new provisions in stride. They knew that in most cases these clauses could be negotiated out of the agreement. But inexperienced attorneys can still walk into traps like this. So if you are an artist, and you do get a record deal, this is yet another example of why you need a good lawyer.

Singles Restrictions. Certain recording agreements, especially those with highly successful artists, may include a provision for the artist to approve any release of a commercial single. Historically, the release of a single was a key marketing decision. Singles were used to promote album sales and define an artist's style and image. Therefore, the artist's attorney often tried and succeeded in getting this consent into the contract. But this restriction has limited the labels' ability to license services such as iTunes, which specialize in selling single tracks.

Artist Relations. Even if a recording contract does not include a right for the artist to approve certain things the label would like to do, such as release digital singles, the label will often ask the artist for consent anyway. The reason for showing such courtesy is that the record label needs the artist's cooperation. The artist's cooperation takes many forms, from delivering an album on time to showing up for a photo shoot. Even if the contract does not require the artist's consent, the label will therefore often at least consult with the artist, and if management or the artist is dead set against digital licensing, the label may have to withhold these masters.

Territory. Generally, recording agreements give the label the right to distribute records on a worldwide basis. Sometimes, however, an artist will have a recording agreement with more than one record company. For example, an artist may enter into an exclusive recording agreement with a label for the distribution of recordings in the United States and Canada, and enter into an exclusive recording agreement with another label for distribution of those recordings in the rest of the world. In this situation, a label must honor the agreement's territorial restrictions when determining whether it can license downloads in a specific geographic region. Although the Internet is a worldwide medium, it's possible to accept orders only from people in countries within the label's territory.

Featured Guest Artists. Among the "exclusive" rights provided for in the standard recording agreement is a provision that the artist may not perform as a featured guest on another performer's record during the term of his or her agreement. If an artist would like to perform on another artist's record, and that artist is signed to a different label, the other label must acquire the consent of the guest artist's record company. Although these consent agreements are generally very brief, they usually include a clause that prevents the release of the track as a single. This is because the guest artist's record company does not want its artist to be associated too closely with another label. The result of this practice, though, is that the track cannot be sold as a single, either as a single CD or as a digital download.

Samples. Using samples (i.e., excerpts of another recording or a song in the creation of a new track) has been a popular form of making records in hip-hop, electronic, and dance music for many years. If a sample involves an actual master as well as the underlying song, generally permission must be obtained from the owner of the master as well as from the owner of the song. The resulting agreements must be scrutinized to make sure that digital downloads of the sample are authorized and, if the track is to be made available as a single download, whether singles rights were granted. Often sampling licenses specifically include a clause that prohibits the sale of the track as a single in any medium. This is a major problem in clearing hip-hop records for sale as single downloads.

Clearing Songs for Downloading and Interactive Streaming

Clearing songs and other musical compositions for downloading and interactive streaming may be divided into mechanical and public-performance rights. First we address downloading, and then interactive streaming.

Downloading

Mechanicals. A mechanical license is required to make a copy of a song embodied in a sound recording. The income that results from these licenses is referred to as "mechanical" royalties. Those royalties (currently the greater of 8.5 cents, or 1.65 cents per minute of playing time or fraction thereof) are paid to music publishers who generally share 50% with the songwriter. As we explained in Chapter 1, the Copyright Act provides a "compulsory" license with regard to mechanical duplication of songs. This means the copyright owner cannot deny consent provided that the song has been previously recorded and released to the public. This compulsory license also applies to downloading of songs. Section 115 of the Copyright Act refers to downloading as "digital phonorecord deliveries" (DPDs). The relevant language is as follows:

> When phonorecords of a nondramatic musical work have been distributed to the public in the United States under the authority of the copyright owner, any other person, including those who make phonorecords **or digital phonorecord deliveries**, may, by complying with the provisions of this section, obtain a compulsory license to make and distribute phonorecords of the work. A person may obtain a compulsory license only if his or her primary purpose in making phonorecords is to distribute them to the public for private use, **including by means of a digital phonorecord delivery**.

> Emphasis added.

As we discussed in Chapter 1, the act provides that parties making and distributing copies subject to the compulsory mechanical license can provide notice and pay the copyright owners directly. But those provisions require monthly accounting and filing with the copyright owner a detailed annual statement certified by a public accountant. However, those who offer downloads of song can, just as those who make and distribute copies of CDs, use the Fox Agency to obtain mechanical licenses instead of complying with these onerous provisions. As we discussed, the Fox Agency acts as licensing agent for the vast majority of music publishers, who in turn represent the interests of more than 160,000 songwriters. Although the rate is the same whether the licensee deals directly with the copyright owners or with the Fox Agency, the license issued by Fox only requires quarterly accounting instead of monthly statements and alleviates the necessity of finding and paying each copyright owner. The Fox Agency does that work for you. And many music publishers depend on the Fox Agency to handle DPD licenses just as they do old-fashioned mechanical licenses.

Public Performance. As we have discussed, ASCAP, BMI, and SESAC represent public performance rights in the vast majority of all songs still under copyright in the United States, and through their agreements with foreign performing-rights organizations, they represent virtually all the songs still protected by copyright that have been recorded throughout the world.

It is not totally clear whether performance licenses are required for downloading music if no sound is heard during the downloading process. Many experts point out that downloading for later playback is the same as buying a record. When you buy a record and listen to it at home, there is no public performance of music. When you play the music at home, it is considered to be a *private* performance. On the other hand, downloading does involve a transmission "to the public," which is one of the definitions of public performance in the act. At the current time, this issue has not been definitively determined. However, the Copyright Office issued an opinion that downloading was not a public performance, and ASCAP and BMI joined in issuing a statement that it "can be said that 'pure' audio-only downloads should not require payment for the public performing right."[3] In any event, the PROs are not actively pursuing licenses for pure downloading at this time. Furthermore, the issue does not arise very often, as most digital music services that offer downloads also offer interactive streaming and/or webcasting, which clearly do require public performance licenses.

---

3. *Joint statement of American Society of Composers, Authors & Publishers (ASCAP), Broadcast Music, Inc. (BMI), the National Music Publishers' Association (NMPA) / Harry Fox Agency (HFA) on Internet uses of music November, 2001. See www.ascap.com/legislation/jointstatement.html.*

Interactive Streaming

Mechanicals. Interactive on-demand streaming is a common model for transmitting music online. With this format you can listen to any song on-demand and make playlists that reside on your computer for as long as you subscribe to the service. The major labels, as we discussed above, chose this model for their initial foray into digital music distribution. We will discuss these services—MusicNet (launched by Universal, EMI, and BMG) and Pressplay (launched by Sony and BMG)—again in our discussion of the history of the labels and digital distribution in Chapter 8. Among the services that presently offer interactive streaming as at least an element of their package to consumers is the new Napster, Rhapsody, MusicNet, Musicmatch, and Emusic.

The advantage to the labels of this form of digital delivery of music, as opposed to permanent downloads, is that streaming does not directly compete with traditional CD "brick and mortar" (i.e., record store) sales.

There was serious debate for some time as to whether mechanical licenses were even required for on-demand streaming because listeners are not permitted to make permanent copies. The music-publishing community vigorously pressed the view, however, that on-demand streaming may displace normal record sales and that songwriters should receive a royalty from streaming to compensate them for lost mechanical income. In 2001 the U.S. District Court for the Southern District of New York confirmed in *The Rodgers and Hammerstein Org. v. UMG Recordings Inc.*, 60 U.S. P.Q. 2d 1354 (S.D.N.Y. 2001), that a mechanical license is indeed required for interactive streaming. The case involved an online music service, Farmclub.com, introduced by Universal Music. Farmclub copied thousands of recordings of musical works to their computer server for on-demand streaming to subscribers, but it did not seek specific permission from the owners of the copyrights in the songs. In response, the Rodgers & Hammerstein Organization and other publishers and songwriters filed suit for infringement of their numerous copyrighted songs.

Universal argued that its existing mechanical licenses to manufacture and distribute records of the plaintiffs' musical compositions permitted it to make copies of those recordings on Farmclub.com's computer servers and to operate its on-demand streaming service. The songwriters and music publishers argued that the licenses did not extend to interactive streaming and tethered downloading. The court agreed and entered summary judgment in favor of the songwriters and music publishers.

Subsequent to the Farmclub decision, in October 2001 the RIAA and the NMPA announced a major deal for the mechanical licensing of on-demand streaming. Under the agreement, the RIAA and its member labels, which at that time owned MusicNet and Pressplay, secured access to every musical work authorized by participating publisher-principals. Under the deal, Fox issued licenses for on-demand streaming and tethered downloads. Pending the determination of the applicable royalty, the RIAA paid the Fox

Agency an advance of $1 million. According to the deal, if the two sides did not settle on a rate during the next two years, the recording industry would pay monthly advances totaling $750,000 per year until a rate is set. Since the time that agreement was made, Universal and Sony sold Pressplay and other major subscription services gained momentum, including Rhapsody, Musicmatch, the new Napster and many others. These services are now dealing directly with the music publishers through Fox. In fact, the RIAA and NMPA have not reached an agreement on a royalty.

Public Performance. Under the Copyright Act, the owner of a copyright in a song has exclusive public-performance rights. This right, as we discussed in the last chapter, extends to public performances of songs on the Internet. It does not matter whether the performance is a noninteractive stream (webcasting), or an interactive stream providing on-demand listening to individual songs. Both are public performances and both require a license from the PROs for performance of copyrighted songs.

In regard to BMI and SESAC, the licenses for interactive streaming are the same as those required for webcasting. See Chapter 3 for a discussion of those licenses, including royalty rates.

ASCAP offers a license titled "Interactive Sites & Services" that is specifically designed for Internet sites and services that allow users to "download or otherwise select particular musical compositions within their Internet transmissions." This license officially ended December 31, 2004, but is still posted in the ASCAP Web site, and presumably ASCAP will continue to offer this license to interactive streaming services, although the rates could change. The minimum license fee for 2004 was $312, compared to the minimum of $264 for noninteractive Web sites. The percentage of revenues was also higher—3% of revenues—instead of 1.165% for noninteractive sites. Similar to ASCAP's noninteractive Internet license, the interactive Internet licensees had additional choices designed to give some flexibility depending on how much music they used. For instance, under the second schedule in the Interactive license, the percentage of revenues is 4.95%, but the amount against which this percentage is multiplied is adjusted to reflect income derived directly from the use of music on the site. (Click on the link to Web pages updating this book in the CD-ROM for information on new rates and/or licenses that ASCAP may offer in 2005 for interactive Internet music services.)

Chapter 5

Music Videos, Audiovisual Concerts & Documentaries

As high-speed Internet connections through cable modem or DSL systems increasingly replace slower dial up services, more and more videos are now featured on digital music Web sites such as Launch.com. More digital music services are playing videos and more people are watching them online because high-speed connections offer the videos in much less time with much greater picture quality.

In addition, as this book went to press there is much talk about a new generation of wireless networks that companies like Sprint and Verizon are rolling out. They are promising direct access to streaming video as well as music through cell phones and other portable devices.

Videos will also becoming increasingly available for on-demand viewing on digital cable systems. For instance, America Online recently rolled out AOL Music On Demand, which offers hundreds of on-demand videos on Time Warner digital cable. AOL Music On Demand is now available in 30 markets, entering New York and New Jersey in January 2005. Digital video-on-demand (VOD) cable systems are delivered through the same cable modem connections as high-speed Internet. Basically the only difference between VOD and the Internet (besides the fact that people generally watch VOD on their TV sets) is that there is a direct connection between you and only one other computer, which is controlled by the cable company, whereas the Internet connects you to a network of computers.

This chapter will summarize the rules with regard to distributing music videos, audiovisual concerts, and music-based video or film documentaries, through both conventional broadcasting and new digital systems.

Synchronization License

A synchronization license authorizes the user to synchronize a song or other musical composition with an audiovisual work. This permission actually consists of two separate elements: the permission to reproduce the music in connection with a particular audiovisual work (e.g., a music video), coupled with certain conditions limiting how the audiovisual work may be used. Such conditions may restrict the medium in which the audiovisual work may be used (such as only on cable TV or only on the Internet), the territory of the use, and the duration of the license. There is no law or statute governing the amount of money that must be paid for a synchronization license. This, as we have discussed, is unlike a "mechanical" license. A mechanical license permits the reproduction of music in a form that may be heard with the aid of a "mechanical" device, without visual images. An example of a mechanical use of music is a standard audio-only CD. If the song has been recorded before, the mechanical use is subject to a compulsory license fee set by federal statute. Each "synch" license, in contrast, must be negotiated individually.

Master-Use License

A master-use license authorizes the user to synchronize a master, rather than a song, in an audiovisual work. In music business parlance, though, master-use licensing also refers to securing rights in masters for audio compilations. Similar to synch licenses, there is no statutory right applying to a master-use license. The owner of the master, usually a record company, or for an unsigned artist, the artist himself, can negotiate any rates and terms the market will bear and refuse to license their masters altogether.

Music Videos

By "music videos" I mean those short-form video clips consisting of one song that MTV used to show all the time, but which are now showing up with greater frequency on on-line digital services such as Launch.com and on-demand cable systems like AOL Music On Demand. Music videos are also referred to as "promo videos" because they promote sales of CDs, and now digital downloads.

For music videos, there is an industry-wide practice on the part of music publishers to grant a free license to show the video on television. This means that the publishers encourage the use of their songs on TV including MTV, VH1, and BET. Sometimes, though, a token charge of $200 or less is exacted. But the publishers (which represent most songwriters, for the purpose of licensing) generally perceive music videos as promoting record sales from which they reap mechanical royalties. Yet many publishers still limit the medium in which a music video may be shown to television because they fear that if the video plays on the Web, people will download the song without paying for it even if the digital service promises to prevent unauthorized downloading. So the publishers will be selective about which services they will deal with and require them to prove that they employ a stringent DRM, or digital management system, that will prevent free downloading and piracy.

A record company is in a much stronger position than other parties, such as a digital music service, to acquire rights in the underlying songs for exploitation of music videos on the Internet and other digital systems. This is due to the "Controlled Composition" clause contained in standard recording contracts. As we discussed in Chapter 1, this provision provides, in relevant part, that with respect to songs that the artist wrote or co-wrote, the artist grants a free synch license to the record company to use the song in any audiovisual work including short-form music videos. Sometimes the contract limits the free license to promotional uses so that if the record company were to release a compilation of music videos on a DVD, they would have to pay for the use of the songs. But the standard recording agreement will generally provide a free license for any "promotional" use of a music video *in any medium.* This means that the record company can license their promo videos to Internet-based digital music services such as Launch.com, as well as on-demand digital cable systems, without paying for the underlying song, provided that there is no charge for watching or downloading the individual video.

It is also important to note another advantage a record company has in using a music video in any media including the Internet: Most music videos are actually silent movies synchronized to prerecorded tracks. The record companies controls those prerecorded tracks. They produce the videos, i.e., the silent movies, on a work-for-hire basis and own them as well. An independent producer who makes a silent movie and synchronizes it to a prerecorded track would not only need a synch license from the songwriter to use the underlying musical composition, but would also need a master-use license from the record company to use the prerecorded musical track. The labels already own both.

Audiovisual Concerts

Another growing area of music on the Web is the transmission of live or prerecorded video concerts. But an audiovisual concert is generally viewed differently than a music video by the songwriting community. A music video, as we discussed, is generally seen as promoting record sales which will result in mechanical royalties payable to the publishers. Music videos are also generally provided to television outlets and digital music services at no charge in the hopes that the exposure will spur record sales and paid downloads. In contrast, producers of audiovisual concerts will generally seek the highest license fee they can extract from television services who wish to air the concerts. Although these fees may only reimburse the producers for the cost of recording the concert, publishers will seek payment for use of their songs because they perceive the concerts as commercial ventures rather than purely promotional. For this reason, producers or owners of audiovisual recorded concerts should expect to pay for a synch license. An exception is a live concert. Copyright law exempts live broadcast concerts from the requirement to obtain a synch license. This rule would apply to live transmission of a video concert on the Internet as well. However, if the audiovisual recording of the concert is repeated, whether on TV or the Internet, a synch license will be required.

If the artist featured in the concert also wrote the songs, the producer may be able to convince the artist or his or her music publisher to grant a free license because the concert will promote the artist's career. But this argument may not work in the case of an established artist or band such as Eminem or No Doubt. In that case, the producer will probably have to pay the standard rate for the synch license, even though the artist or the band wrote the music. Standard synch fee depends on the nature of the rights requested. For U.S. basic cable, those fees will range in the hundreds of dollars for a term of, for example, one year. A network television synch license will cost more because the networks still attract more viewers than most cable stations.

For the Internet, the fees will vary depending on the manner and duration of use sought. Certain publishers, however, will still not grant licenses for concerts on the Internet because of fears of piracy and the fear that making a concert available on the Web could cannibalize record sales. A concert producer must also decide whether to seek digital cable video-on-demand rights. Currently most producers do not even try because VOD systems have focused on movies and popular TV series such as *The Sopranos*. They have not shown much interest yet in music except for music videos. However, this may change soon because Music Choice, which is present on every large cable operator's system, has announced plans for rolling out concerts on demand. In any event, there are no standard fees for synch rights for video concerts on cable VOD systems yet.

Record companies, which occasionally produce, or hire production companies to produce, music concerts for their own artists, are in a much stronger position than most independent producers to secure publishing rights for digital transmission of video concerts. Once again, this is due to the Controlled Composition clause. As stated earlier, under the terms of a standard recording agreement, with respect to songs that the artist wrote or co-wrote, the artist grants the record company a free synch license to use the song in any audiovisual work that the record company produces. Thus, if the label produced the concert, it may be entitled to a free license, at least in songs that the artist wrote or co-wrote. Generally, these clauses are written very broadly and cover transmission *in any media.*

We have already discussed the record companies' rights in prerecorded masters for use in music videos. But record companies also have other rights that come into play in the recording of concert programs. Generally recording contracts prohibit an artist from recording music for anyone else, including audiovisual renditions of songs, without consent. Thus, if an independent producer records a concert without the label's permission, the producer may run afoul of the artist's contract with the record company, subjecting the producer to a claim of "interference with contract." However, a record company often wants to support an audiovisual recording of a concert in return for particular rights. Support could come in the form of providing for the artist's travel and accommodations, rehearsal fees, and the like. The record company may even contribute to production costs in return for certain rights, such as home video. Who would control the Internet rights would be subject to negotiation.

Performing-Rights Societies

Even if a producer succeeds in securing synch licenses for transmission of a short-form music video or a video concert on the Internet, the producer is not totally in the clear. The producer should make sure that the Internet service transmitting the concert or music video has a public-performance license to play the songs. As discussed in the prior chapter, a performance of music on the Internet is considered a public performance, and each of the three PROs offer blanket licenses to Internet music services. The producer should get the Internet service transmitting the video or concert to warrant and represent that it has secured licenses from the performance-rights societies, and assume all responsibility for their payment, including reasonable attorney fees in case of litigation.

Music-Based Documentaries

These programs may be very complicated to clear for the Internet. They usually involve many more elements to be cleared than just music. For instance a music based documentary may involve, in addition to music, prerecorded performance footage, excerpts from old TV shows, and footage from old movies. All of these elements would have to be cleared. At present the movie studios, for instance, are very reluctant to license footage for the Internet. This may change in the course of time and as the studios receive more requests for this kind of use.

Chapter 6
Music-Licensing Fundamentals

T his chapter is designed to provide an overview of music licensing. Songwriters, composers, labels, and artists can make significant income from licensing music for audio compilations, television, motion pictures, and other media. We will outline the fundamentals of music licensing for:

- Audio compilations
- Television
- Motion pictures
- DVDs
- TV advertising

We will also provide some general tips for licensing music.

Audio Compilations

Compilations can consist of a collection of new tracks by different artists. Compilations are also a popular way of selling old music in new packages. Time-Life, for instance, licenses and sells compilations of various types of music such as *Legends, The Ultimate Rock Collection* or *The Ultimate Love Songs Collection*. These are the compilations you see being pitched on late-night television.

Songs. If a compilation consists of songs that have previously been released, they are subject to the compulsory mechanical license. As we discussed in Chapter 1, the Harry Fox Agency is set up to issue mechanical licenses that incorporate the statutory mechanical rate of 8.5 cents per unit per song (or 1.65 cents per minute or fraction thereof for musical compositions over five minutes). All you need to do is to fill out forms provided by Fox indicating the names of the songs, the writers, and the publishers. Here are the exact requirements:

1. Song title
2. Songwriter's name(s)
3. Publisher name and copyright percentage splits
4. Record company name and address (if you have a contact name or phone number, this would also be helpful)
5. Catalog number (usually on the spine of a recording) and configuration (CD, LP, cassette, etc.)
6. Playing time for each selection (especially if the song is over five minutes in length)
7. Release date
8. Artist name
9. Title of album
10. Sign your name in the "Publisher's Approval" section

When completed, return the forms to Client Relations and the Fox Agency. If you have any questions, contact a Client Relations representative at 212-833-0100, or clientrelations@harryfox.com.

The Fox Agency, as we pointed out in the first chapter, also has a database, www.song-file.com, that you can use to find the writers and publishers, as well as ASCAP, BMI, and SESAC for their respective songs. Upon securing a license, the distributor can pay after the record is released. In the rare occasion that the Fox Agency does not represent a song, you will have to go to the publisher. Of course, if the song is in the public domain, as most of the classical repertoire is, you will not need permission. However, new arrangements of PD songs may be protected by copyright, and in that case you will need a license. Check for an arrangement credit on the packaging of CD, cassette, or vinyl record from which you derived the music.

Masters. You must negotiate with the owners of the masters for compilations. There is no "compulsory" rate. As a licensee, if you can get 10 cents for commercial release per track, that would be very good. The labels may request a percentage of the retail price of the compilation such as 10% plus a floor of 10 cents or more. In addition, they will seek advances. For instance, an advance of 10,000 units is commonly required. Sometimes a more difficult problem than establishing a fair rate is getting a license at all. Record companies are extremely reluctant to license tracks that are still selling well. They fear the compilation may compete with their own albums or "best of" records. Since there is no compulsory license for use of masters, they can just deny permission, and frequently do. Finally, each record company will usually ask for Most Favored Nations protection. This means that if label X insists on more money than label Y agreed to accept, and label Y conditioned its consent on MFN treatment, you would have to pay Y the additional amount. Since almost all labels want MFN, one master can screw up a reasonable rate that you have negotiated with for all the others.

Television Programs

Licensing for television can be a source of income for new songwriters as well as established ones. Companies such as LoveCat Music (www.Lovecatmusic.com) specialize in representing new music to TV producers and music supervisors who are looking to spice up cutting-edge shows such as *The Sopranos*, and humdrum shows as well. I specialize in working with TV producers in clearing music for television as well as home video. Typical fees are in the hundreds of dollars for basic cable. They can be in the thousands for network airings. If you are a producer using a prerecorded master rather than a new recording of a song, you must also clear the owner of the master as well, usually the record company. In addition, if a program includes new performances rather than just archived footage, you have to make a deal with that performer. If you are clearing pre-existing footage, then you have to make a deal with the owner of the footage.

Songs. A license of a song for inclusion in a television program is a kind of synchronization license. The fundamental terms of any TV synch license are:

The Synch Fee. The fee payable for the use of a song in a TV program will vary primarily in accordance with the rights requested. For instance, a license to use a song in a program for all forms of television will be expensive. Limiting the usage to U.S. basic cable, for instance, will considerably reduce the fee.

Duration. Publishers will generally want to limit the use of a song in the program for a specific period of time. The television service for which a program is produced, for instance, A&E, a network, or HBO, may require a producer pursuant to contract to clear a song for a specific period of time. Producers should try to limit this period in their deals with the television service. Otherwise, the synch fees could go way up, or it may even be impossible to acquire the duration required by the TV service.

Media. This term refers to the different forms of television that are requested. Choices are all forms of TV, network, cable, Pay TV, foreign TV, pay-per-view, and now VOD (see Chapter 5). As we stated, all forms of TV will be the most expensive. The producer should make sure that his or her deal with the television service limits the rights that the producer must secure to the narrowest possible form of television. For instance, if you are producing a program for A&E, the music rights that you are responsible to secure should be limited to basic cable.

Options. Options can be used to keep costs in check. Suppose the producer is not sure that he or she will get a deal for foreign TV. Instead of paying for foreign TV up front, the producer can request an option. The deal would be that *if* the producer releases the program on television in foreign countries, *then* she will pay the prenegotiated option fee.

Usage. Use of an excerpt of a song may cost less than use of a full performance. Also, if a song is heard but no one is seen performing it ("background use"), the song may be cheaper to license than if someone is depicted singing or playing an instrument ("visual vocal" use).

Promotional Use. If you are seeking to use a song in a TV program you should also ask for "promotional rights," i.e., the right to use the music to promote the show. Many publishers will limit promotional use to "in context" promotion. This means you are allowed to use the music to promote the program only by using excerpts of the program including the music—you can't strip the music and use it in a different way than it is actually used in the show.

Most Favored Nations. Music publishers will insist on MFN treatment. This means if publisher x agrees to enter into a license on a certain set of terms including fee, duration, and rights, if any other publisher receives better terms, then those terms must be applied to the deal with publisher x. Sometimes, MFN can be used as a way of securing all the music in a program on reasonable terms. Suppose a publisher controls a number of songs in the program and grants a favorable rate, that rate can then be used to secure the same rate from the other publishers. On the other hand, if one publisher demands more than all the others, you may have to pay more for all the other songs or delete the high-priced song.

Masters. All the rules above apply to masters. Generally the owners of the master will insist on MFN treatment with the owners of the songs.

Special Rule for Public Broadcast Stations. The Copyright Act provides for special rules for use of copyrighted materials, including music, on public broadcasting stations. Generally producers are not obligated to clear songs or masters for programs produced for PBS or other public broadcasting stations as defined in the act. The relevant section of the act are Sections 114 and 118.

In regard to songs, Section 118 provides for a statutory license subject to federally prescribed rates. PBS, on public TV producers' behalf—with funding from the Corporation for Public Broadcasting—will pay the federally prescribed fees to the copyright owners. But Section 118 does *not* provide for a statutory license with respect to the use of the songs in the home video distribution of the program or foreign TV. So producers have to acquire synch licenses for these uses.

In regard to masters, Section 114(b) reads in relevant part:

> The exclusive rights of the owner of copyright in a sound recording… do not apply to sound recordings included in educational television and radio programs…distributed or transmitted by or through public broadcasting entities… *Provided*, that copies or phonorecords of said programs are not commercially distributed by or through public broadcasting entities to the general public.

Note that the last sentence means that if the program is released as a DVD, the producer will have to secure master-use licenses. For instance, a documentary on Broadway musicals may have a lot of prerecorded music that would have to be cleared. (See the discussion of clearing music for DVDs below.)

Motion Pictures

The price of clearing music for movies will be primarily determined by the budget and the potential audience for the film. For instance, publishers and labels know that student or "art" films with budgets in the thousands of dollars and a potential audience of thousands of people or less cannot afford to pay dearly for music. Of course, they may decide not to grant a license at all, but if they do, the price will be commensurate with the budget and potential audience. The cost of including one song in a major motion picture, on the other hand, can and often does exceed six figures. Even with a student or independent art movie, the publishers and labels may include a clause that requires additional payments should the movie actually generate a substantial amount of income.

Rights. The most expensive license for music in a movie is one for "broad rights." Broad rights generally refers to all rights including theatrical distribution, all forms of TV throughout the world, home video, and the Internet. Because this grant of rights is all-encompassing, even an obscure song or master for a low-budget movie can be very expensive. Again, to save money you can use options.

Use. Another important factor in determining price is how the music is used in the movie. The cost of using a song over the opening credits, for example, will generally cost more than using that song as background music during a scene. The use of a brief excerpt of a song, to present another example, may cost less than using the full song.

Options. If you are a producer, you can use options to decrease your music-clearance costs. Suppose you are still looking for a theatrical distributor for your film. You may or may not find it. You may only get a TV deal. Or perhaps the only form of distribution you will be able to find is home video. Obviously you will not need broad rights. You need only the rights in the music that are necessary for the method of distribution you actually use. You can structure the license to give you options for each of these media—for instance, home video, foreign TV, U.S. cable TV, etc. You only have to "exercise" the option, that is, pay for the rights, once you have secured your deal. So you can save a lot of money by negotiating options instead of paying for rights you may not need. I know a producer who made deals for broad rights for all the music in his movie. Sadly, he never got a deal for distribution. He paid close to $50,000 for music for a movie that is still sitting in his loft.

Festival Licenses. Most music publishers and labels will give producers the right to show their movies at festivals for $250 or less for each song or track. When you secure a festival license you can save time by negotiating options for other rights.

MFN. A record company will usually insist on MFN treatment with the owners of the song embodied in the master. The music publisher of a song will also usually insist on MFN treatment with the owner of the master of that song. But with some skill and luck you can avoid MFN treatment between different songs and masters. Both labels and publishers recognize that the use of a song or master over the credits is much more important and therefore should be more expensive than other uses of music in the movie. The value of music in a movie also depends on how much is used, whether it is played in the background of a scene or someone is depicted as playing a song, how much of the song is used, and whether it is used as a theme in the movie, etc. Because of the multiple ways music can be used in a movie, you can sometimes, but not always, avoid MFN licenses. As we discussed, MFN can be a problem even if only one licensor asks for more money.

If you want to keep the song, then you have to pay everyone else at least as much, which can drive your budget way up. A strategy that a producer can use if a music copyright owner insists on MFN is to limit favored-nations treatment based on use. For example, if a song is used as background music, the producer may be able to negotiate that the price will not go up if another copyright owner insists on more money for a song that is used over the credits.

Music-Based DVDs

At a time when the recording industry is suffering a drastic decline in sales, due at least in part—according to many experts—to unauthorized downloads facilitated by the Internet, record companies are gaining a measure of solace from an increase in sales generated by another relatively new technology: digital video discs, or DVDs. The music business online news journal *Digital Music News* (www.digitalmusicnews.com) ran a story in October 2004 titled "Music DVDs Continue to Overachieve." The article reported that just as ringtones pleasantly surprised a weary record industry (see the next chapter for a discussion of ringtone licensing), so too are music DVDs. The positive sales story actually started in earnest in 2003, with revenues from music-specific videos hitting $369 million, according to the RIAA, a 56% increase from the year before. Some point to the trend starting with a Led Zeppelin double-DVD live performance that sold over one million copies.

The trend continued into 2004 after a major sales surge between January and June, with the global market growing 20%. The increases indicate that consumers are interested in purchasing music but may feel that DVDs provide a better value. DVDs, like motion pictures, are also far more time-consuming to share and download on free P2P services than are audio files.

In December 2004 the *New York Times*, in an article titled "Music Labels Look to DVDs as Sales of CDs Decline," reported that DVDs also offer a way of "wringing money out of the untold number of hours of concert footage owned by the music industry." The article cited Live Aid as an example. Initially released as a TV show featuring U2, Paul McCartney, and Madonna, *Live Aid* was first televised in 1985. Warner Music released the program as a DVD in 2004, and the DVD sold about 100,000 copies, according to Nielsen Soundscan. It's not Eminem numbers, the article stated, still "the label is happy." "*Live Aid*," the article pointed out "is one example of the growth in sales of music-related DVDs, a welcome piece of news for major labels still suffering from decline in CD sales."

DVD vs. VHS. Music DVDs, like VHS cassettes, feature live music concerts or compilations of promotional video clips. DVDs, however, feature more-brilliant visuals and higher-quality sound, are capable of containing more content than VHS cassettes are, and, similar to CDs, include "random selection" so that you can watch and listen to particular videos or performances without forwarding or reversing.

Bonus Material. Record labels can enhance sales by adding so-called "bonus" materials to each DVD release. Such bonus content usually consists of items such as photos and other images, bonus promo videos, audiovisual excerpts from TV appearances, biographies, and discographies. But the inclusion of such extra materials in DVDs raises a host of rights clearance issues.

Photos and Other Images. Bonus materials consisting of photos or other images fall into two basic categories: pictures of the artist and pictures of others. If the image depicts the artist, the record label, which has the exclusive right to distribute DVD for their current artists (see Chapter 1), generally does not need releases because recording agreements usually permit the record company to use images of an artist to promote the sale of records and videos. Of course, as a matter of artist relations, it makes good sense to allow the artist to veto the inclusion of any pictures the artist doesn't like.

Even if the only person depicted in an image is the artist, the label must make sure that it has the permission of the owner of the copyright in the image, unless it is in the public domain. Often marketing people at the labels will want to use photos from magazines, books, or newspapers. However, the labels generally do not own these images. Unless the copyright holders in these images consent to their inclusion in the DVD, the label can be liable for copyright infringement and be subject to an injunction against further sales.

There is no standard fee for the use of images in a DVD, so each clearance is a separate negotiation. This is assuming the owner can even be found. On the other hand, the labels may own the right to use images from album art or shoots that the label commissioned. Even in that case, unless the images were created by an employee, the record company must have a contract transferring the copyright to the label or granting rights covering the use of the images in the DVD.

If people other than the artist appear in an image, the label must not only clear the copyright in the image, but may also have to secure releases for those people. Because a DVD is a commercial product, the people depicted in the picture could have a right of privacy claim if the label fails to secure their permission. Even if the label can locate releases that were signed at the time that the picture was taken, that document may not be sufficient if the language of the release allows the use of the picture for promotional purposes only. In that case, a label may have to try to identify and locate the individual and enter into a new release allowing the commercial use of the image. On the other hand, if the image focuses on the artist, and the other people in the picture are not recognizable, then a release may not be required.

Music Videos. Typically, a label will commission an independent production company to produce a promotional music video. A great deal of money is invested in these promo clips. Some, particularly those featuring superstars such as Eminem or Beyoncé, may cost more than $1 million each. In exchange for a production fee (generally 15% of the "below-the-line" costs in the budget, that is, all costs except a limited number of expenses such as director and producer fees, and insurance), a production company will produce a promo video on a work-for-hire basis. This means that the label can use the video for any promotional or commercial purpose without any additional payment to, or consent from, the production company.

However, certain people appearing in the video—for instance, side-musicians, vocalists, and dancers—may be entitled to additional payments pursuant to guild agreements. Obviously the artist will generally be entitled to royalties for the DVD under his or her recording agreement. The bottom line, however, is that because the label usually owns the copyright in promo videos, their use in a DVD involves fewer clearance hurdles than the use of other bonus materials.

Written Materials. Often a label will commission a writer to create liner notes for the release of a CD. The label may want to include these materials in the bonus section of the DVD. If an employee of the label wrote the liner notes, the label would own all rights in them. If the record company commissioned them from a freelance writer, the contract would usually grant the company the right to use them in all media. But if a magazine article or newspaper review is sought, then the label will have to clear the writing from the owner, which may be the publication or the author.

Audiovisual Excerpts. Sometimes marketing and other creative types at a record company will want to include in the bonus section of a DVD footage of an artist's performance in a television show such as *Saturday Night Live*. Trying to get permission from one of these shows can be difficult because the program's producers may not want their show to be associated with the record label. However, the show may be more likely to respond favorably if the management for the artist pursues the clearance. The producers of the show may wish to stay on favorable terms with the artist.

If consent is obtained, payment is usually required. These deals usually involve an advance against a certain per-unit royalty. If the orchestra from the show or the in-house band played with the artist during the television performance, the release of the performance in a DVD may require additional union-mandated payments. Finally, if the audiovisual footage was shot at a venue such as a concert hall or stadium, other union-required payments could be triggered to labor groups such as the stagehands.

Discography. Discographies usually consist of the titles of each previous album and home video of the artist featured in the DVD. The original packaging and artwork for each such album and home video may also be shown. In addition, each song contained in the prior record and home video may be listed. By clicking on the title of each song, the consumer may be able to hear a brief excerpt of that song, or in the case of a home video, the viewer may hear and see an audiovisual excerpt.

In regard to album artwork, the labels almost always acquire the right to use such artwork to promote sales of the record in any media. Using the artwork in discographies arguably promotes sales of the old records. With respect to playing excerpts, the labels generally own the masters and the videos. But the issue is whether the labels must acquire additional licenses from the owners of the underlying music. The record companies have generally taken the position that playing small excerpts of music to promote sales of a catalog does not require additional publishing licenses. To the knowledge of this writer, the songwriting community has not challenged this position. Further, if the artist wrote or co-wrote the song, the labels would generally have the right to use the music for this purpose under the "Controlled Composition" clause (see Chapter 1).

Internet Transmission and Video on Demand. Although music-based long-form programs embodied in DVDs are not generally offered for streaming and/or download because of bandwidth limitations, as technology becomes more sophisticated and more powerful, they soon may be. Thus a producer's lawyer or clearance person should think about clearing the various forms of content discussed above for these media, as well as home video. Such deals may be structured as options and not to be paid unless and until the producer is ready to distribute the DVD as a stream and/or download. In addition, as digital cable video-on-demand systems roll out to more households, this may be another medium for distribution of music-based long-form programs, and therefore another option that should be structured into licenses for content.

DualDiscs. At about the time this book goes to press, the major labels were expected to start a major marketing push for DualDisc, a new format that contains a traditional music CD on one side and a music-based DVD on the other. The idea is to give consumers a big incentive to buy a CD. It is also impractical for people to freely exchange the content in DualDiscs on free P2P services.

Negotiating a License for Use of Music in Television Advertising

We are all familiar by now with the use of pop music in national television commercials, such as the Rolling Stones' "Start Me Up" for Microsoft. Due in part to the success of these campaigns, popular songs are being licensed for TV spots with increasing frequency. This section addresses the financial parameters of these licenses, key deal points, and practical tips for negotiation.

The Song. The most important element in determining the fee for which music may be licensed in a television campaign is the song itself.

Contemporary Mega-Hits. As one may expect, the highest quotes, or fees charged, may be for recent smash hits. There may be little room for negotiation here, because once a song is licensed, its value to another sponsor is radically reduced. Therefore, the copyright owner, who is usually either the publisher and/or the writer, may hold out for the highest royalty price, assuming that the writer is even willing to license the song for a commercial use. The only meaningful leverage is to solicit lower quotes for comparable songs. In any event, the going rate for such hit songs may be a million dollars or more.

Catalog Songs. An advertiser may be willing to settle for a song that may be recognizable but not currently on the charts. Of course one can expect to pay less for a catalog song than for a contemporary smash hit, but a routine call to a publisher asking for the "standard fee" for use of such a song in a national television campaign may well precipitate a response such as: "We will not license any song in our catalog for less than $150,000 to $250,000 for a one-year period" (a typical duration for a license of music for a television campaign discussed below). A pop standard such as "Strangers in the Night," or "Wicked Game" (which was used in a television campaign by Jaguar), may garner prices well beyond the "standard" range. The bottom line is that the more popular the song, the more it will be in demand for commercial use, and the higher the demand, the higher the royalty price. On the other hand, there are many songs in the catalogs of major and smaller publishers alike that, although recognizable when originally released, have neither received significant television or radio airplay nor have been used in movies or commercials for some time. The fee for such songs, which are of proven quality and which may work perfectly for a client's product, may well be negotiated lower than the standard range. The bottom line is that an offer, even if less than the publisher's standard, is better than no money at all. A publisher may also be hopeful that the advertising campaign will rekindle interest in its song. For instance, the Gap's use of K.C. and the Sunshine Band's "Get Down Tonight" revived catalog sales for the band's records. In addition, the tips that appear in the last part of this section may be helpful in getting the lowest possible rates for songs in this category.

There are also certain sections of a publisher's catalog composed of jazz, new-age, and R&B songs that are catchy but which have never had any real commercial success. The publisher may be eager to make a deal for these underutilized songs. Although the songs never received a great deal of public play and would not be recognizable to the consumer, they may fit the spirit and texture of an advertising campaign quite well. These songs may be secured for substantially less than the standard range. However, one can still expect to pay more taking this approach than by going to a music library or "jingle" house and licensing or commissioning a work specifically for a commercial.

Baby Bands. Publishers also represent songs by unknown artists. They may want to use a national advertising campaign to gain exposure for such baby bands (just as they may wish to gain exposure for older songs that have not been popular for years). If this is the case, one has a reasonable chance to negotiate a deal well below the standard range.

Other Criteria. In addition to the identity of the song itself, there are several factors that will be key ingredients in the quote provided by the publisher. As in any negotiation, the initial quote will probably start on the high end. If any of these factors favor the advertiser, however, they may be used to reduce the initial quote.

Manner of Use. If one only needs a song to play in the background while, for instance, a spokesman is making a pitch, one can argue for a reduced rate. In addition, sometimes the lyrics to a song are not needed. Since, in effect, one is only using half of the song, one may be able to negotiate a reduced rate.

Branding. Publishers may start off with a quote that includes the concept that an advertiser will use no music other than the licensed song to promote the product or services. This is sometimes referred to as "branding." If an advertiser will actually use different music for different commercials, this should be emphasized as a possible way of reducing the fee.

Radio and Other Media. A publisher will often demand an extra 5% to 15% for use of a song in radio spots. This charge is usually negotiated as an option to run concurrently with the television advertisement. However, for obscure, catalog, or baby-band songs, it may be possible to include radio without an additional charge. This may provide the song with some much-needed publicity and public-performance income. (See the conversation of public-performance income in the first Practical Tip below.) This may be used as leverage to get as many media as possible (such as theatrical use preceding movies) without an extra charge. Securing Internet rights however, particularly when one is not willing to pay additional fees, may be more difficult (see the conversation on clearing music for new media in the next chapter).

Territory. The quotes above assume that the territory for an advertising campaign is limited to the United States, its possessions, and territories. Of course, one can dramatically reduce the initial fee where an advertisement is targeting a specific geographic market. For example, a very low fee may be negotiated for use in just one geographical market. Sometimes, an advertiser may wish to start a commercial in specific cities, and if the commercial proves to be successful with viewers, expand the commercial to the entire country. In that case, one may structure an option for the entire United States for a one-year period after the initial limited run.

Publishers will generally try to negotiate an additional 10% to 20% charge for the use of commercials in Canada. If a song is less than a major hit or a pop standard, it may be possible to negotiate Canadian rights into the basic fee, or at least reduce the standard increase.

Options for Extending the Term. The quotes referred above are also based on the assumption of a one-year license. This gives an advertiser time to roll out its campaign and generate momentum. Of course, those fees may be negotiated down for a shorter period. Options generally cost 5% to 15% for each additional period. For instance, if the fee is $10,000 for a 13-week period, a publisher may ask for $11,000 to exercise an option for the next 13 weeks. Or the additional charge may be avoided by paying, for example, $20,000 up front.

Master Use. Sometimes publishers will make a recording of a song for the purpose of licensing the music. In that case it may be possible to include the right to use the master produced by the publisher for no additional payment. Generally, the master will be controlled by a record company. In that case, one may expect that the record company will insist on a fee equal to that of the publisher. For the use of popular recordings by big-name artists, this could double an already substantial payment. Use of and payment for the master can be avoided by rerecording the song.

Practical Tips

Note: Publishers Are Paid Twice. The publisher, and the writers it represents, will get paid twice if an advertiser uses a song; first by the advertiser when the ad is produced, and then by the publisher's performing-rights society (ASCAP, BMI, or SESAC) when the ad is broadcast. The societies pay the publisher and writer based on public performances of the songs on television and radio, as well as in other public venues. The income generated by these performances can be substantial when the commercials appear on network television and in television syndication. If a publisher does not license the song, it has that much more to lose, so it is important to reaffirm what it has to gain when negotiating a deal.

Give Them a Budget. Some publishers will work with you if you let them know how much you or your client is willing to spend. As discussed above, ask a publisher for a standard range for a catalog song and the publisher will start with $150,000 and up. If you suggest $50,000, the publisher may suggest songs that are in your or your client's price range. In fact, the publisher may give you CDs containing those songs to listen to and choose from.

Consult the Experts. There are music-clearance professionals who are very experienced in negotiating these deals. You may wish to avail yourself of that expertise.

Approach the Writer. If you know the writers or composers, it may be better to approach them first. Writers may be more eager to make a deal for a song than publishers who represent many other writers whose work may bring in higher fees. In certain cases, the writer may be able to make a deal without the publisher's consent, but even if the publisher is the exclusive agent for making the deal, the writer may be your advocate for a reasonable rate.

Don't Focus on the Number of Spots, Unless You Are Producing Only One. The publisher may ask for more money for the use of a song if it focuses on the fact that the producer plans to make more than one version of a commercial containing the song. You may want to avoid the issue and hope that the license provided by the publisher will not limit your right to use the songs in more than one television spot. If you focus the publisher on the notion that you want to make a dozen different spots using the publisher's song, the publisher may ask for more money. Of course, more-sophisticated publishers will bring up this point during the course of negotiations. If you only wish to use the music in one spot, however, it is to your advantage to emphasize that in an attempt to reduce the fee.

Consider Using Stock Music or a Jingle House. If you are not looking for a recognizable song, you may be better off not approaching a music publisher at all. There are many music libraries and jingle houses that may be able to provide music composed on a work-for-hire basis that will work for your commercial. They are also more likely to control the masters as well.

Interview: Tips for Music Licensing

Entertainment Law & Finance, January 2003

In the following interview, I respond to questions from *ELF* about practical considerations involved in music licensing.

ELF: What kinds of projects do you work on?

Steve Gordon: TV, movies, documentaries, compilation albums, DVDs, and Internet-based projects. I recently worked on several interesting jobs in cooperation with Universal Media Inc. [a company specializing in finding footage and music]. These projects included a documentary on Latin jazz for the Smithsonian Institution, a companion record album for Smithsonian Folkways Recordings, a network TV special featuring the music of Elvis Presley, and a PBS special featuring Frank Sinatra's duet performances from his old TV series, to be released as a home video and on foreign TV. Currently, I'm working on an independent movie about a serial murderer who targets punk-rock fans, containing more than two dozen songs and masters. I also represent a publicly traded Internet content provider that is continually securing rights in all kinds of content, including music, videos, and computer games.

ELF: What is the process for securing copyright clearances?

SG: The process is basically the same for any kind of project. Research the songs, strategize with the client, negotiate the terms, and review or, in certain instances, prepare the licenses. In regard to the last item, music publishers and labels will usually provide their own licenses. However, occasionally a small label, publisher, or unsigned artist will request that you draft the license.

With respect to research, the kind of material to be cleared will dictate the nature of research to be performed. For instance, for musical compositions, the ASCAP and BMI databases are excellent sources for identifying the writers and music publishers. Each of these databases may have to be explored because each performing-rights organization provides information only on the songs in its own repertory. SESAC also administers certain songs that will not be included on the ASCAP or BMI sites. In addition, the Harry Fox Agency provides information concerning songs that it represents [see www.Songfile.com]. If your client is using musical recordings, the packaging and liner notes can supply information such as the name of the record company and artist and the release date. If the client is using excerpts of TV, movie, or video footage, someone should view the credits from the original TV program, movie, or music video to determine the TV service, studio, or record label that controls the copyright in the footage. The musical artists, actors, and other persons (or their estates) appearing in the footage may also have to be cleared depending on various circumstances, including whether there is a musical performance in the footage.

Once you have identified those who control rights in the material to be used, you are almost ready to approach the owners and negotiate terms. [A sample license follows this interview.] But first you must strategize with the client. This conversation should include what rights will be required, that is, media, territory, duration; what you think it will cost; and what to propose to the licensors. This process is the real "art" of licensing. With knowledge of the applicable business practices and pricing, you can advise your client on the approximate amount of money he or she will have to pay for clearances; alert him or her to potential problems, such as material that may be too expensive and may have to be replaced; and develop a letter addressed to the owners accurately reflecting the precise rights that your client needs and proposing the lowest reasonable fee or royalty. The proposed payment, which obviously must be approved by the client, should be as low as possible and include a cogent explanation of the reasons that the owner should accept such a rate. At the same time, the proposal should not be so out of whack with standard business practices that the owner feels insulted.

The negotiation process involves a discussion with the copyright owner or its representative about the project, plus continual follow-up. Many of the projects on which I work will not make a great deal of money for any individual copyright owner. For that reason, many of these requests usually are low-priority items to the people from whom I am seeking permission. To do this work, therefore, a combination of courtesy and persistence is recommended.

Ultimately, if the licensor doesn't accept your terms, you will have to negotiate compromises or even advise the client to drop the desired music. For instance, trying to get a hit song for an independent movie may not happen because the song owner may not like your client's project, or may not wish to license it to anyone at any price, or may propose a fee well beyond your client's ability to pay.

Finally, the owner will send the license, and it is my responsibility to make sure that the terms in the license exactly match the understanding between my client and the owner.

ELF: What issues arise specifically in the case of independent movies?

SG: From a clearance point of view, the most important difference between an independent film and a major studio production is that an independent producer usually has a lot less money to spend on anything, including music. Therefore, an independent filmmaker may have to curb his or her desire for securing "name-brand" talent. For instance, if your client wants to use "Satisfaction" under the opening credits, that is going to cost big bucks indeed, unless he or she happens to be a personal friend of Mick Jagger, and even then, don't assume a huge discount.

Even if Mick Jagger is your client's best friend, the people who administer the Stones' copyrights may never have heard of your client. Music publishers and labels generally will adjust their rates downward based on the size of a movie's budget. But don't expect to pay a nominal fee for a hit song just because your client's budget is modest. Independent film producers should also understand that no matter how popular or recognizable the music in a movie is, people don't watch movies to listen to music. A lawyer or clearance person can work with a savvy producer to create a great soundtrack without busting the budget. For instance, many music publishers, labels, and managers may be eager to place new songs written by "baby bands" that will be more reasonably priced than songs written by established acts. Another alternative is a "stock" music house. Generally, these firms can license both the song and the master, and therefore offer one-stop shopping as well as low prices. Finally, a composer or songwriter/producer can be hired to write music for specific scenes, or a complete score. There are many talented but hungry songwriters who would be happy to work on a client's project for a credit and a reasonable fee.

Another way to work within a client's budget is to set up the quote request as a series of options. Generally, a film festival license can be secured for a small fee because music publishers and labels recognize that festivals are not commercial enterprises. Additional rights such as theatrical, free TV, cable, and home video can be requested as options. Each one may be exercised by paying a specific fee. "Broad rights"—which include theatrical, TV, and home video—can be expensive. In case your client does not succeed in securing commercial theatrical distribution, these options will allow him or her to gain exposure for the movie (on cable TV, for instance) for a reasonable fee without paying for unnecessary rights.

ELF: Please describe the deal points (e.g., term, territory, royalties, or fees).

SG: The term will vary depending on the nature of the project. Of course, you always would like to secure perpetual rights for your client. But that may not always be possible. For instance, in regard to a TV project, music publishers and labels will customarily limit the term to three to five years. A longer period will cost a lot more money. One way to accommodate future uses is, again, to set up options. The original term can be three years, with an option for another three. That way, your client doesn't have to pay the additional fees unless he or she actually exploits the program for a longer term. Movie and TV producers will generally seek worldwide to maximize the audience for, and income from, their projects. Producers of album compilations, on the other hand, may wish to target the U.S. and Canada market only. So the scope of the territory provision will depend on the business interests of your client. Of course, the most important item in virtually all clearance licenses will be the money. Generally, flat fees will be required for TV and movies because that is the standard business practice. On the other hand, if you license a song or master for an album or a home video, you can expect to pay a penny rate per unit. How much you pay will depend primarily on the nature of the project. In regard to a compilation album, although there are exceptions, the owner of the track (generally a record company) will require a per-unit penny rate against an advance. If the penny rate is 10 cents, then an advance payment of $1,000 may be required, with a "rollover" payment of another $1,000 for sales exceeding 10,000, and additional rollover payments after that for each block of 10,000 units. The underlying song will be subject to a statutory mechanical license, currently 8 cents per unit, although it may be possible to secure reductions from such rate in certain circumstances (if a charitable purpose is involved, for example). Clearing music for a motion picture is a whole different ball game because there is no compulsory license for use of musical compositions in audiovisual works. The money demanded for even a never-quite-famous song can easily reach six figures for a movie to be distributed by a major studio. The owner of the master, usually the record company, probably will want at least an equal amount for the master recording.

ELF: What is meant by the phrase "Most Favored Nations"?

SG: Also referred to as "MFN," this is a business practice that can affect all the terms of a license. It means that you cannot treat the owner or licensor of content less well than any other owner or licensor of content used in a similar manner. The practice is very common in regard to concert TV programs featuring a dozen full-length musical performances. No one who licenses any song for such a program wants to get less money or give more rights than any other licensor. MFN also plays a big role in audio compilation albums. It exists but is less common in regard to clearing music for movies, because in a movie each piece of music is often used in a different way. For instance, one song may be used over the credits, another song may be used for only a few moments in the background of a scene, and another song may be heard as a theme throughout the movie.

ELF: What are some reasons that a copyright clearance cannot be secured?

SG: Money is the most common reason. In regard to a movie, although some baby bands, composers, or songwriters may love the exposure that your client can create, established artists and bands may not need the exposure. They already have it. Therefore, the price can be prohibitively high. To give a recent example from my own practice, we could not get the price of a Bee Gees song down for an independent movie. So we replaced it with a new song composed by my client. Another problem is that the copyright owner, or his or her representative, may not wish to be associated with your client's project for whatever reason. I once had a problem with getting permission to use "Macarena" for a Chipmunks video. Apparently, the composers did not relish the idea of their song being performed by cartoon characters.

ELF: What are the possible penalties if copyright clearances are not secured?

SG: Perhaps the worst-case scenario is an injunction, which is available as a remedy for copyright infringement. Your client's project could be shut down completely. If it's yanked out of distribution, not only are potential profits lost, but there also could be serious expenses incurred in retrieving the product from warehouses or retail outlets (as there would be if a DVD were involved). Of course, copyright owners have other remedies available to them, including statutory damages and attorney fees, if they properly registered their works. Therefore, the price of using a copyright without permission can be quite steep indeed.

ELF: What is the role of a music supervisor?

SG: A good music supervisor can identify music that could enhance your client's project. But due to budget constraints, experienced music supervisors make their living working with big studio productions. When they can be afforded, they have knowledge and contacts that could prove valuable, especially when it comes to finding new, cutting-edge music. The client can't depend on lawyers or clearance people to be his or her "ears." Depending on the budget, therefore, the client may have to be his or her own music supervisor, although a knowledgeable lawyer with good industry contacts can be very helpful.

ELF: What is involved in licensing music for Internet-based projects? How is it or other new technologies an emerging area for clearances?

SG: New technologies, including the Internet, have created new uses for all kinds of content. New business practices and forms of licensing have also emerged. The issues and rules can be quite complex, depending on what you are trying to do (e.g., webcasting, streaming, or downloading) and the kind of content you are trying to clear (interactive games, music, etc.). Perhaps the fastest-growing areas of music licensing are interactive webcasting and video on demand. Already, satellite systems and digital-cable modem services are offering content on demand. Concert specials accommodate themselves beautifully to these new technologies. Eventually, concert videos may also be available on the Web on an on-demand basis. Therefore, in addition to clearing a concert special for TV and home video, clearance people will find themselves clearing for on-demand uses. This will entail educating the licensor as to the new technologies and, in the case of webcasting, assuring copyright owners that your client will protect the owners' copyrights with encryption technologies to prevent piracy.

Sample Clause for Synchronization License

Basic Cable Television
Date: _____

In consideration of the terms and provisions of this agreement as hereinbelow set forth, we hereby license to you, the nonexclusive right to record the musical selection set forth below in synchronization or timed relationship with the single television production known as "_____" in the territory and for the purposes hereinbelow described.

    This license shall apply and be limited to the musical composition and type and duration of usage set forth below, and as compensation therefore you agree to pay and we agree to accept the sums indicated.

TITLE: _____

COMPOSER(s):   _____

TYPE OF USE: _____

PERFORMING RIGHTS ORG.   _____

FEE: $_____

OWNERSHIP SHARE: %_____

    This license herein granted is limited specifically to use in connection with the origination, transmission, and public exhibition of said production by means of Basic Cable Television, provided, however, that production will not be exhibited by so-called pay, subscription, or commercial television, or similar method, and will not be recorded or exhibited on audiovisual cassettes or any other sight-and-sound device, without our prior written consent, it being understood that such usages shall require licensing and payment of additional fees to be negotiated between us. No sound recording shall be manufactured, sold, licensed, or used separate or apart from said film or videotape.

(1) Basic Cable Television shall mean exhibition throughout the Territory of the Program performing the Compositions by means of cable television, whether such programming is transmitted by wires, cables, satellite, or other communication channels, for which members of the public may pay for the transmission service provided by the cable system, but do not otherwise pay a premium for the programming transmitted by such cable system.

(2) The license herein granted is a license to synchronize and record only and does not authorize or permit any other use, it being understood that performing-rights licenses must be secured from any performing-rights society or other entity having the legal right to issue such licenses as the owner of or on behalf of the owner of such rights in any licensed territory in which the music as recorded hereunder may be performed. All rights of every nature and description not herein expressly licensed to you are reserved by us for our use and benefit.

continued . . .

(3) You shall have the further right, but at your sole cost and expense, to edit, arrange and re-arrange the music and lyrics for purposes of recording hereunder, provided that no substantial music or lyric changes shall be made without our prior written consent. This license shall not be deemed to include any right to parody the original music and/or lyrics of the songs. Any new arrangements hereunder shall be made only by persons acting as "employees for hire," but at your sole cost and expense, and all copyrights therein and all renewals, extensions, and reversionary rights interests thereof throughout the world shall be deemed assigned to and owned by the copyright owner of the underlying composition, subject to your use under this agreement.

(4) The license herein granted shall be for and limited to the territory of _____.

(5) Your rights for use covered by this license shall commence on the effective date of first broadcast in _____ for a period of two years.

(6) On expiration of such term, all rights licensed hereunder shall revert to us without further notice and in their entirety.

(7) On completion of production, you shall furnish to us two copies of the music cue sheets for said production (if such a cue sheet has not been furnished previously with regard to the production).

(8) No warranty or representation is made in connection with this license except that we warrant that we have the right to issue this license subject to the terms and conditions hereof. In any event, our total liability under such warranty is limited to the amount paid by you hereunder.

(9) This license shall run to you, your successors, and assigns, provided that you shall remain liable for the performance of all the terms and conditions of this license on your part to be performed, and provided further that any disposition of said film or videotape of any copies thereof shall be subject to all the terms hereof.

(10) License will become null and void if payment not received within 60 days of dated license.

(11) This is the entire agreement between the parties with respect to the subject matter hereof. No modification, amendment, waiver, termination or discharge of this agreement shall be binding unless in writing and signed by the party to be charged. No waiver of any provision shall be a continuing waiver thereafter. This agreement shall be deemed to have been made in the state of New York and its validity, construction, performance, breach, and operation shall be governed by the laws of the state of New York or, if applicable, the United States copyright law.

IN WITNESS WHEREOF, the parties have caused the foregoing to be executed as of the date first above written.

PUBLISHER   LICENSEE

By: _____   By: _____

Chapter 7

Licensing Music for New Media

igital technologies have created some exciting new possibilities for licensing both prerecorded music and songs. This chapter explores legal and business issues pertaining to licensing music for:

- Web sites
- Ringtones
- Video games

Background Music for Web Sites

This section is written from the point of view of those who wish to license music for use in their Web site. Of course, if you are an artist or indie label you will use your own music. This section is intended for people who are not artists but would like to add music to their site.

Free. Licensing music for a Web site is easy if you write and record your own music. You own it; you can use it any way you want. You can also ask a musician friend to write and record music for the Web site in exchange for a prominent credit.

Public Domain. You can also use "public domain" music (see Chapter 1) for free. But be careful—even music by Mozart—whose compositions are in the public domain—may be embodied in a recording that is still protected by copyright. The solution is to rerecord the PD music to avoid using a copyrighted master.

Small Fee. You can easily find a local musician to write and record new music for your Web site. Craigslist.com and local music schools are good places to start your search. You can also go to a music library and pay a small amount for a license to use various forms of music.

Expensive or Impossible. If your heart is set on having a famous song such as "Satisfaction" playing in the background of your Web site, you may be setting yourself up for heartbreak instead of satisfaction. If you have read the previous chapters, you know that if you wish to use the Stones' recording of "Satisfaction," you will have to deal with at least two different copyrights: the owner of the copyright in the master and the owner of copyright in the song. Many record labels and publishers of hit songs will flatly refuse to license the music for a personal Web site. They are often afraid that the song will be in digital form and could be illegally copied. They may think the administrative hassle involved in licensing your Web site for the price you can afford to pay is not worth their time and may have a pre-existing policy simply not to issue any license for background use on Web sites. Or they may have a policy of charging a minimum fee of at least several thousand dollars. This policy would only allow well-heeled corporations or individuals to license music for Web sites.

Even if you rerecord a hot song, you will still need the agreement of the music publisher. There is no compulsory license available for use of the song because, unlike a mechanical royalty using music as background to your Web site is a synchronization. The compulsory license available for the rerecording of a song only applies to audio-only uses such as rerecording of a song for CD.

If you feel you really must at least try, you can ask for quotes yourself. The advantage of using a clearance professional is that they have relationships with the licensors and can at least get them to respond to a request. Once you have a quote you can decide if it's worth it.

Background Music for Video Producers of DVDs of Weddings and Holidays. I have received a number of calls from people who produce videos for weddings and holidays. They often want to use music in the background of their Web sites which promote their wedding DVD business. All the comments above apply to this kind of use. Moreover, if they want to use well known songs in their DVDs, they have the additional problem of getting a synch license from the publishers for use in the DVD and a master use license for the record. Again I would recommend composing your own music, or commissioning a friend or music student, or licensing music from a music library.

Ringtones

The Business. Ringtones are those little snippets of music that people are using more and more instead of an ordinary ring to announce incoming calls on their cell phones. Although some may find them annoying, in the U.S. market alone, total sales have doubled from approximately $150 million in 2003 to more than $300 million in 2004. Worldwide use of ringtones is, however, truly amazing. Consect, a provider of mobile market research and analysis, announced in its 2004 Mobile Music Report that global mobile phone ring-tone sales will total $4 billion in 2004! Mark Frieser, Consect's CEO, said: "Ringtone sales are becoming a significant component of the music industry's business, exceeding that of digital music downloads even at this early stage of the market."

Clearances. Ringtones started with polyphonic MIDI files composed of rerecordings of popular songs—not the original recordings themselves. Therefore, the only clearances were for the songs. Since new recordings were made by ringtone services such as Zingy and Modtones, they owned the new masters. They would then turn around and license the music to cell phone service providers such as Verizon and AT&T. Now "mastertones" are gaining in popularity. Mastertones are the original sound recordings, generally in an MP3 format. Their use, of course, requires the permission of the owners of sound recordings, generally the record companies, as well as the owners of the copyrights of the songs. Some record companies are now creating their own ring- and mastertones. Since the record companies control the masters under the recording agreement with the artists, they generally do not need permission. However, powerful artists may have clauses in their contracts that require their consent.

The music is usually approximately 30 seconds long and plays when someone calls you. The tones are generally available for purchase by the cell phone subscriber for the life of the phone. The cost to the consumer varies, but typical prices are $1.99 for MIDI poly-phonic tones and $2.50 for mastertones.

Cell phones made before 2002 usually cannot play ringtones, but phones made within the last two years generally can, and the newer crop of phones can play master-tones. Mastertones are expected to dominate the market as people replace their old cell phones with new ones.

Songs/Mechanicals. After several years of continuous negotiation between ringtone companies and labels on the one side and the music publishers on the other, this is still a very volatile and controversial area of music licensing. Most ringtone companies and labels would like to pay the same rate that applies to digital downloads: 8.5 cents. Some publishers have agreed to this rate. But others have insisted on higher rates. Ringtones are not considered to be subject to a compulsory license, perhaps because Section 115 requires that a person may obtain a compulsory license "only if his or her primary pur-pose in making phonorecords is to distribute them to the public for private use, in-cluding by means of a digital phonorecord delivery." Ringtones are arguably not "private" as they can be heard anywhere the telephone happens to ring, including pub-lic places.

Most deals for rates can be divided into polyphonic MIDIs and mastertones. The deals for polyphonic MIDIs generally range from 8.5 cents to 10 cents. The deals for mastertones generally vary from 10 cents to the greater of 10 cents, or 10%. Since mastertones can cost $2.50, 10% would be 25 cents. The record companies and the ringtone middle-man companies hate this because they have to pay the publishers out of what they receive from the cell phone services. Publishers also sometimes require "server fixation" fees that are in addition to the per-sale royalty. These fixation fees vary from nominal to significant depending on a number of factors, including the policies of the individual publisher and the identity and number of songs requested.

Ringtone services or record labels that wish to obtain licenses to make and distribute ringtones can apply to the Harry Fox Agency for a license. The process involves the following steps: The prospective licensee proposes a rate for monophonic tones or polyphonic tones and a server fixation fee. The prospective licensee then enters into a written agreement with HFA. Next, HFA sends a notice of each deal to its publisher-principals, who may then choose whether or not to participate in the agreement. The ringtone service or record label must then request licenses for songs it wants to use as ringtones on a song-by-song basis. (HFA does not offer blanket licensing.) HFA will then issue licenses only for portions of musical compositions owned or controlled by those publisher-principals who have indicated that they wish to participate in a particular agreement. If an HFA-issued license does not cover 100% of a musical composition, the licensee is responsible for obtaining a license from the publisher(s) controlling the remaining interest.

Songs/Performing Rights. The PROs take the position that ringtones are public performances. This position is justified by the definition of Public Performance in the Copyright Act, reading in relevant part that to perform a work "publicly" means:

> . . . to transmit or otherwise communicate a performance or display of the work to a place specified by clause (1) or to the public, by means of any device or process, whether the members of the public capable of receiving the performance or display receive it in the same place or in separate places and at the same time or at different times.

ASCAP, BMI, and SESAC all offer licenses specifically for ringtone services. Ringtone providers can secure a blanket license just as background music services such as Muzak do. The licenses are based on a small percentage of revenue, just as most of the other licenses offered by the PROs.

Masters. As we discussed, if ringtone providers rerecord popular songs for MIDI polyphonic use, they do not need the permission of the owners of the masters. But ringtone companies who seek masters for use in mastertones have to negotiate with the labels. The deals are extremely varied and can depend on the popularity of the artist. With respect to stars, the labels will consult with these artists even if they do not need their permission under the recording agreement. The deals are also highly confidential, but the range is generally a percentage of the retail price with the low end at 20% and going up to 40% or even higher. Out of this fee the label must pay the artist pursuant to the recording agreement. Generally, the artist will be entitled to payment of 50% minus authorized expenses incurred by the labels. However, if the artist is not "recouped," that is, if the artist's records have not sold enough copies to reimburse the label for recording costs and other recoupable expenses, the money otherwise payable to the artist will be "allocated" to his account.

The Future of Music and Cell Phones. A parallel development to ringtones is using your cell phone as if it were an MP3 player. In September 2004 Microsoft announced plans to move into the mobile space, with plans ahead to integrate audio and video software in upcoming handsets. That could include a mobile-version of the new MSN Music download offering, allowing consumers to grab tracks between calls. As phones evolve to accommodate media like full songs and video, alliances have cropped up between Loudeye/Nokia and iTunes/Motorola. While Microsoft has taken its time entering the digital music store space, it may not waffle as next generation mobile handsets come to market. Comments Windows Digital Media director Erik Huggers to Reuters, "The sales numbers (of mobile phones) are staggering. It's obvious that it's our goal to sign up all major handset makers."

If your cell phone is also an MP3 player containing your music library, you might have the capacity to make any music in your record collection into your ringtone. The challenge for content providers would then be to find ways of making consumers pay for the privilege. To the present date, digital right management technology (DRM), which is composed of a variety of technical systems designed to protect and facilitate payments for music on the Internet, has not provided solutions to eradicating piracy or free music. Although DRM could be used to pay for music if consumers played by the industry's rules, the sharing of billions of songs by millions of people over P2P services demonstrates that many people are not willing to play by those rules.

Video Games

The Increasing Importance of Music to Video Games and the Increasing Importance of Video Games to the Music Business. The sale of video games is a huge business. The income from sales of a successful game can rival the financial success of a major motion picture. An article in the *New York Times* dated November 14, 2004, and titled "Hollywood Would Kill for Those Numbers" by Michael Marriott, reported that Microsoft estimated that first day sales of Halo 2—its best-selling video game that plays on Microsoft's Xbox console—were $125 million. According to Marriott, Microsoft "executives gleefully note[d]" that this amount "topped the opening weekend of the animated-film-of-the-moment, *The Incredibles*, by some $55 million." Last year, the sales of video games exceeded $20 billion worldwide.

Paralleling the growing popularity of video games has been another pattern: Many of the hottest video games are using more music, both previously released tracks (including those by superstars as well as underground hits), and music specifically composed, produced, and recorded for particular games. In the midst of dwindling opportunities to break new music on commercial radio or MTV, and the slump in CD sales, both indie artists and major record companies see opportunities. Video games are becoming both an important resource in breaking new talent and an important new source of revenue for big labels and established artists.

The first page of the Business Section of the *New York Times* on November 15, 2004, carried an article titled "Hey, Cool Music. And There's a Video Game Too?" by Noah Robischon. The first paragraph reported:

> When the rapper Snoop Dogg's version of the 1971 song "Riders on the Storm" makes its debut tomorrow, it will not premiere on MTV or on the radio. Instead, the song, which was recorded with the surviving members of the Doors and includes outtakes of Jim Morrison's vocals, will be heard on Need For Speed Underground 2, a video game from Electronics Arts.

The article's main point was that video games have become an important avenue for the marketing and distribution of music. Robischon explains that the Doors were looking for a "way of reinventing their catalog for a new generation," and Snoop had long wanted to cover and release "Riders." Certain record company executives now believe that many listeners are no longer discovering music via radio or even MTV. Instead they are learning about and listening to new artists through new media such as the Internet, satellite radio, and now, video games.

Due to the steep decline in sales of CDs in the last several years, video games have also emerged as an important source of revenue for record companies and recording artists. For instance, Robischon reports that when Electronic Arts was creating the 21-song lineup for Madden NFL 2005, one of their most popular games, the labels sent 2,500 songs for consideration. In addition, songwriters and those who compose original music for video games are also benefiting from the coalescence of video games and music.

Now that we know that music is a vital element in many video games, and that video games are a more and more important player in promoting new music and in offsetting the decline of traditional revenues, what are the parameters of the deals?

Licensing Parameters. Music in games is used in various ways. Often, for instance, music plays in the background of many scenes in a game. Another example is that music is used as a control. For example, every time you hear a guitar playing a certain theme, the player is prompted to do something else in the game. This kind of music is generally commissioned on a work-for-hire basis. That means that the musicians/composers who create this music generally transfer all their rights in the music and the recordings to the producer. The price of this kind of job is often paid based on the amount of music composed and delivered. Generally the price can be $1,500 per minute and up. Respected composers/musicians with a track record for composing for games can make quite a bit more. Note that these work-for-hire agreements generally apply to both the master and the underlying musical composition.

Some video games employ music in an entirely different way. For instance, the Madden 2005 game will feature prerecorded masters, some of which have already had considerable success. This is similar to a movie that uses certain highly recognizable music to conjure up a style or an era. Use of highly successful songs in major motion pictures can fetch six-figure fees and up each for the song and the master. Licensing of famous songs and masters in video games may never reach these levels because video games do not have as many "windows" as a movie. For instance, a movie can be theatrically released, placed on pay cable, network, and home video. However, as games gain in popularity and in production budgets (some are rumored to cost almost as much to produce as major movies), the price of these licenses may eventually rival the prices for use of popular music in blockbuster movies. Also similar to licensing prerecorded songs for movies, and unlike composers who are commissioned on a work-for-hire basis, the rights conveyed under these licenses will generally be limited, and the copyright in the master will generally be reserved by the artist or his record company, and the copyright in the underlying music will remain with the composer and/or his music publisher.

Another way that music is used in video games is that certain video game producers are engaging highly successful artists to create new recordings specifically for their games. A good example is the Need For Speed game discussed above, which will contain a new Snoop Dogg version of the Door's "Riders on the Storm." This song will be a featured part of the video, and you can bet it cost more than $1,500 per minute to acquire the rights! You can also safely assume that Electronic Arts did not secure the copyright in the master. The underlying composition is already controlled by the Doors' publishing company, and no doubt they retained the copyright in the song.

Note that the compulsory license rate of 8.5 cents per song per copy does not apply to the use of musical compositions in a video game because, as with movies, these are audiovisual uses and the compulsory license applies solely to audio-only uses.

Soundtracks. There have been instances where game producers have spun off soundtracks based on music contained in their games. So far these soundtracks have not met with great success. Robischon reported in his article:

> Stand-alone video game soundtracks have not proved particularly successful. The critically acclaimed orchestral soundtrack for Halo by Microsoft sold only 40,000 copies, although the accompaniment to Halo 2 is expected to sell better. And the seven-CD box set for Rockstar Games' Grand Auto Theft Auto: Vice City, which featured a slew of 1980s radio hits, sold fewer than 30,000 units.

On the other hand, video game soundtracks are winning awards. In 2004 the MTV Video Music Awards started giving out an award for the best soundtrack from a video game. Perhaps the award was to acknowledge the taste of many in the MTV audience who love these video games, as much as it was to recognize the success of the soundtracks.

The compulsory license and the rate established by Copyright Act would apply to the inclusion and distribution of songs in these audio soundtracks. But the record companies generally demand a higher rate than 8.5 cents for the masters, plus a hefty advance.

Chapter 8

The Recording Industry in Crisis

I n the last several years, sales of recorded music and revenues have declined approx-imately 20% in the U.S., according to the RIAA's income and sales reports.[1] World-wide sales and income are down commensurately throughout the rest of the world. Although sales and income improved a bit in 2004, according to a quote by Cary Sher-man, the President of RIAA, published in October 2004, "We lost a third of our sales in four years." Critics have charged the RIAA with manipulating the numbers in order to bolster its case against music downloading. And the year 2004 will be the first in four that the music business has managed to increase income from sales of recorded music in the U.S. But sales and income are up only about 2% from last year, compared to the previous year's 6% decline. Any way you look it, the situation isn't pretty and the future of the in-dustry remains uncertain. In 2003 Time Warner sold Warner Music, at one time the lead-ing record label in the world, to private investors. Elektra Records, one of the most innovative labels of all times, was shuttered; many people lost their jobs and artists were dropped. In September 2004 Sony Music merged with BMG. A reported 2,000 people, some of whom are personal friends, were let go.

Many in the business blame unauthorized file sharing and CD burning for the recording industry's woes. In his testimony before the California Senate Select Commit-tee on the Entertainment Industry in March 2003, Eric Garland, the CEO of Big Cham-pagne, the leading firm measuring activity for peer to peer networks, reported:

> Consider this: song for song, more music was acquired on peer-to-peer networks last year than through retail sales of compact discs

---

1. *Total U.S. income for sales of prerecorded music in all formats including CD, cassettes, LPs, DVD, etc. were at an all-time high in 1999 at nearly $14.58 billion. By the end of 2003 that income was $11.85 billion, and this loss does not account for inflation. CD sales also declined more than 20% in that period of time.*

worldwide. Or, to put it another way. File sharing is bigger than the record business.

This chapter recaps the brief but brutal history of the record industry's battles with unauthorized music file sharing and its own customers.

Whatever problems the music industry may face at this time, music itself is in fact more popular, more diverse and is being listened to by more people than ever. There is more and more music in our lives, on the Internet and on our MP3 players now, as well as at clubs, on the radio and TV. What the crisis in the recording industry does mean is that the traditional music business is being replaced by something else. One of the big questions is whether the major record labels, which still control approximately 80% of world's distribution of recorded music, will survive. In the mid '80s multinational corporations began gobbling up independent labels to create vast multinational money machines. The business was very tempting. Rock 'n' roll was continuing to capture the public's imagination and many bands were selling in the millions. And superstars, led by Michael Jackson, were selling tens of millions of records. An album may take a million dollars to produce and a couple more million to market and promote. But if a record sold, for example, at $7 dollars wholesale, the payoff for a successful album was spectacularly lucrative. In his recent book *Howling at the Moon*, the former president of CBS Records, Walter Yetnikoff, reports that when he got to CBS Records in the early '60s the most popular artists were Mitch Miller and Jerry Vale. Gross sales were only $250 million. When he left in the late '80s sales exceeded $2.5 *billion*. No wonder a business that consisted of hundreds of independent companies became co-opted by five multinational corporations. The accountants saw money in the music and rushed in to reap the profits for their stockholders.

Because the profits are no longer abundant, the multinational corporations that own two of the major labels, EMI and Universal Music, are contemplating merging or selling off their record divisions. Sony and BMG have already merged, discarding many employees and dropping artists. Time Warner sold off Warner Music in 2003. It is possible that we will have a world where the record business will go back to small entrepreneurs once more because the multinationals will get out of the business.

Electronic Frontier Foundation defines itself as the nation's leading nonprofit interest group devoted to protecting American freedoms in the digital environment. Although it does not condone the widespread copyright infringement going on over the Internet, it does criticize the recording industry for the way it has responded:

> Five years have passed since the original Napster demonstrated that American music fans were ready for digital music choices beyond the CD. But rather than rushing to address that marketplace demand, the

music industry dragged its feet, hid behind its lawyers, and branded music fans "thieves."

EFF Web site (www.eff.org) August 2003

There is some truth in this criticism but it doesn't tell the full story. This chapter attempts to give a succinct but balanced view of the history of the record industry's struggle to come to terms with digital music and the Internet.

SDMI: Labels vs. Electronics Business

This section deals with the labels' failed attempt to place a "digital lock" in computers to stop unauthorized distribution of music.

The Secure Digital Music Initiative (SDMI) was a forum which brought together more than 200 companies and organizations representing the major record labels, consumer electronics and computer manufacturers, security technology, information technology, and Internet service providers (ISPs). It started functioning in earnest at the beginning of 1999. According to its Web site, SDMI's charter was to develop "technology specifications that protect the playing, storing, and distributing of digital music such that a new market for digital music may emerge." The open technology specifications released by SDMI were supposed to: "reflect … the legitimate needs of the record labels for security of digital music." The Web site stated: "Record companies have identified the lack of a … standard for security as the single greatest impediment to the growth of legitimate markets for electronic distribution of copyrighted music. Likewise, technology companies developing computer software, hardware and consumer electronics devices that will handle new forms of digital music have realized that an important part of these devices is the presence (or absence) of adequate security for electronic music." Evidently, the electronics companies ultimately preferred the absence of standards because in 2001 SDMI went out of business.

The SDMI Web site concluded:

> Based on all of the factors considered by the SDMI plenary, it was determined that there is not yet consensus for adoption of any combination of the proposed technologies. Accordingly, as of May 18, 2001, SDMI is on hiatus, and intends to re-assess technological advances at some later date.

What happened? The content owners could not get the electronics industry to play ball. The labels wanted them to voluntarily include in their computers and CD burners codes that would prevent transmission and download for content that was not marked as kosher by the content providers. This would have made those computers and other devices less appealing to consumers. One of the problems is that the content owners themselves were partially owned by the electronics business. Specifically Sony Music is owned by one of the world's leading manufacturers of gadgets including computers, blank optical discs and all kinds of digital devices to record and copy music. You can imagine how difficult it must have been for the Sony Music executives to strongly advocate for systems that could make their parent company less profitable.

Napster & Grokster Cases: The Labels vs. P2P Services

This sections tells the story of a big win, followed by a bitter loss, followed by desperation.

In the late 1990s, Napster started to gain popularity and users beyond the small group of college students who adopted it in its infancy. It was no big deal until record company executives found out that people throughout the country, including some of their own kids, were downloading hundreds or thousands of songs for free. The record companies and their lawyers decided that file sharing was a problem they could throw money at and litigate away. They marshaled their resources, economic and legal, and sued Napster. *A&M Records, Inc. vs. Napster, Inc.*, 239 F.3rd 1004 (9th Cir. 2001). Napster created and released software that allowed people to make music files on their hard drives available to others in cyberspace who were using Napster's service. The Ninth Circuit determined that the plaintiffs, who included the major record companies, were likely to prevail against Napster on a theory of contributory infringement. The court's analysis was heavily influenced by the fact that Napster itself created a system that was not only overwhelmingly used for acts of infringement (trading copyrighted songs and masters without the permission of the copyright owners) but that Napster was able to control, access, or block infringement by end users. The court emphasized that Napster's ability to control the illicit conduct was "cabined by the system's current architecture." At a minimum, the Ninth Circuit noted, Napster had the ability to locate infringing material listed on its indices and had the right to terminate users' access to its system. The Court held that Napster was under a duty to police its service and remanded the case to the District Court. On remand the District Court enjoined Napster from engaging in or facilitating others to engage in, copying, downloading, uploading, transmitting, or distributing copyrighted sound recordings. After that Napster hobbled along for short period of time until BMG put it out if its misery by buying what was left. Shortly thereafter it closed forever. (Although Roxio bought the name and the famous logo which it uses today for its music service, the new Napster has nothing to do with the original.)

Unfortunately for the labels, things just got worse notwithstanding their legal victory over Napster. The P2P community and technology was, and this had become a pattern, one step ahead of the law. While the record companies were litigating Napster to death, a new and even more powerful form of P2P burst on the scene. These services were typified by Kazaa and Grokster. Just like Napster, these services allow people to trade music files without paying a cent, but unlike Napster they proved to be more resilient to the labels' legal fire power. This is the reason why: these services did not control a central data base or index where every song was available. Instead they merely allowed people to download software that allows their subscribers to trade files directly with each other. This was the legally decisive fact in the *MGM vs. Grokster* decision.

In *MGM Studios, Inc. vs. Grokster, Ltd.*, 269 F.Supp.2d 211 (C.D. Cal 2003), a district federal court in California ruled that because Grokster, unlike Napster, did not control a central database containing music files, Grokster did not violate copyright law. Since Grokster could not delete copyrighted music even if it wanted, the court reasoned, this new file sharing service was as lawful as a VCR. Like a VCR, the court reasoned, Grokster just provided tools (i.e., software) that customers could use to trade both legal public domain materials as well as copyrighted materials. Grokster could not be held responsible, as it had no control over the traded content.

In the next chapter we will explore the Ninth Circuit's recent affirmation of the Grokster decision and the upcoming Supreme Court review of that decision.

RIAA's Lawsuits Against Kids and Grandmothers

Shortly after the Grokster decision, facing ever mounting decreases in CD sales and income, the record industry did the unthinkable. They started suing their own customers. As Cary Sherman recently said about the industry's dramatic loss in income in the last several years, "You worry more about survival and a little less about popularity."

Among the defendants in the first round of lawsuits was a 12 year old and a grandmother. The grandmother reportedly got off when her son-in-law, an attorney, was able to demonstrate that the RIAA had made a mistake. Her computer was incapable of downloading or uploading the songs she had been accused of stealing. In the next chapter on latest legal developments we will report on the latest group of lawsuits by RIAA against music file sharers and we will discuss whether they have achieved the RIAA's goal of reducing unauthorized music file sharing.

Suing Verizon So You Can Sue More of Your Own Customers

Although the labels would have loved to have made the Internet Service Providers liable for carrying pirated works, the ISPs (which are controlled by companies much bigger than the labels) have been able to immunize themselves from liability under federal law. Therefore, even though they provided access to P2P services such as Grokster and Kazaa, they are not responsible for their activities. Some believe this is unfair; they argue that the ISPs could take down such unauthorized services if they chose to do so.

The labels were able to succeed, however, in inserting a provision in the Digital Millennium Copyright Act that they thought would entitle them to obtain names of ISP subscribers who download and upload unauthorized music files. However, in *RIAA vs. Verizon Internet Services*, 351 F.3d 1229 (D.C. Cir. 2003), the D.C. Circuit granted Verizon's motion to quash a DMCA subpoena served to identify a pseudonymous alleged infringer. Verizon had refused to divulge the subscriber's identity, claiming that the provision didn't cover alleged copyright-infringing material that resides on individuals' own computers, only material that resides on an ISP's own computer. The Court agreed, finding that the act did not authorize the issuance of a subpoena to a service provider acting solely as a conduit for communications not actually stored on its own service.

Although the Verizon case temporarily slowed the pace of RIAA's lawsuits, as we shall see in current developments in the next chapter, it did not stop them.

MusicNet and Pressplay: The Labels Enter the Digital Music Business

This is the story of the label's unsuccessful initial attempts to enter the digital music business.

I recall being present at a business affairs conference at Sony when the original Napster was still active. One of lawyers gave a presentation on digital downloading. She presented Napster first with the aid of a projector. We could see the service offered a seemingly unlimited music collection. She requested a title from the audience and someone suggested a popular rock song. She typed into her keyboard and the title came right up, available for download. Then she asked for another request from the audience. This time it was an obscure blues tune. Again, it came up instantly. Also available for download. And not only, she said, could anyone download it for free in a few seconds—they could transfer it to any other computer they had and send a copy to their friends.

Then she showed what Sony Music had to offer. In order to buy a Mariah Carey single online, you would have to wade through several Web pages in the Sony Music Web site. Each page was loaded with ads, promotions and hype. When you finally got to the page where Mariah's music was offered for download, only several of her songs were offered for download, and each cost more than $3. Although you could download the song to your hard drive, due to the miracle of digital rights management, you could not transfer the music to any other computer. My heart sank. I thought, how could anyone be so dumb? By the time anybody actually found the Web page for Mariah's downloadable singles, they would probably be so irritated they might figure that perhaps the labels deserved not to get paid at all. Looking back on this episode, I think now the labels didn't really want to compete with Napster. They wanted to kill Napster and discourage online delivery of music by keeping the price high and the content difficult to access. They wanted to retain the old way of doing business that made the labels so profitable in the first place.

When the record companies started hemorrhaging money and litigation failed, they finally launched their own legal alternatives to the pirates. Warner, EMI and BMG started MusicNet. Sony and Universal launched Pressplay. Both were introduced in 2002 and both were miserable failures. They failed because (1) neither allowed the user to download any music; (2) neither allowed their customers to transfer the music to any other device; (3) each service offered music only from their label parents (so Pressplay, for example, had no music except from Sony and Universal artists); and (4) even in regard to the music of their label parents, a lot was missing because major artists had either not consented or because of restrictions in guest artist contract and sampling licenses (which is still a major problem for contemporary digital services as we discuss in the next chapter).

Universal and Sony sold Pressplay. MusicNet continues in a different form today. For instance, it includes music of all the major labels and indies as well. The point that I am trying to make here is that the labels were not focused on creating the future when they birthed MusicNet and Pressplay. They were too busy trying to kill the future. As we will see in Chapter 10 when we look at the Induce Act and fresh lawsuits aimed at consumers, they are still at it.

What Is the Future of the Music Business?

The number of U.S. broadband subscribers tripled between June 2001 and December 2003, growing from 5.9 million to 20.3 million, according to a recent report from the Federal Communications Commission. The report found that cable modem connections accounted for 58% of broadband lines, while DSL represented 34% and other technologies made up the remaining 8%.

These facts can spell further trouble for the music business as higher speed Internet connections will only facilitate more P2P trading. In the next chapter we offer solutions to the recording industry, especially the major labels whose fate may be hanging in the balance, suggesting that they embrace and profit from the new technologies rather than trying again and again to sue them out of existence.

Another problem for the labels is the implicit approval by the electronics industry for distributing free content. They have in fact given consumers the ability to get free music easily. Major computer manufacturers such as Dell, Compaq, Gateway, Apple and yes, even Sony, which also owns a record company, advertise their products as home entertainment centers. One of them even carried the motto: "rip mix and burn your own music!" They also sell CD burners in almost every new computer and manufacture blank optical discs. I recall that at the Sony electronics store, which is in the same building as the headquarters for Sony Music, there was a display above some new recording devices that actually said "burn your own music." (Eventually the sign was taken down.)

If I were to offer my prediction for the future of the music business, I would start with where we are now: Income from recorded music has declined approximately 20% throughout the world in the last several years. Many blame unauthorized file sharing. But others blame the bad economy, competition with other diversions such as video games, the ending of the CD boom of replacing vinyl and cassette collections, and finally, the diminishing quality of the music. My opinion is that file sharing is a factor contributing to the music industry's decline, but that it has been exacerbated by artificially high prices for CDs and the record companies' slowness in embracing new business models made possible by the new technologies.

Rock 'n' roll revitalized pop music starting with Chuck Berry and then Elvis and growing into the era of the Beatles and the Rolling Stones. During those years the music business grew approximately tenfold. The music became a more important component in our culture and our identity than ever before. The music became part of the boomer generation's identity and their vision of the world and their future. Rock 'n' roll is by no means dead, but it no longer is at the vanguard of our culture. To some extent hip-hop music has replaced it and music no doubt still plays a key role our lives. Perhaps that is why the music business is still a multi-billion dollars business instead of the cottage industry it used to be.

So what is the future? Internet and wireless digital delivery of music will continue to grow in both the legal and unauthorized forms. The real issue is how and when the labels will secure the cooperation of the ISPs and the electronics industries to pay them and their artists for all the music that is being transmitted, downloaded, burned and shared. My view is that the kids are not to blame for "free" music: It's the huge corporations that control the pipe through which they receive free music, and the machines that allow everyone to listen to and keep free music (computers containing CD burners, MP3 players and all those other new gadgets which are about to be released such as cell phones that play music). As Eric Garland stated in his California Senate testimony:

> The tools of the digital age are de facto tools of infringement: e-mail, instant messaging, the world wide Web, search engines, wireless technology. Any communication technology, any desktop computer, any portable storage device can and will be used … for infringement, often on a massive scale.

The electronics industry and Internet service providers have been able to avoid liability for allowing people to use the Internet to get and make permanent copies of free music. And part of the reason they've been able to get away with it (in addition to their political and economic leverage) is the content owners themselves. If the labels' strategy included getting a reasonable royalty from the ISPs and the electronics business instead of, or at least in addition to, suing kids and grandmothers, the record companies might be able to get the voluntary cooperation of the ISPs and computer manufacturers. The ISPs and electronics business would no doubt pass the cost on to the public. But since so many people buy these products and services, the cost could be quite small to each consumer and at the same time would compensate the record companies and the artists for lost sales.

This cooperation is more likely to take place as a more technology-friendly generation of executives takes over the helms of the major labels. I see a statutory or "blanket" license like those implemented by ASCAP and BMI which allow radio and TV stations to play their entire catalog of songs in return for a percentage of the stations' income. This means that file sharing will be legal in exchange for payments to the labels and artists by the ISPs and the electronics industry. The result will be more music for the consumer for less money, and at the same time fair compensation for the labels and the artists. We discuss these ideas in more depth in the following chapter.

Chapter 9
Proposed Solutions

T his chapter begins by setting forth the proposal that I originally advanced in a commentary in *Entertainment Law & Finance*. *Billboard* magazine republished the commentary in August 2003. The proposal is for a statutory license legalizing file sharing. This idea was in large measure the inspiration for the entire book. The proposal is a solution for the big record companies and how they can survive. The rest of this book is meant to provide solutions for independent artists and entrepreneurs.

Legalize File Sharing

Commentary on Legalization of Music File Sharing. The original title of my commentary in *ELF* was "How Compulsory License For Internet Might Help Music Industry." *Billboard* retitled it: "Technological Advances Have Led to a Market Breakdown: Licensing Could Solve Internet Piracy." The beginning of the commentary notes:

> Sales of recorded music in the United States and throughout the world
> have declined for three consecutive years. Three of the five major
> record companies are now reportedly for sale."

Since the publication of this piece, Time Warner sold off Warner Records to a group of private investors, and two of the other majors, Sony Music and BMG, have merged. The commentary continues:

> Layoffs are decimating record industry professionals. The International Federation of the Phonographic Industry blames the situation
> on CD burning and unauthorized Internet file sharing.

One of the primary causes for the industry's present woes can be traced back to the Digital Millennium Copyright Act of 1998 (DMCA). In negotiations surrounding the passage of the act, the record labels agreed that the ISPs would receive certain "safe harbors" designed to shelter them from the infringing activities of their customers. In exchange the content owners received certain concessions including the right to subpoena the ISPs for names of alleged infringers (see discussion of the *Verizon* case in the last chapter). Due to this accommodation, when unauthorized file sharing became a huge problem shortly after passage of the act, the labels could not force the ISPs to shut down "pirates" such as Napster. Instead the labels had to pursue the unauthorized file sharing services themselves. But this strategy, as we discussed in the last chapter, hit a brick wall in the *MGM vs. Grokster* case. At that point the labels started to sue the only people left to sue, those who were actually trading music files, that is, their own customers. This strategy, as we shall see in the next chapter, has not solved the labels' problems either.

The solution to the music industry's woes is a federal law providing for a statutory license that would legalize the sharing of music online while compensating copyright owners for lost sales. A federal law implementing a statutory license could legalize the transmission of all recorded music for purposes of sharing music over the Internet and downloading permanent, portable copies. Fees would be paid by those directly profiting from file sharing, that is, the makers of CD burners, including computer manufacturers, and the Internet service providers (ISPs) whose subscribers already pay in part for access to such services as Kazaa. As CD sales continued to decline due to an ever-increasing number of households acquiring computers and high speed Internet connections, the amount payable to the fund could be adjusted upwards.

Apple has reported that sales of iPods are through the roof. Sales of other MP3 players, CD burners, and computers continue unabated. High-speed Internet subscriptions are at an all-time high and growing dramatically. These segments of the economy, as opposed to the record companies, are doing very well. What is really happening is a redistribution of consumers' dollars away from those who sell music to those who sell electronics and high-speed Internet connections.

Moreover, to many consumers "free music" does not seem free at all. For example, many consumers spend hundreds if not thousands of dollars each year on computer equipment and maintenance, plus monthly Internet service. When they download music, even without paying for individual songs, it does not seem free because they already spent a great deal of money on the technology that made getting the music possible.

The commentary continues with a description of how a statutory license would work.

> The contribution of each ISP and computer manufacturer would be determined by a body designated by the U.S. Copyright Office. The payments would be delivered to a central administrator on behalf of the labels and the artists. This fund would be allocated based on downloads of each master as tabulated by digital rights management technology similar to what the performing rights societies already use to count the performances of songs on broadcast radio and TV. The fund administrator would then pay each label and artist on a 50/50 basis, just as ASCAP and BMI pay songwriters and music publishers. (There

would also be a separate fund for music publishing. In fact, the rate for downloading songs is already subject to a compulsory license of 8 cents [now 8.5 cents] per song under the Copyright Act.)

The commentary also pointed out that a statutory license could cut through a major obstacle in the labels' capacity to compete in the digital music world. That obstacle has to do with contract restrictions. As I pointed out in the commentary:

> Some artist's contracts do not allow record companies to put the artists' music online. As a consultant for one of the major authorized online services, I had to delete approximately 80% of hip-hop music because sampling agreements typically do not permit sales via the Internet or as singles of tracks on which samples are used. Third-party artists who record with other artists often include the same restrictions. And many major artists who are justifiably afraid that they will not be adequately compensated by the labels for use of their records online threaten not to record another album or with some other form of retaliation, even if they are contractually obliged to allow the labels to use their music in any media. A statutory license could cut through these knots while guaranteeing fair compensation to the artists.

These contractual problems have had a strong negative impact on the record companies' ability to compete with unauthorized P2P systems. Kazaa and eDonkey, to name just a couple of the dozens of unauthorized services, are only limited in the amount of music that they offer by the number of songs that their subscribers make available to each other. These contract problems will also impede the labels' efforts in establishing authorized P2P systems. See the subsection "Will the Labels Embrace P2P?" later in this chapter.

The commentary concludes:

> The proponents of a free market would argue that the market is the best device in establishing a fair price for all private property, including music copyrights. However, the technological advances created by the Internet have led to what economists call a "market breakdown" in the recording business. Without a compromise—such as a compulsory license—between the competing economic interests (i.e., hardware versus content), everyone will lose.

The crux of my proposal is that a statute legalizing file sharing, in return for a levy on the technologies that make "free music" possible, would help everyone: the public would have access to more music without the threat of lawsuits, the labels and the artists would be fairly compensated, and the technology companies would still have the labels around to find, produce and promote music to attract more subscribers to high speed Internet services, and more customers for computers, CD burners, MP3 players and other digital devices.

Interview on NPR Radio with Cary Sherman of RIAA. I reiterated these views in a recent interview on a National Public Radio program. NPR also interviewed Cary Sherman, President of the RIAA, for the same program. Here is the transcript of that interview including Mr. Sherman's remarks.

INTRO: The past few years have been dismal for the major record labels. Their trade groups say there has been a slight improvement this year. But in the previous two years sales tumbled by more than 20%. This is the third and final part of Rick Karr's series on alternative revenue models for the music business. Today he examines an idea whose advocates say could make up for that crash.

NPR: There is a spirited debate about the cause of the major labels' crash. The record firms and their allies say that it is the result of people downloading music from the Internet without paying for it. The labels' critics say the economy and changing musical tastes are to blame. But for former Sony music executive and current New York music attorney Steve Gordon, the important question is not why is this happening, but rather who benefits.

Steve Gordon: The ISPs are getting rich selling high-speed connections. Also, the manufacturers of computers, blank optical discs, CD burners, and MP3 players are making a huge sum of money by facilitating unauthorized file sharing and CD burning. It seems to me that these are the people who should be made to compensate the record business for lost sales and lost income.

NPR: With an opinion piece for the trade magazine Billboard, *Gordon joined a small but growing group of music industry observers and insiders who want to tax those software and hardware firms and Internet service providers. That revenue would then be paid out to songwriters, musicians, and record companies in amounts proportional to how much of their music is being copied online. To make that happen, Gordon says, Congress would have to pass a law known as a statutory license.*

SG: A statutory license is a law that permits the use of copyrighted materials such as songs without the consent with the copyright owner in return for a predetermined payment.

NPR: Gordon says there are already statutory licenses that apply to the music business. One allows any artist to record any song that has already been recorded. So that when the members of the band Yes decided to record the song "Something's Coming" from the musical West Side Story, *the law gave them the right to do it without asking permission from composer Leonard Bernstein and lyricist Stephen Sondheim, as long as the band paid a legally required royalty of a few cents for each copy that sold. Steve Gordon says that is because a statutory license would circumvent the need to ask for permission. It would get the major labels out of a bind.*

[At that point in the interview I said that after I left Sony, I worked as a consultant for another major label. That label wished to license its catalog to MusicNet, at that time a new digital interactive streaming service owned by BMG, Warner, and EMI. My job was to pore over hundreds of agreements and to figure out which artists' works the label could make available to MusicNet.]

SG: I deleted 80% of Puffy's records because they included samples.

NPR: In other words, short snippets of other artists' work.

SG: And although he got permission to use the samples, he didn't get permission to sell the songs on the Internet.

NPR: Gordon says that complications in the major labels' contracts with artists have prevented the release of millions of older songs.

SG: The record companies have their hands tied behind their backs. They can't put up all of their content, and they are at a severe disadvantage with the unauthorized services that can allow *anything.*

NPR: A statutory license would trump those contracts and make every piece of music ever recorded available online. The major labels can't stand the idea of a statutory license. Carey Sherman is president of the trade group Recording Industry Association of America, or RIAA. He says it would be something like the government taking over the record business.

Cary Sherman: Do you really want the government regulating art? Do you want the government deciding the value of art? Do you want the government deciding whether a song from Frank Sinatra is worth more or less than a song from Eminem?

NPR: What's more, Sherman says, once the government levies a tax for music, it would have to do the same for movies, software, video games, books.

CS: And everything else that can be digitized and sent around the globe on the Internet. So are we going to have a compulsory license now for the entire cultural output of the U.S.? And how much would consumers have to pay to subsidize the hundreds of billions of dollars represented by the copyright industries? We account for more than 5% of the GDP now. It's the number one export of the United States.

NPR: Supporters of the statutory license admit that it would engender a huge new bureaucracy. Ultimately the decision falls to Congress. A couple of trial balloons have been floated over Capitol Hill, but those efforts haven't come to much. Instead, Congress looks likely to pass another controversial bill that would make it more difficult for electronics firms and software companies to create computers, blank optical discs, CD burners, and MP3 players. Devices that the bill's supporters, including the RIAA, say induce copying. Rick Karr, NPR News.

Responses to the Criticism of a Statutory Model. Here are my thoughts on the points Carey Sherman raised in the NPR interview.

CS: Do you really want the government regulating art?

Advocates argue that a statutory license would not be government regulation of art. Making those who profit from facilitating the free transfer and ownership of music pay for their raw materials has nothing to do with regulating who makes the music or what the music may be.

CS: Do you want the government deciding the value of art?

Clearly, the major record labels are facing market failure because of technologies no one could have predicted. A statutory license taxing the electronics business and the ISPs would not decide the value of art, say advocates—it would merely compensate the labels for lost sales. Fees would be distributed to copyright owners and artists based on their popularity. Therefore the public would be deciding the value of the "art," not the government. For example, if I recorded "Happy Birthday" and Beyoncé Knowles also recorded "Happy Birthday" and her version was downloaded a million times more than mine, she and her label would receive a million times more income than I would.

CS: Do you want the government deciding whether a song from Frank Sinatra is worth more or less than a song from Eminem?

In the world of physical CDs, they are already the same amount. A mechanical license is 8.5 cents per copy sold for both a song recorded by Eminem and a song recorded by Sinatra. Also, if the recordings of both songs are webcast, as we discussed in Chapter 3, they are treated as equally valuable by SoundExchange in distributing payments to the record companies and the artists (or in Mr. Sinatra's case, his estate). All the proposed license would do is extend this principal to the P2P world, in effect treating ISPs like webcasters.

CS: Once the government levies a tax for music, it would have to do the same for movies, software, video games, books.

I agree with Mr. Sherman that it would not make sense to impose a statutory license on other cultural products such as movies. It does not seem fair to treat in the same manner a low-budget documentary and, for example, a major Hollywood movie that cost $50 million to produce. Perhaps this is the reason that the movie business has never had anything similar to a statutory license for mechanicals or a blanket license for public performance royalties. On the other hand, a song recorded by Eminem and a song recorded by Sinatra are comparable, and the law already recognizes that.

The following point was made by the moderator rather than Mr. Sherman.

NPR: Supporters of the statutory license admit that it would engender a huge new bureaucracy.

As advocates of the license point out, no new "bureaucracy" would have to be created; it already exists—it's called SoundExchange. As we discussed in Chapter 3, SoundExchange is a nonprofit organization controlled equally by the labels and artists' representatives that collects fees for webcasting of master recordings and distributes the money equally to labels and artists. SoundExchange would have to expand its operation beyond webcasters but basically the infrastructure is already in place.

Legislative Model. Even the basis for the legislation for a statutory license is in place. The 1992 Audio Home Recording Act, which we discussed in Chapter 2, already imposes a levy on certain digital copying equipment. This legislation immunized home copying on these devices for personal use from prosecution or liability for copyright infringement. The fees collected from the manufacturers of the covered devices are distributed in turn to the copyright owners and the artists. If this sounds like what I am proposing that's because it is precisely what I am recommending except that the levy should be expanded to cover a new generation of devices and technologies that facilitates and encourages the sharing of "free" music. Ironically, the recording industry, led by the RIAA, was the principal proponent of this legislation.

All that would have to be done is to expand this legislation to cover the new devices that facilitate and encourage sharing free music, that is, MP3 players, high speed Internet connections, CD burners and the new powerful generation of computers that are being marketed as home entertainment systems. As we discuss below, Professor William Fisher at Harvard has done a careful economic analysis of how much the business has lost and is poised to lose. The levy could be calibrated to compensate the business for those losses. In that way the record companies, which discover, nurture, promote, market and distribute new music, could survive and even prosper.

Another Benefit of a Statutory Solution. Another nice thing about a statutory solution is that the artists and musicians would, if the division of income were the same as that applied to statutory royalties from webcasting, receive 50% of the income. The statute would supersede the recording agreements between the labels and the artists which generally provides for a royalty of 10–15%. In addition, under the standard record agreement, an artist does not even receive this royalty unless her account is "recouped" (that is, her records have sold enough units to pay the label back for production costs and other recoupable expenses). Further, even if the artist is recouped, the artist's royalty is subject to all kinds of deductions as we discussed in Chapter 1.

Proposals by Professors Neil Netanel and William Fisher. For those who would like to further explore what the details of a compulsory license would look like I encourage you to read the pioneering article by Professor Neil Netanel, "Impose a Noncommercial Use Levy to Allow Free Peer-to-Peer File Sharing," *Harvard Journal of Law & Technology*, Vol. 17, 2003, in which he sets out in detail how such a scheme would work. The following is an abstract of the article.

> Noncommercial users of peer-to-peer systems, such as Kazaa and Gnutella, should be free to distribute and modify files as they wish. But providers of services and devices the value of which are substantially enhanced by such P2P file-swapping should be charged a statutory fee—what I term the Noncommercial Use Levy ("NUL")—set as a percentage of gross revenue. Likely candidates include Internet access, P2P

software and services, computer hardware, consumer electronic devices (such as CD burners, MP3 players, and digital video recorders) used to copy, store, transmit, or perform downloaded files, and storage media (like blank CDs) used with those devices. Once collected, levy proceeds would be allocated among copyright holders in proportion to the popularity of their respective works and of user-modified version of their works, as measured by digital tracking and sampling technologies. I estimate that an average levy of some 4% of annual retail revenues of P2P-related goods and services would be sufficient to compensate copyright holders for the lost revenues they suffer as a result of NUL-privileged activity, at least for the next 5 years. . . . My proposed NUL is not a panacea. But a balance of trade-offs favors it over the alternatives."

Professor William Fisher of Harvard completed a brilliant economic analysis of alternative collection and compensation models in his book *Promises To Keep: Technology, Law and the Future of Entertainment* (Stanford University Press 2004). Chapter 6 is entitled "An Alternative Compensation System" and can be read at http://tfisher.org/PTK.htm.

The thesis of the book is that changes in the technologies used to make and store audio and video recordings, combined with the communication revolution associated with the Internet, have generated an extraordinary array of new ways in which music and movies can be produced and distributed. Professor Fisher points out that both the creators and the consumers of entertainment products stand to benefit enormously from the new systems. He argues, however, that the entertainment industries have failed thus far to avail themselves of these opportunities. Instead, too much energy has been devoted to interpreting or changing legal rules in hopes of defending older business models against the threats posed by the new technologies. These efforts to plug the multiplying holes in the legal dikes are failing and the entertainment industry has fallen into crisis.

In Chapter 6 of his book, Fisher provides a comprehensive economic analysis of the losses suffered by the recording industry in the last several years. He proposes a plan that would redress those losses which would include (1) watermarking all music content capable of digital transmission; (2) systems to monitor how many copies of each song and/or master were distributed; and (3) on the basis of those numbers, compensation to the copyright owners and the artists. The income would come from a tax on the Internet service providers and the electronics business.

Voluntary Collective Licensing

Another possible solution to the recording industry's current economic crisis is voluntary collective licensing. Under this model, copyright holders would voluntarily join together and offer "blanket" licenses. As we discussed in Chapter 1, this is how the songwriters and publishers who created ASCAP, and later BMI and SESAC (the "PROs"), decided to deal with the problem of securing compensation from the tens of thousands of users including broadcast radio and television stations, cable, satellite, background music services, nightclubs, hotels, arenas, etc. Now the PRO's license Internet-based music services as well (see Chapters 2 and 3).

As discussed, there are now many P2P services which offer software that makes it possible for millions of people to trade music files with each other. Many of these services have expressed an interest in gaining a license that would make it legal for their users to listen to and download music. The PROs do offer their Internet licenses to any service which applies. The major labels do not. Even before being shut down by the labels, Napster was trying hard to negotiate for such a blanket license from the major labels.

As the Electronic Frontier Foundation (a nonprofit organization dedicated to defending freedom of thought and expression for new technologies, such as the Internet and the World Wide Web) has suggested, blanket licensing would not require any changes to copyright law and leaves price-setting to the copyright owners. According to the EFF, "Something much like this could be developed for file-sharing [for masters.]" Copyright owners could offer blanket licenses on nondiscriminatory terms, either to ISPs, software vendors, or consumers directly.

The problem, of course, is that this solution has been available to the labels all along. It only works if virtually all copyright owners cooperate and forego lawsuits in exchange for a reasonable piece of the pie. So far, the big record companies have shown no interest in pursuing a voluntary "collective licensing" plan.

It is worth noting, and one would hope that the major labels have noticed, that while the labels struggle not to lay off more employees and artists, the PROs are doing better than fine. For instance, BMI reported revenues of $673 million for the 2004 fiscal year—6.8% more than the prior year. This translated into royalties of more than $573 million for its songwriters, composers and music publishers. The revenues and royalty distributions were the largest in the company's history. In addition, new media revenues, including the Internet, were up 70%. This kind of success is especially remarkable in a period when market forces and technology continue to batter the record business. BMI also traversed this period without a single business-related layoff compared to massive layoffs at the big labels.

Will the Labels Embrace P2P?

In October 2004, there were signs that the RIAA and their major record company members were beginning to consider licensing masters for P2P transmission. In an article in *Wired* magazine called "Toe-to-Toe Over Peer-to-Peer," Michael Grebb reported that "Amid the recent collapse of talks over the Induce Act in Congress, record labels are closing in on deals to enable several new peer-to-peer services to emerge—with the sanction of major record labels that have so far derided P2P as a haven for piracy. At least one record industry representative predicted that such sanctioned P2P services will start to proliferate in the next several months."

"We are going to see three or four of these in the very, very near future," said Mitch Glazier, senior vice president of government relations and legislative counsel at the Recording Industry Association of America. Glazier said the new services will be consumer-friendly and enable the portability that digital music consumers demand, all without running afoul of copyright law. "P2P technology is great," Glazier said. "It can be harnessed for good or harnessed for bad." *Wired* also reported that Glazier said "it's still unclear whether consumers will be willing to pay for P2P services, but companies such as Wurld Media … are trying to wrap up deals with various record labels to try out new service models."

I asked former President of Grokster, Wayne Rosso, if Glazier's comments signaled a shift in policy on the part of the recording industry towards P2P. Rosso replied: "Let's face it. The RIAA is losing the battle. They HAVE to start changing their tune. P2P is here. There's no way to kill it off. The challenge is to legitimize it. And that will take some forward thinking record company CEOs. Fortunately there is one out there who is progressive and wants to break the mold and try to create a new marketplace through leveraging P2P traffic. That day will come very soon."

In fact, the dynamic seems to be changing. Continues Rosso, "The future is going to be an amalgamation of several different licensed schemes that each P2P will bet their futures on. But the problem is that even though the opportunities are starting to arise now and the record companies are reaching out, many of my colleagues are backing off, afraid that if they play ball they'll lose their traffic. I happen to think that after you've been screaming to the high heavens for years claiming that you want to work with the labels if they would only license P2P, and when presented with the opportunity many P2P players then only want the licenses on their terms, it's totally dishonest. You can't change things unless you're in the room with the top guys. You have to start somewhere. And let's face it, copyright owners deserve to be paid for their content. I've always maintained that."

In December 2004 a company called SNOCAP announced that it has signed a landmark agreement with Universal Music Group to provide technology and database services for authorized P2P online distribution of the company's entire catalog. SNOCAP promised in the press release that it "will expand the digital music marketplace by finally making available on authorized services the broad and deep selection of content that has made peer-to-peer services so popular." One of the principals of SNOCAP is Shawn Fanning, the legendary founder of the first great P2P "pirate," the original Napster. Neither the press release nor current news stories, however, were very clear as to exactly how SNOCAP would actually work, or how it could compete effectively with free P2P services such as eDonkey or Kazaa. Other reports indicated that Wayne Rosso's new company Mashboxx was forming a strategic partnership with SNOCAP.

The continuing existence of free file-swapping services that operate beyond the reach of U.S. authorities, however, will present significant competition for any service like SNOCAP, according to Peter Menell, a law professor at the University of California at Berkeley. SNOCAP is "certainly a nice idea and it's serving at least a public-relations benefit for the copyright industries, but I don't think they're banking on it as their savior," Menell said. "I think we could spend a lot of time developing business models that meet all of the needs of the major players, but no one really wants to buy it."

But Wayne Rosso is confident that people will flock to a network that lets them share songs without having to worry about lawsuits from the RIAA or the Motion Picture Association of America, or about "spyware" programs that are sometimes packaged with files downloaded from free services. Still, the number of legal downloads is dwarfed by unauthorized transfers. In November 2004, file swappers traded nearly 1.4 billion tracks over free networks, according to Atlanta-based BigChampagne, a company that monitors peer-to-peer services.

Rosso believes that companies such as Mashboxx and SNOCAP have a better shot of luring long-time P2P users than a pure download service like Apple's iTunes because they will offer the ability to participate in an online community, share files with other members and browse from a vast library that includes rare tracks often not available from the big download stores. "Record companies need for me to succeed as much as I need to succeed," Rosso said. "I want to be an agent for change. I think this is a big win for me. I'm about to get everything I've been fighting for and frankly so is the record industry."

You can read my interview with Wayne Rosso in Chapter 20 in which the conversation focuses on the history, present, and future of P2P. Also, for current developments in regard to the major labels' plans to cooperation with new authorized peer-to-peer services, click on the link to Web pages updating this book in the attached CD-ROM.

Other Solutions

The following alternative solutions are from the Electronic Frontier Foundation's Web site (www.eff.org). My comments follow.

Individual Compulsory Licenses. "If artists, songwriters, and copyright holders were required to permit online copying in return for government-specified fees, companies could compete to painlessly collect these fees, do the accounting, and remit them to the artists. The payment to each artist need not directly reflect what each consumer pays, as long as the total across all artists and all consumers balances. Anyone could start such an intermediary company. Some companies might charge a flat rate per month, some might charge per song or per bandwidth, some might offer a single lifetime payment. Consumers would have the option to sign up with whichever of these services was most convenient or least intrusive for them. Consumers who don't download music, or don't mind the risk of a lawsuit, would not be required to buy a license."

This idea parallels the proposal for a statutory license which would legalize file sharing in exchange for a levy on the ISPs and electronic devices which facilitate copying music, including computers and MP3 players, in order to compensate the labels and artists for lost sales. The EFF's proposal, however, envisions independent entrepreneurs collecting the levy on behalf of copyright owners and artists instead of a governmental agency or nonprofit such as SoundExchange.

Ad Revenue Sharing. "Sites like the Internet Underground Music Archive, EMusic.com, and Artistdirect.com provide an online space for fans to listen to music streams, download files, and interact with artists. In the meantime, these fans are viewing advertisements on the site, and the revenues are split between the site and the copyright holders. Like radio, the money that funds the pie comes from advertisers, not consumers. But unlike radio, artists are rewarded directly. And since these sites often host a page for member artists, other payment methods are possible at the same time. IUMA, for example, compensates artists for both ad views and song downloads."

As this paragraph points out, advertising is already a key component of many digital music services, especially those focusing on independent music.

P2P Subscriptions. "P2P software vendors could start charging for their service. Music lovers could pay a flat fee for the software or pay per downloaded song. The funds could be distributed to artists and copyright holders through licensing agreements with studios and labels or through a compulsory license. In 2001, Napster and Bertelsmann AG were considering such a *subscription service*. Although Napster's legal battles with the recording industry removed it from the playing field, recent attempts at a subscription service (such as Apple's iTunes Music Store) show that consumers are willing to pay for downloaded music."

This model depends on the cooperation of the record companies, which has thus far been lacking. However, an individual artist with an established fan base could consider starting a closed P2P network on a subscriptions basis. The fans would be able to share that artists' music from records and live concerts without fear of reprisal from the artist.

The artist would be responsible for paying any third party stake holders such as third party songwriters, producers and side musicians.

Digital Patronage and Online Tipping. "Direct contribution from music lovers is a very old form of artist compensation, ranging from a simple passing of the hat to the famed patronage of Florence's Medici family. As content has moved to digital form, so has the form of payment. With an online tip jar such as the Amazon Honor System, artists can ask for donations directly from their Web sites, in amounts as small as one dollar. Patronage sites such as MusicLink have also emerged, which allow consumers to seek out the musicians and songwriters they'd like to support. Either way, consumers are given an easy, secure method to give directly to the artists they admire."

The independent online record company Magnatune incorporates this concept in their business plan except they start with a floor for the purchase price of downloads of their artists' music. Customers are invited to pay more than the minimum. See my interview with John Buckman, CEO and founder of Magnatune, in Chapter 15.

Microrefunds. "As a twist on online tip jars, Brad Templeton introduced the interesting idea of making 'opt-out' the default for paying for copyrighted works. The system, called 'microrefunds,' would collect small fees for each copyrighted work accessed and total them into a monthly bill. Upon reviewing the bill, charges that seemed too high or were for songs the consumer did not enjoy could be revoked. Instead of making a purchasing decision every time they want to hear a song, consumers could review their charges periodically. The billing could fit into a P2P subscription system, or as part of a music service such as the iTunes Music Store."

We discuss another system involving low-priced purchases such as downloads of single tracks in Chapter 17. I am referring to micropayment systems. They are designed to reduce transaction costs for the vendor, that is, the owner of the digital music service. Chapter 17 also contains an interview with Rachel Gravengaard, the General Manager of Mperia.com, a music store incorporating micropayments.

Bandwidth Levies. "Several people have nominated ISPs as collection points for P2P. Every Internet user gets Web access from an ISP, and most have a regular financial relationship with one as well. In exchange for protection from lawsuits, ISPs could sell "licensed" accounts (at an extra charge) to P2P users. Alternatively, they could charge everyone a smaller fee and give their customers blanket protection. The latter model would, however, charge people whether or not they download music."

At least one major ISP, Verizon, publicly announced that they would consider paying such a levy if the record labels agreed to stop suing their customers. The record companies have not publicly supported such a levy to date. They do not want to relinquish control over pricing. Again the plan advanced at the top of this chapter would include a levy on ISPs as well as the electronics business in order to adequately compensate the labels and artists.

Media Tariffs. "Another place to generate revenue is on the media that people use to store music, also known as a 'media tariff.' Canada and Germany tax all recordable CDs and then distribute the funds to artists. In the U.S., we have royalty-paid recordable CDs and data CDs. It's difficult to pay artists accurately with this system alone, but other data (statistics from P2P nets, for instance) could be used to make the disbursement of funds more fair."

Measuring the popularity of downloads of individual tracks in P2P is subject to precise measurement according to the folks at Big Champagne. For more information on how this is accomplished, listen to the interview with Eric Garland and Joe Fleischer of Big Champagne in the CD-ROM included with this book.

Concerts. "Concerts are a huge source of revenue for musicians. Some, like the Grateful Dead and Phish, have built careers around touring while encouraging fans to tape and trade their music. P2P dovetails into this model nicely, providing a distribution and promotion system for bands who choose to make money on the road."

Before they disbanded, Phish offered downloads of their concerts to their fans for a moderate price. They reportedly had the consent of their record company. Unsigned artists would not need permission. They would, however, be responsible for mechanical payments in case they did not write their own music.

Conclusion. According to the EFF, "There are many options available to make sure that artists receive fair compensation for their creativity. Today, convoluted and outdated copyright law is being used to claim that 60 million Americans are criminals. It's time to look seriously at the alternatives and start a dialogue with Congress to bring copyright law in tune with the digital age."

Weed

Another possible solution for how artists and labels can get paid for online music distribution involves a type of digital rights management called Weed. Weed allows artists to monetize their music for sale on P2P systems. The following is an article on how Weed works, which we have reprinted with the permission of the author. Following the article I clarify some points.

THE FUTURE OF MUSIC DISTRIBUTION. The revolution has already begun and it's called Weedshare. So, what is Weed and how does it work? Weed (as in "spreads like a") is a very pro-artist and pro-file-sharing group co-founded by John Beezer (formerly with Microsoft) of Shared Media Licensing, Inc. based in Seattle, Washington, consisting of a group of musicians and software developers. Simply put, it is a new music distribution business model with a radically different perspective regarding Internet file-sharing. In much the same vein as other digital music services, users can preview a track on their PC (up to three times) after downloading it for free before being invited to purchase it. Then after the 3rd play, if you like the song and decide to buy it, the purchase experience is extremely simple via PayPal. Once purchased, the file is "unlocked," and users can then play the track on up to three computers, burn to CD and/or download to a portable MP3 player. According to Craig Anderton, a writer for *EQ* magazine, "Weed aims to obsolete the concept of a record company altogether by de-centralizing A&R, promotion and distribution. . . . Essentially when you forward a file you've bought, you're acting as the A&R person, promoter and distributor." Weed principal and mastering engineer Steve Turnidge explains, "one of our highest aims is to ensure the legality of the music on the Weed System and that 50% credit goes to the right party." However, there are a few surprising twists with this innovative new business model.

Twist Number One: The price is set by the artist.

Twist Number Two: Buying a song makes the user eligible to earn a share of *future sales*. Instead of trying to shut down file-sharing, Weed thinks people should be paid for it, and uses Microsoft Digital Rights Management (DRM) to achieve that goal. Instead of punishing fans who don't respect artists' rights, Weed thinks it makes more sense to actually reward those who do. The resulting Weed files are a brand-new music file format that will soon revolutionize the entire global music industry and here's how it works ...

1. Download music files from any "Weed-Enabled" Web site.
2. Play any Weed file three times for free on any software that can handle Windows Media Audio (Windows Media Player, RealPlayer, etc.). If you don't like the music, just delete it. But if you like it, then you are automatically invited to buy it. [Editor's note: This process is repeated for any new user. If you buy the song and "unlock" the file, the song does not remain unlocked when you upload it to a friend—that person would have 3 free listens, and then must buy the song to hear it again.]
3. Install the free Weed software and get an immediate $5 credit.
4. Use the Weed software to buy the songs that you like, then play, burn, and share to your heart's content. That's right—play it *forever* on your computer, burn multiple CDs for your stereo, boombox, and car and also download the tunes to your portable device.
5. Share your Weed files with everyone you know—if anyone eventually buys Weed music through your own distribution and promotional efforts, *both you and the artist* make money.

Sweet! But it gets sweeter. Take the song you just bought and create your own Web site, burn CD-ROMs or e-mail it to your friends. Every time they buy a song you turned them on to, you get paid! Listen closely . . . *You* get paid to listen to music and turn your friends on to hot new tunes by independent artists from around the world.

Using Weed, artists can distribute songs freely over peer-to-peer networks and fans can listen to each song 3 times with no charge. If you like what you hear, you can buy the song for whatever price the artist sets (i.e. $.99). Then 50% goes to the artist, 35% goes to the people who actually *shared the file*, and Weed takes 15%. While there are other models that use DRM (digital rights management), none are as clever as Weed, incorporating a sense of community, fairness, and "give-back" mentality. While many other online music business models are trying to fight or manipulate P2P, Weed takes advantage of this disruptive technology. And as a general rule, you can tell the shady online music ventures from the respectable ones simply by seeing whether they are honest and open about where the money goes.

Here's how everyone gets paid with Weed:

- The artist always gets 50% of every sale
- You get 20% for passing around your own Weed files
- The person who shared the file with you gets 10%
- The person who shared the file with that person gets 5%
- Weedshare gets 15% for inventing the whole thing

The entire Weed concept does not sink in immediately to most people because it is such a radical departure from the traditional music business and a true paradigm shift, one which will take some time to digest and percolate. Weed has the potential to truly contribute to the success of independent artists with its community-based feeling of membership and its viral propensity to efficiently multiply. The Weed concept is truly optimized for independent artists and for people who use file-sharing to satisfy their thirst for musical variety. Only time will tell if it *spreads like a weed* across the Internet, but it is definitely a business approach worth watching.

Written by Todd B. Beals at www.creative-media-services.com, a privately held company that provides solutions for the protection, management and distribution of digital content.

As Beals states, the artist sets the price and receives 50% of income from each sale of a Weed file. Artists should recognize, though, that they are responsible for all required clearances. For instance, if they did not write the song they are by law obligated to secure a mechanical license. If the song was previously recorded and released, the artist would be entitled to a statutory license—but the rate is 8.5 cents and the artist would be liable for that payment for each sale. In addition, the artist is responsible for clearing and paying for any samples included in any Weed encoded recording. Further, if the artist fails to obtain all the necessary clearances, each Weed user who copies or distributes an unlicensed track would also be legally liable for infringement.

In December 2004, *Digital Music News* ran an article titled "WeedShare Inks Partnership with CD Baby." The article reported that independent online retailer CD Baby brokered a distribution agreement with WeedShare, with 70,000 tracks slated to go live by January 2005. For a detailed description of CD Baby, the largest online retailer of independent artists, see Chapter 17.

Chapter 10
Latest Cases & Legislative Initiatives

T his chapter sets forth the latest legal developments regarding digital music. Check the CD-ROM accompanying this book for a link to Web pages that will update this chapter.

MGM vs. Grokster: The Ninth Circuit's Decision

In August 2004 the Federal Appeals Court in the Ninth Circuit upheld the controversial District Court decision that file-sharing software programs such as Grokster are legal. Following the lead of the District Court, which we discussed in the last chapter, the Ninth Circuit decided that peer-to-peer software developers were not liable for any copyright infringement committed by people using their products, as long as they had no direct ability to stop the acts. *MGM Studios, Inc. vs. Grokster, Ltd.*, 259 F. Supp. 2d 1029 (C.D. Cal., April, 2003) aff'd.—F.3d—(9th Cir., Aug. 19, 2004).

The ruling means that companies that write and distribute peer-to-peer software can't be shut down because of the actions of their customers. But the Circuit Court did *not* find that file-trading itself is legal, and other courts in the United States have said individual computer users are breaking the law when they trade copyrighted files without permission. But the ruling does lift the cloud of potential liability from defendants Grokster and StreamCast networks, as well as from many of their rivals.

"The (record labels and movie studios) urge a re-examination of the law in the light of what they believe to be proper public policy," the court wrote. "Doubtless, taking that step would satisfy the copyright owners' immediate economic aims. However, it would also alter general copyright law in profound ways with unknown ultimate consequences outside the present context."

The decision marks a substantial—if not entirely unexpected—setback for the major record labels, which have tried hard to win legal rulings that would clamp down on anarchic peer-to-peer networks such as Kazaa or eDonkey. "Irrespective of what any court says, a debate has crystallized: it's legitimate versus illegitimate," said RIAA Chief Executive Officer Mitch Bainwol in a statement. "It's whether or not digital music will be enjoyed in a fashion that supports the creative process or one that robs it of its future. That's the online future of music."

Copyright holders have been more successful in the past, forcing companies such as Napster, Audiogalaxy and Scour to shut down their file-trading networks. But those companies had distributed software using an earlier model of file sharing, in which searches and indexing of available files all took place using a central server operated by the software company. That meant that all the millions of search requests that took place on the original Napster network involved small bits of data flowing through computers operated by the company itself—and that was enough to make the company liable for the copyright infringement. By contrast, most modern file-trading networks involve vast, decentralized webs of PCs that talk only to each other—and not to any central computer. When someone using Grokster searches for a file, the search request goes to another personal computer and ripples out through the network, like a rumor being whispered from one person to the next. When the correct file is found, a direct connection is made between the computers at the beginning and end of that chain—but Grokster itself is never involved. That decentralized system means that Grokster has no direct knowledge of individual file transfers and has no direct ability to stop transfers, the court said. As a result, it cannot be held liable for the infringement any more than Xerox can be held responsible for people using a photocopy machine to copy pages of a book. Like photocopiers, the file-trading networks could be used for many legal, noninfringing activities, the court noted. They cited rock band Wilco's use of the P2P networks to voluntarily distribute its music for free to gain attention for its music after the band lost a record contract. This fact helped establish the software itself as legal, even if the vast majority of its use turned out to be for illegal activities, the court said.

Attorneys for the copyright holders had argued that the file-trading companies could be ordered to change the way their software worked in order to exert some control over their users' illegal behavior. The court dismissed this argument, however. Only companies that had already been found liable for infringement could be ordered to block that infringement, it said. Attorneys for the file-sharing companies welcomed the decision. "This is a big win for innovators generally—not just peer-to-peer," said Fred von Lohmann, an attorney for the Electronic Frontier Foundation who represented StreamCast in the appeal. "The court (said) you have no general duty to design only software that entertainment companies approve." Von Lohmann also remarked that "the same principle means that people who make crowbars are not responsible for the robberies that may be committed with those crowbars."

An attorney for Kazaa parent Sharman networks, which is facing a parallel lawsuit in Los Angeles federal court, said he would immediately ask the record labels and movie studios to dismiss that case, or ask the lower court to rule immediately against the entertainment companies.

Like the lower court, the Ninth Circuit implied that any ability to hold software developers liable for copyright infringement might have to come from Congress rather than from the courts. Indeed, the RIAA is already pursuing that goal. It's called the "The Induce Act," and we will discuss it later in this chapter. The Appeals Court included in its decision words that some technology lawyers are interpreting as a cautionary note to Congress, as it debates that bill.

> The introduction of new technology is always disruptive to old markets and particularly to those copyright owners whose works are sold through well-established distribution mechanisms. Yet history has shown that time and market forces often provide equilibrium in balancing interests, whether the new technology be a player piano, a copier, a tape recorder, a video recorder, a personal computer, a karaoke machine or an MP3 player. Thus, it is prudent for courts to exercise caution before restructuring liability theories for the purpose of addressing specific market abuses, despite their apparent present magnitude.

U.S. Supreme Court Review of the Ninth Circuit's Decision

In October 2004, the plaintiffs in *MGM vs. Grokster*, representing virtually every major record company and Hollywood studio, as well as the National Music Publishers Association (NMPA) which represents all the major publishers, petitioned the U.S. Supreme Court to overturn the Grokster ruling. The plaintiffs joined in the 46 page petition asking the Supreme Court to overturn the ruling that peer-to-peer file-trading networks cannot be held liable for copyright infringement. In November 2004 40 state attorneys general filed a separate amicus brief urging the Supreme Court to review the Ninth Circuit's decision. The attorneys general argued that P2P networks are becoming "havens for non-copyright-related criminal activity" such as child pornography.

In early December 2004, The Supreme Court announced that it would review the Ninth Circuit's decision. According to *Billboard* magazine, the Supreme Court's decision "will finally clarify the industry's ability to control peer-to-peer technology through existing law." *Billboard* also noted that "entertainment industry lawyers say" that the Court's decision "will influence the industry at every level, including its ability to invest in artists and songwriters…" (*Billboard* magazine, December 25, 2004).

Certain experts, however, argue that even if the Court were to reverse the Ninth Circuit, the decision would not have a major impact. These experts argue that, in terms of P2P trading of songs, the train has already left the station. They point to off-shore P2P services that operate beyond the legal jurisdiction of U.S. law including certain countries, such as Canada, in which P2P is legal. They also contend that there are certain P2P systems that operate without any central control or owner. In other words, when it comes to these systems, there is no operator who could be sued. The only effective way of dealing with them, these experts argue, would be to force the ISPs to weed them out. But the content owners are not and cannot seek that relief. It would violate the ISPs' immunity from liability under DMCA and force them to spy on their customers and to censor content.

Oral arguments before the U.S. Supreme Court were expected to be scheduled for March 2005, and the Court's decision is expected before it adjourns for the summer of 2005.

The CD-ROM accompanying this book contains a link to Web pages updating the book. Those Web pages will give the current status of this case, will report on the Court's decision as soon as it is announced, and analyze the decision's impact on the music business.

More RIAA Lawsuits

You might think that perhaps that the Ninth Circuit's decision would finally persuade the labels to stop suing people, including its own customers, and work with the ISPs and the electronics industry to negotiate a statutory license which would legalize file sharing and at the same time provide fair compensation to the labels and their artists. In that case, you would be wrong.

What strategy did the recording industry decide to pursue? Apparently, more lawsuits. In the last days of September 2004 the RIAA continued its flurry of legal actions. It announced that it initiated lawsuits against another 762 individuals suspected of copyright infringement on peer-to-peer file-sharing networks. As of December 2004, the total number of people the record label trade group has filed suit against is 7,706. The new lawsuits included 26 against university students. For the RIAA, the latest round is part of a consistent string of suits that started the year before. The RIAA also said it sued 68 defendants whose identities had been revealed as a result of past "John Doe" suits, and had declined out of court settlements. The RIAA has offered to settle its copyright infringement suits against file-swappers for an average of $5,000 each. RIAA President Cary Sherman was quoted as saying about the lawsuits that because sales of prerecorded music have declined so precipitously, "You worry more about survival and a little less about popularity. We also knew if we did nothing, the damage would get far, far worse." According to marketing specialist Adam Hanft, however, the recording business "has done nothing right." Instead of criminalizing file sharing, "the industry should have put a focus on how we can cooperate with hardware and software manufacturers to create legal alternatives."

While the intended effect is to reduce illicit file-sharing and encourage legitimate music purchases, it is unclear if the trade group is actually "winning." P2P traffic levels appear to be steadily increasing. Eric Garland, CEO of Big Champagne, whose California Senate testimony we cited in Chapter 8, was reported as stating, "The RIAA has been effective at stigmatizing the downloading behavior that people don't want to talk about it, which is different than people giving it up." According to Garland, Big Champagne research as of October 2004 shows that illegal peer-to-peer is actually slightly higher than it was before the RIAA launched its campaign. Their research also shows that, at a conservative estimate, 4 million people are online at any given moment happily swapping 1 billion files every month, at the very least. Garland estimates that in November 2004 alone, file swappers traded nearly 1.4 billion tracks over free networks. (The CD-ROM accompanying this book includes an interview with Mr. Garland, and his Big Champagne colleague, Joe Fleisher.)

Is an even more massive enforcement effort needed? The RIAA says yes, and is looking towards proposed legislation called the "Piracy Act" (not to be confused with yet another piece of proposed legislation called the Induce Act discussed in the next section) to give the government jurisdiction to prosecute file-swappers in civil courts. According to outgoing Senate Judiciary Committee Chairman Orrin Hatch, the Piracy Act could provide some serious enforcement muscle, as "tens of thousands of continuing civil enforcement actions might be needed to generate the necessary deterrence."

I received permission to reprint the following e-mail exchange from a prominent record company executive to Peter Fader, a professor at the Warton Business School, on the issue of the wisdom of the RIAA's course of legal action:

> From: [Record Company Executive]
> Sent: Tuesday, September 21, 2004
> To: Fader, Peter
> Subject: Question
>
> Off-the-record. If you were to be asked the impact of the lawsuits—whether there was another route to take, etc.—what would your answer be?
>
> From: Fader, Peter
> Sent: Wednesday, September 22, 2004
> To: [Record Company Executive]
> Subject: RE: Question
>
> The lawsuits have been a disaster for the industry, particularly with a view towards the long run. Ten reasons:
>
> 1. They alienate customers (including many of the biggest/best ones).
> 2. They force customers to focus on and talk about stupid counter-productive stuff instead of focusing on music, per se.
> 3. They destroy any possible goodwill/brand equity that the labels could have with their customers.
> 4. They make the industry look very foolish (and desperate) in the eyes of influential outsiders (e.g., journalists and investors).

5. They "prove" to customers that file-sharing/downloading is the best way of getting music. Forbidden fruit.

6. They encourage outsiders to come up with new (and largely unauthorized) technologies and business models to obtain music in stealthier ways.

7. They are an enormous waste of corporate and industry resources.

8. As a result of this enormous waste of resources, they keep the industry from investing time, money, and creativity into productive outreach activities (such as promoting subscription models).

9. They make people skeptical about the bias and validity of any statements (e.g., sales numbers) that come out of the industry.

10. They encourage industry executives to cling to (and invest in) the old, outdated business model instead of looking ahead towards new ones.

I find it very disheartening that interesting new initiatives (like the latest version of Musicmatch) are largely unnoticed by any music fans. I'm amazed at how few people have tried any subscription services—or can even identify any of them.

You guys are shooting yourselves in the foot (and more sensitive places), and the bleeding isn't going to stop for a long time.

Despite all this, I'm still on your side—wanting to see music customers do the right thing. I just believe more in carrots versus sticks.

It would be great fun to have a forum to discuss these points openly and honestly. The bunker mentality isn't working.

In addition to suing more music lovers in the wake of the Ninth Circuit's ruling in the Grokster case, the RIAA also helped launch a major legislative initiative aimed at overturning the decision.

Induce Act

Proposed legislation titled the Inducing of Copyright Infringement Act of 2004, and better known as the Induce Act, was introduced last summer by Senator Orrin Hatch (R-Utah), himself a songwriter. There were also powerful co-sponsors from the other side of the aisle, including Tom Daschle (D-South Dakota) and Patrick Leahy (D-Vermont).

The act provided that "any party who intentionally induces, or intentionally aids, abets, counsels or procures any violation of the Copyright Act shall be held liable as an infringer." This language was so broad that it raised a lot of concern among the consumer electronics and computer industries. The Electronic Frontier Foundation lodged a mock complaint against Apple on behalf of record companies, stating that Apple's ad for a 40 GB iPod that can hold up to 10,000 songs *is* in fact inducement under the act's all-encompassing language. Since most Americans don't have a CD collection containing 10,000 songs, the iPod would "induce" them to download free music. Focusing on the dark-side of this joke in terms of its potential impact in the electronics business, the Consumer Electronics Association pushed very hard to amend the language.

As a consequence of this criticism, the Senators who co-authored the Induce Act are seeking to overhaul aspects of the legislation. That process has involved Register of Copyrights Marybeth Peters coordinating high-level meetings with music, movie, technology and even P2P companies. A letter requesting Peters' help was signed and delivered by Senate Republican leader Bill Frist (R-Tennessee), Democratic leader Tom Daschle (D-South Dakota), Judiciary Committee chairman Orrin Hatch (R-Utah), and committee senior Democrat Patrick Leahy (D-Vermont).

"Technology companies are concerned that claims for intentional inducement of infringement might be misused frivolously against entities who distribute legitimate copying devices or programs such as computers, CD burners, personal video recorders, and e-mail services," wrote the Senators. The letter continues with a not so subtle stab at P2P firms: "We are open to any constructive input on how Congress can best frame a technology-neutral law directed at a small set of bad actors while protecting our legitimate technology industries from frivolous litigation."

As of the time this manuscript was delivered, the Senate Judiciary Committee had officially postponed a vote on the Induce Act, with bill sponsor Orrin Hatch initiating another round of negotiations in order to "perfect" language in the bill. Looking forward, it is unclear whether or not the bill can be narrowed to only target P2P networks. One industry executive who opposes the legislation noted that groups like the RIAA normally start with overly broad pieces of legislation, seeking far more piracy protection than what is needed. In a recent report titled "Induce Act Stalls, Lame Duck Possibilities," the *Digital Music News* (www.digitalmusicnews.com) announced in November 2004:

> After an 11th hour breakdown in negotiations . . . the Induce Act was withheld from a Senate Judiciary Committee vote. Bill sponsor Orrin Hatch postponed the vote, fearing eventual lack of support for the initiative. Heavy opposition from the CEA and other technology groups dimmed the possibility of the bill surviving. While Hatch did follow through on a promise to hold closed-door, marathon sessions between entertainment and technology interests, discussions were fruitless. According to one source to *Digital Music News*, the gulf between industry groups like CEA and the RIAA actually widened, with no compromise in sight.

A report on the Induce Act published on December 25, 2004 in *Billboard* announced that "Congressional Insiders and industry players say that federal lawmakers will put [the Induce Act] S. 2056, on hold next year until the Supreme Court renders a decision in the Grokster case, expected in June." (See the discussion earlier in this chapter on the Supreme Court's review of the Grokster case.) For an update of the status of the Induce Act, visit the Web pages updating this book by clicking on the link provided in the menu in the attached CD-ROM.

Recent Developments in Other Countries

Various forms of recording equipment are subject to a levy in more than 40 countries, including the United States under the AHRA. The fees are generally collected by government or nonprofit agencies on behalf of copyright owners and creators, and then distributed to the copyright owners and creators in accordance with government approved formulas. Generally, the fees are distributed on a 50–50 basis to creators and copyright owners, but the specifics vary from nation to nation. These levies generally do *not* include computers or MP3 players. With the dramatic popularity of using computers and MP3 players to make copies of and listen to music, there have been calls for expanding the levies to cover these machines. Some of the most interesting recent developments have occurred in Canada and Germany.

Developments in Canada

Levies on MP3 Players: A Step Forward, and a Step Back. Before the Canadian Copyright Act was amended in 1998, copying any copyrighted sound recording for almost any purpose infringed copyright in Canada. The 1998 amendment legalized copying of sound recordings for the personal use of the person who makes the copy. The 1998 amendment also imposed a levy on certain forms of recording equipment. The amendment mandated the Copyright Board of Canada to develop allocation formulas to compensate copyright holders for "private copying." In 2000, the Board imposed levies on recordable CD media, having already applied one to blank audiocassettes. Manufacturers and importers are responsible for paying the levy on covered items that they sell or otherwise dispose of in Canada.

The fees collected from these levies go into a fund to compensate songwriters, recording artists, and record labels for revenues lost from personal copying by consumers. The Canadian Private Copying Collective (CPCC) was designated as the collection and distribution body for the amounts generated by private copying levy. The CPCC collected approximately $24 million for 2003. The money is paid in accordance with the Board's allocation formula to songwriters and music publishers, recording artists, and record companies. Royalties collected for 2001 through 2004 were allocated as follows:

- 66% to eligible songwriters and publishers
- 18.9% to eligible performers
- 15.1% to eligible record companies

According to the CPCC Web site,

> [S]ince no inventory of privately copied tracks exists, distribution is based on representative samples of radio airplay and album sales, which are given equal weight in the distribution. Together they provide a proxy for determining the titles that Canadians typically copy for private use. Samples are regularly used by copyright collectives because the cost of capturing and analyzing all available information would be excessive.

In December 2003, the Copyright Board took the controversial step of expanding levies to MP3. As everyone knows, many people rip their personal CD collections and make copies in their iPods for portable listening. Since this is a hugely popular form of "reasonable copying," the Board decided to make MP3 subject to the levy. They demanded that MP3 player manufacturers cough up $2 for each player with a capacity of less than 1GB, $15 for 1–10GB players and $25 for devices with storage of more than 10GB. Not surprisingly, MP3 player manufacturers weren't too happy about this, and took the Board to court. The case eventually ended up in the Canadian Federal Court of Appeal.

That court shot down the levy on MP3 players in a decision rendered in December 2004. The court decided that Canada's levy on blank media, authorized under the amendment to the Copyright Act, did not apply to MP3 players. Judge Marc Noël admitted that the Board was acting from an understandable desire to compensate copyright holders for revenue lost when copies of their work are downloaded from P2P networks, but stated "the authority for doing so still has to be found in the act."

Organizations such as the Canadian Private Copying Collective, which distributes the proceeds of the levies to artists and recording companies, are pondering whether to take the case to Canada's Supreme Court in a bid to have Judge Noël's ruling overturned. At the very least, they are likely to lobby the Canadian government to amend the Copyright Act to take into account MP3 players and perhaps, and personal computers.

Canadian Federal Court Rules That Downloading and Sharing Music Online Is Legal. In March 2004 Justice Konrad von Finckenstein ruled that sharing music files on P2P services is legal under Canadian copyright law (*BMG Canada Inc. et al. v. John Doe, Jane Doe*, Docket.)

Numerous record companies, through the Canadian Recording Industry Association ("CRIA"), the Canadian version of RIAA, sued 29 individuals who had over 1000 downloaded recordings on computer file sharing services such as Morpheus and iMesh and who downloaded songs and made their music files available to others on these services. These individuals had only been identified by their Internet addresses, and CRIA sought a court order to compel their Internet service providers to disclose their names and addresses.

The Court denied the order based on its opinion that file sharing did not infringe Canadian copyright laws. It held that downloading a song for personal use was not an infringement because private copying sections of the Copyright Act expressly permitted the making copies of music for personal use. But the court went beyond this and also ruled that the CRIA hadn't shown copyright infringement by these people even though they allowed their music files to be *uploaded.* The decision means that in Canada individuals who share personal copies of music files on the Internet are immune from prosecution and liability. This goes well beyond the Ninth Circuit's decision in Grokster. The Grokster court only found that the defendant P2P services did not infringe. In dicta that court stated that individuals who download unauthorized music, let alone upload it, were *not* immune from copyright infringement.

"No evidence was presented that the alleged infringers either distributed or authorized the reproduction of sound recordings," von Finckenstein wrote in his 28-page ruling. "They merely placed personal copies into their shared directories which were accessible by other computer users via a P2P service."

The music industry in Canada wanted to shut down Internet file sharing of music, blaming it for plummeting sales of compact discs. As expected, this decision is being challenged by the Canadian Recording Industry Association. The CRIA filed an appeal which is pending as of the date of this manuscript submission. For the current status of the case, go to the Web pages updating this book by using the link in the accompanying CD-ROM.

German Court Imposes a Levy on Computers

In a landmark decision that could have wide ramifications for the electronics business in Europe and perhaps the U.S., a German court in January 2005 ordered a computer manufacturer, Fujitsu Siemens, to pay copyright royalties for each computer it sells.

The suit was first brought by VG Wort rights society, a copyright management society. VG Worth argued that Fujitsu Siemens' hardware can be used for copying, and therefore infringes the rights of its members. VG Wort administers a levy on blank recording media which was designed to compensate rights holders for lost royalties. In 2003, VG Wort collected about 83.53 million euro in royalties and distributed the funds to 260,000 authors and 6,500 copyright owners. VG Wort had originally sought a levy of 30 euros for each new PC sold.

The Munich District Court ordered Fujitsu Siemens, a joint venture between Japanese and German electronics makers, to pay a levy of 12 euros per new computer sold in the country. The court reasoned that Fujitsu Siemens should pay a tax—just as the makers of blank audio and video cassettes have to pay—given that its computers can be used for unauthorized copying. The money will be used to reimburse copyright holders—artists, performers, recording companies, publishers and movie studios.

This decision marks the first time a European court has imposed a copyright levy on new PCs. The decision could pave the way for lawsuits against other PC makers, and is likely to be challenged by the computer industry.

Roundtable Discussion

This is a conversation about the latest legal developments with:

> Ariel Taitz, Esq., V.P. Legal and Business Affairs, Atlantic Records;
> Stan Soocher, Professor, Univ. of Colorado; Editor, *Entertainment Law & Finance*
> Eric de Fontenay, Editor, MusicDish.com and mi2n.com

> The conversation was recorded in September 2004.

Steve Gordon: Let's start with the technology that some people perceive as the end of the music business—at least as we've known it. I'm talking about peer-to-peer file sharing. A huge development, as we all know, is the Ninth Circuit's decision just a few days ago, in the MGM v. Grokster *case. Stan, as our resident legal scholar, what was the difference in Napster and Grokster cases? That Napster* had *control and could* have filtered out copyrighted *material?*

Stan Soocher: That's absolutely right, Steve. They found that there was control by Napster in that case. Also, let's keep in mind the fundamental issue which courts regularly will find, that people who are doing the downloading are direct infringers themselves. So the first issue is that you have to find *direct* infringement in order to find vicarious or contributory infringement. But they were not found in the *MGM v. Grokster* case, and the Ninth Circuit ends its ruling by telling the music industry and the entertainment industry, "If you want to do anything about this, you really need to go to Congress and ask for help."

SG: I'd like to go around the table and ask whether you agree or disagree. Ariel, was the case correctly decided?

Ariel Taitz: I don't presume to be a copyright expert or a copyright professor, but my sense is that the court placed far too much emphasis, and I think frankly maybe was a little bit—fooled is too strong a word—but *confused* by the so-called non-central server aspect. . . . I think despite the fact that the software was created to be different from Napster and its so-called central server, I think it's very hard to understand how the court can conclude that there is neither actual knowledge nor material contribution to infringement here. I think had there *not* been substantial non-infringing uses, then they'd simply have constructive knowledge. I think that as to both vicarious liability and contributory liability, those with success in this lawsuit, Grokster, etc., are largely dependent on their creation of software that was able to . . . effectively not have any central server, but in fact it still contributes materially to the infringement. And they clearly have actual knowledge of the vast majority of uses for their software, which is to infringe copyrights.

SG: Let me read the very first paragraph of the opinion, which I think is the essence of the decision. "From the advent of the player piano," Circuit Judge Thomas wrote, "every new means of reproducing sound has struck a dissonant chord with musical copyright owners, often resulting in federal litigation. This appeal is the latest reprise of that recurring conflict, and one of a continuing series of lawsuits between the recording industry and the distributors of file-sharing computer software." It seems to me, Eric de Fontenay, that this case was about a clash between content and new technologies. Do you think that the court did not strictly apply the relevant rules because it wanted to establish that you can't impede the new technologies or the creation of something that might be of great benefit to the public?

Eric de Fontenay: I disagree. For me, it's the question of, Is it the gun that's committing the murder, or is it the murderer? If you presume that it's the gun, then you go after gun manufacturers, something that hasn't been very successful, by the way.

AT: But it has been for the tobacco industry.

EF: Because they explicitly had a strategy of misleading. I think in this case the industry was aware that this tactic of attacking technology was very dangerous. It was very dangerous for innovation, and I feel it's fundamentally wrong. Basically what you have to do is go after people that are using the application in an illegal manner, and that's what the RIAA has been doing very aggressively with what we call the "John Doe suits." And we've seen very recently, right after the Grokster case, that the Department of Justice is bringing criminal charges. Now the issue is: Is it a war than can be won when you're talking about a population of 20 million or more "infringers"?

SG: Eric, just to clarify, the court did not *legalize uploading or downloading of copyrighted files. So although Grokster's technology is legal, the court did* not *legalize the sharing of copyrighted files. So the RIAA is free to continue enforcing.*

Ari, looking back to the Sony Betamax case, Jack Valente thought that VCRs and home copying were going to kill the movie business. Instead VCRs have turned out to be a major source of income for the movie studios. In fact, they make more money from home video than they do from box office receipts. Ari, is there any possibility that the record labels can embrace P2P on any level, or is it just anathema and it has to be shut down?

AT: The court told it exactly right—every new technology brings about fights between copyright owners and technological innovators. That is an historical fact. Typically, as with the VCR and many other technological innovations, it's brought new sources of revenue for copyright owners. I don't think that this round of technological innovation is going to be any different.

SG: It's just that no one has figured out a way to compensate the labels yet, but hopefully that idea will emerge.

AT: I think that it's a very difficult problem. Cassette tapes didn't have that sort of complexity to them. It's a particularly difficult challenge, and it's taken its toll on the music industry. There's no doubt that the music industry has suffered as a factual matter. Record sales are down worldwide . . . basically about a 10% decline in revenue in the U.S. in the last three consecutive years. This year we're starting to see a leveling off and a slight increase in the number of units sold, but interestingly it's not increasing revenue because the sales of CDs have gone down dramatically.

SG: Stan Soocher, would the Induce Act countermand the decision in the Grokster case?

SS: Well, it would certainly help the music industry from that point of view. In a nutshell, what the act states is that "any party who intentionally induces, or intentionally aids, abets, counsels, or procures any violation of the Copyright Act shall be held liable as an infringer."

SG: That's pretty broad, isn't it?

SS: It's very broad, and that has raised a lot of concern among the consumer electronics and computer industries, who would like to see this, if passed at all, to specifically be limited to P2P file-sharing.

SG: Even if it was limited to P2P, in either case it would still shut down Grokster and this kind of technology, wouldn't it?

SS: That's the intent of the legislation, and that's really the fallback position of the entertainment industry after losing the federal appeal in the Grokster case. Now the computer and electronics industries have to act fast because Orrin Hatch has indicated that he intends to move this as quickly as possible through Congress. Again, he has a vested interest, being a songwriter, so he's got an emotional side to this issue as well as a political side.

SG: Right, because the way it's phrased now, I would think that it's broad enough to capture iPods or all MP3 players in its net. It seems that broad.

EF: In fact, we've seen a letter from the Consumer Electronics Association to the leading Senators and sponsors of the bill, proposing amendments to the language which would narrow it to commercial computer applications that are specifically designed for wide-scale piracy on digital networks. What's interesting with that nuanced proposal is that possibly the Grokster case is in fact saying: "No, this software is not specifically designed for piracy because it has sufficient non-infringing uses." And so Grokster *could* pass under the umbrella.

SG: It was drafted so broadly that I would think that everybody anticipated that the electronics business would be very disturbed by the language, and that they would be on the scene. Was it broadly drafted, Stan Soocher, just to get attention? They'd have to expect that it would have to be narrowed.

SS: With legislation there's often give and take. But one of the things that really caught the ire of the electronics industry was their claim that this legislation was drafted in secret between the RIAA and Orrin Hatch's staff. So, right away they're angry.

AT: People are telling me that there's tremendous momentum for this particular legislation. Obviously there will be some compromise, there'll be some revision. In a more narrow version, I think something like this *is* going to pass. I've been told that it's on the fast track.

SG: So you're optimistic that there will be legislation that will reverse the Ninth Circuit's decision, Ari? Or will it be watered down so much that Grokster may get in under the wire as Eric de Fontenay discussed?

AT: Yes, I think Eric's point is well-taken. It will be interesting to watch.

EF: We also have to realize that we're in an election year and we may end up with a slightly reshuffled Senate, and I think that the Consumer Electronics Association has its own friends in the Senate. The Induce Act certainly has some momentum, but I wouldn't count on the other side not creating a coalition of Senators to advocate protecting the tech industry.

SG: As the Grokster court pointed out, it's really a conflict between content owners and technology, and the technology sector has a great deal of money, which translates into political power.

Stan Soocher, notwithstanding the decision in Grokster, it's still a violation of copyright law to upload or download unauthorized music files. Can you give us a snapshot view of the RIAA's lawsuits against those who upload and download copyrighted music? And has Attorney General Ashcroft joined the fight?

SS: The record labels through the RIAA have been going after consumers. The first battle was whether they could bring a John Doe subpoena and get the courts to reveal names of users, direct infringers who are downloading, without having to go to a court hearing. There was a case that came out of the District of Columbia that said that the RIAA had to go to court, to a judge and not just a court clerk, to find out the name of users. [See Chapter 9 for a discussion of the *Verizon* case.] We've had other cases coming about like this, but the RIAA continues to be determined, even after the Grokster ruling, to go directly after infringers by serving subpoenas on them. I don't think that's likely to change. The widespread importance of this issue has caught the Justice Department's attention, but I'm not sure how much they're going to run with it. I think that there will be more criticism the more heavy-handed that they get.

SG: I read in the New York Times *that Ashcroft is going after Internet crime, but the article didn't specifically mention P2P file-sharing. Eric de Fontenay, did you hear anything about that?*

EF: Yes, they have launched the first enforcement action against the P2P, through the FBI, I believe. There were search warrants that were issued and I believe there have been some criminal charges lodged. And there have been a lot of complaints, even in Congress. There is another statute called the No Electronic Theft, or NET, Act that also has some severe penalties, which I believe the government has only used once in trying to enforce it.

The problem that the government faces here, again, is almost analogous to the problem with drugs. If so many people are using it, what type of real enforcement can you provide? With the industry at least—and the Department of Justice has not been this clear at least in their actions—they've been going after what have been clear infringers: people who make 800 songs available for other people to download.

SG: Tiny Napsters, if you will.

EF: Yes, and there is a logic to the theory. In general, in any network 5% of the users account for 85% or 90% of the files made available. So you can slice off the dragon's head, [and] you may be able to dry the well of illegal music coming onto these networks. What's been interesting is that although the John Doe suits *did* have an initial impact on file-sharing, it didn't last very long. I believe that file-sharing is now exceeding where it was prior to those lawsuits, because most people know that they're not within that parameter of bad behavior.

AT: I think that over the long-term they are having a small impact. I don't by any means think that they're any sort of cure-all. I think it's part of a much larger strategy. They can play a small part in trying to encourage people to choose legal alternatives to unauthorized file-sharing. The obvious more important part of the larger strategy has got to be offering alternatives that people like—viable alternatives to get files over the Internet, to purchase, download, stream, to do the things that people want to do, legally, for a small fee.

SG: Everybody thought that iTunes was going to be the answer. How many songs have they sold?

AT: They've sold over 100 million now. [As of December 2004, approximately six months after this interview, sales were over 200 million.] They're selling over 2 million a week. Plus with Napster, Rhapsody, and some of the other ones, I think we're starting to exceed 3 million downloads a week. It's a growing business, [but] it's still a tiny fraction of the overall music business.

SG: It's growing, but as someone pointed out, Norah Jones sells more records just on her own than all of iTunes, because 100 million songs if you divided it by the number of songs on an album . . .

AT: Yes, it's about 9 or 10 million albums. But the point is that there *are* legal alternatives out there that are really starting to gain subscribers. iTunes is a tremendous service. I use it, I love it. Everyone who has an iPod who has tried iTunes loves it. Napster and Rhapsody are starting to offer monthly subscription services that are starting to gain some appeal.

The other thing that nobody's mentioned yet about the P2P systems are that they are very popular, tremendously popular, but they're not perfect. There are a lot of problems with them. There is a potential for getting viruses when you use these services, and also a potential for [when] you think you're getting a new Madonna song or a new Christina Aguilera song, it turns out that you're getting a file filled with dead air.

SG: But Ari, that's partially due to the record companies' hiring other companies who "spoof" and send fake files out there. That's public record.

AT: But the point is, whatever the reason, if you talk to any teenager nowadays they'll tell you that the heyday of file-sharing is kind of over. And they're having to find different and newer file-sharing systems and networks to get what they used to get.

SG: On the other hand, file-sharing has whetted the appetite for new music and free music, and instead of Kazaa, which is riddled with spyware, kids are going to services like eDonkey, which promise no spyware, and technologies are developing that will prevent the spoofing to the extent that it occurs. And these kids who turned out to be so brilliant in developing these new technologies—Napster was developed by a 19-year-old; the Kazaa technology was developed by another teenager—it just seems that the kids will find a way of averting the measures of the content owners, and that the content owners are losing the battle. Eric de Fontenay, do you agree with that?

EF: We are not talking about a homogenous market. The people going to iTunes are people who know what they want, and they don't have time to deal with all of the problems that have just been mentioned. They want to find it fast, and they don't mind paying for it. I think there is always a segment of the population—and it seems to be a relatively large segment—that still feels that whatever the problems that they may have with P2P, that they're still getting more bang for their buck—if effort can be translated into money—than paying 99 cents for a download. First of all, we have to look at what would the demand for music on iTunes, etc. be if the songs were 50 cents. That is the real question.

SG: Isn't Rhapsody implementing a 50-cent download?

EF: Yes. I don't believe it's permanent. The record industry has a lot of problems because on the one hand they're trying to protect revenues from CDs, so the downloads can't undercut that, otherwise in their eyes they're really losing revenue. But they're not really taking into account what is the real demand at various price points. I think that's where you're going to see more demand coming out of a little more competitiveness. But to do that, we have to also deal with royalty issues, etc., because 50 cents just won't make it unless the distributors are willing to distribute the music at a loss, which, in the case of Apple, maybe leads to 15% more iPods being sold.

AT: File-sharing is never going to disappear. Just like it's a fact that people copy software—there will always be people who are copying Microsoft Word from their friends in their dorm rooms and from their friends at work and from trading stuff in their classrooms, etc. Just like there are people with illegal cable boxes, there are people getting pirated movies, there are people doing all sorts of things. Maybe the file-sharing is more than that, it's a bigger chunk of the population, but in the end the software industry survives despite piracy, the cable industry same thing, and ultimately the reason that they're successful is all the same reason. If you offer quality, consistency, and accountability for a reasonable price—maybe 99 cents isn't quite there, maybe 89 cents is there. Maybe $10 a month for all you want is a better model. There will be a point where we find the right price, and enough people will be buying music legitimately.

SG: Ari, as we wait for that successful business model to emerge, thousands of people are being offered early retirement at the major labels, artists are being dropped . . .

AT: From the software point of view I think it's incorrect. The software industry, how they fought piracy has been by creating a relationship with the customer. If you want to update to the next Word, well, if you're already an existing customer here you go. And I think there are all types of embedded things—when you buy the software initially, what you're in fact acquiring is value over the life of the software. In music we haven't been able to do that. Funny enough, DVDs sell like crazy because at the price point they're viewed as a bargain among all of the entertainment products available. So that's what I'm talking about—pricing, but it's also about value. The old CD is not going to make it, not at this price. Just plain downloads that you play that give sound are not sustainable, not at 99 cents, not at least to grab a large enough market no matter how well you deliver the file.

SG: Maybe the key is the relationship with the customer. The customer of the music business is now being sued by the music business, which does not help customer relations. Plus, here's what I think is going on in terms of psychology. When a kid has his parents buy a new Dell computer with speakers and blank optical CDs, and they subscribe to a high-speed Internet connection, they have relationships with Dell or AOL or Verizon. So they pay a lot of money already to use this stuff, and what does the stuff allow you to do? To download music. In other words, the customers have already paid a lot of money to get so-called free music. And you're up against technology that is absolutely brilliant. So here's what I'm suggesting as a compromise between the content owners, the music business—which has lost $3 billion of $14.5 billion in the United States alone—and the competing industry which is not *Kazaa or Grokster, but is Verizon and Dell and Compaq and Microsoft and MP3 players and the electronics and ISP businesses. Perhaps a compromise could be worked out either by having those businesses that are profiting from illegal file-sharing pay to compensate the content owners for their loss, or a blanket licensing system could be established, as ASCAP and BMI have done. Ari, is that out of the question?*

AT: I think they're very interesting ideas. Some of them are even quite compelling. The problem is when they come up against reality. I just don't see it coming about so quickly. The licensing of music and the purchasing of music is such a complex web. For better or for worse, for sales of recorded music, there's no statutory rate like with musical compositions, which is one of the things that determines this web of complexity. There are so many players that would have to come together to reach some sort of a set fee. I mean, how much money would have to be paid into this big fund? How would they set it per stream, per download? How would the money be split up among composition owners…

SG: I know that there are a lot of problems, Ari, but we have models that have *worked.*

The ASCAP and BMI models offer blanket licenses for performing songs, and now SoundEx-change, which administers a statutory blanket license for masters for webcasts.

AT: The ASCAP and BMI models are child's play compared to what you're suggesting.

SG: But we already impose levies in many countries, including the U.S., for various forms of recording media like blank audio and digital tape. It's not just theory.

AT: There is no statutory rate for the sale of recorded music. There are statutory rates in the U.S. and Europe and Canada for underlying compositions.

SG: I was mentioning these levies that are applied to consumer electronics, a tax if you want, that is collected and paid to copyright owners and creators including labels and artists.

Ari, on a personal note, at Sony Music they've been downsizing for the last three years. Last week many friends of mine got severance packages, and they're wondering where they go next. Because nobody's going to hire them because everybody is downsizing. And on the other hand, Ari, people at ASCAP have never been more secure, because they're making more money there than ever because of blanket licensing. So from a personal point of view as a music industry professional, I hope that this becomes a more viable solution to the recording industry, because a lot of people in the business are suffering.

AT: There's no question about it. The combination of Atlantic Records and Elektra Records when I started there four and a half years ago had probably about 600 or 700 people working there. Now we've combined completely and now we have about 200 people in one company for the last four years. So we've basically cut over 60% of the staff in four years.

SG: My point of view is not to attack the record companies because I think that they've always performed a useful service by promoting artists' careers, and I would love to have the record companies around in the future. That being said, Ari, what new business models are you excited about in terms of new technologies and the record business's abilities to exploit those new technologies?

AT: It's your favorite topic: ringtones.

SG: A $3 billion business!

AT: Actually, what's going to start being well-known in the U.S. and is already a big thing in Europe are "ring-back" tones. People are quite willing to pay $1.99 and sometimes even $2.50 and more to have their cell phones play a song instead of making a ringing noise. People who buy them buy multiple ringtones, and sure enough your phone will not only be able to designate what song it will play when your phone is ringing, but you also get to designate what song will be playing when people call you. So when someone calls your cell phone, instead of hearing a ringing noise, they can hear a song and vice versa. There is a lot of personalization of mobile devices with music. It's no longer just an idea—we're talking about real money.

Sales of ringtones were over $100 million in 2003 in the U.S. alone, but were estimated to be close to $3 billion worldwide. That's because Japan and Europe are two or three years ahead of us. They're looking at massive exponential growth, and they think that within a few years the ringtones sales business will be over $1 billion in the U.S. alone. To put that in perspective, that's roughly 10% of total recorded music sales in the U.S. So it's just a massive business, far outstripping digital downloads and iTunes. And that's part of my overall point, which is that, despite file-sharing—which I think will always be around—there are still people who are going to buy CDs and people who are going to buy digital downloads, people who are going to sign up for subscription services in growing numbers, and there are going to be a lot of new sources of revenue. Ringtones and ring-back tones are one of the biggest examples.

People are going to be able to access video on their phones as well. So just like you can buy a ringtone for $2, you can buy a 30-second clip of a video for a couple of bucks. We're experimenting with subscription models where you pay one fee and you get a whole bunch of ringtones and wallpaper and images for your phone, and videos.

SG: I believe there is a company called iRiver that is now manufacturing gadgets that are basically MP3 players but also play video.

AT: There are a lot of exciting opportunities for new revenue sources. I think that in the end we're going to find that music is consumed more than it ever was, by more people, at a cheaper price than it ever was. Music will be everywhere—it will be a part of your phone, a part of your identity, a part of all your wireless devices—and people will still buy CDs. People are now experimenting quite a bit with offering companion DVDs, so that you get an audio CD and a free DVD, and there's a new product that we're putting out very shortly called the Dual Disc, which on one side is a regular audio CD but on the flipside it's a DVD which can contain a DVD-audio version of the album, photo galleries, video, anything that you would find on a DVD.

SG: You can listen to the latest U2 album and on the other side see a live concert . . .

AT: These are ways that the record companies are trying to add value to something. We've already seen an increase in sales of recorded music this year, the first increase in four years. I think that's due in part to the decreased price *and* the added value. But we're also starting to see additional business from ringtones and sales of video for wireless devices and all of the things I've mentioned, plus the exponential growth we're seeing on iTunes. Small as it is still, in a couple of years I think it's going to be big enough to make up the difference that we've seen in the lost sales from the past few years.

SG: Well, I hope so, Ari, because I make my living by helping people comply with the law and paying copyright owners what they deserve. The issue is harnessing this new technology.

EF: Can I just make one remark on the issue of growth? The recording industry has kind of been the black sheep of the music business. It should be noted that the music industry as a whole *has* been growing. ASCAP and BMI are seeing historically high revenues from licensing music, largely due to the emergence and growth of new media platforms such as satellite TV. The recording industry has historically been selling physical units.

The problem is that it's not clear whether the Internet is in fact a per-transaction, per-unit type of environment, or whether it's pay [one fee] and you're able to use as you want. Looking at ISPs, most of them revolve around the latter, and I think that's part of the problem for the recording industry. That is an adjustment they'll have to make.

AT: I think that's a good point, and one of the other new business models is a subscription-based model. For a couple of decades now, the only thing we've really done is sell physical product containing recorded music, either a cassette or a vinyl album or a CD. We're now looking very seriously at going into merchandising, into possibly getting a piece of touring, into fan clubs, into basically being a part of the growth of the music industry as Eric correctly points out. I think that you'll start to see the record companies evolve into something more than they were, a combination of merchandising companies, record companies, and marketing companies, and making money from selling physical goods as well.

SG: Well Ari, as long as the artists are fairly compensated, that may be a positive development, because the one thing that the record companies have done that the publishing companies and ASCAP and BMI have not done so much is promote and market their artists' music. The record companies put a lot of money into creating recordings, marketing, and publicizing, and nurturing and developing artists. So if they become even more proactive, that's a positive development as long as the artists are getting their fair share.

I want to return to the subject of blanket licensing to get Stan Soocher's take. Do you have a point of view on whether it would work?

SS: It might work because the model is already there, but you're talking of course about the interactive services, because for webcasting we already have it. I'm more neutral on that issue. I think that the sound-recording copyright owners would like the ability to negotiate. They could still, I suppose, try to do that somewhat with a blanket license. I also want to mention something that we haven't talked about that's really looming on the horizon: that is, the coming of digital broadcasting and the receivers that will be able to select songs to record in a digital format, and the fight that's beginning in that area with the record industry being highly concerned. This would also apply to music publishers too, people being able to pretty much take songs and trade them with each other. They've got good digital copies that they have gotten off of their broadcast service. It remains to be seen how damaging that would be, but that is another factor to add.

SG: You're talking about digital radio?

SS: Digital radio broadcasting. It's beginning to roll out. The FCC has already said, and this is just an initial decision, that they are not going to require, at least in the beginning, any kind of copyright protection technology.

SG: Now, why would a conservative administration permit that?

SS: It's a wait-and-see attitude. I think they will need to see true damage.

SG: Would digital radio stations have to pay royalties to the record companies? I think they would—all digital broadcasts of music are subject to payment to the owners of the recordings under DPSRA, and the rates to be paid are provided under the DMCA. Perhaps that is why encoding is not an issue—because the record companies and the artists will be compensated. Ari, I think the record companies would make money from this.

AT: Yes.

SG: Well, that may be one reason why the FCC does not seem to be in a hurry to prevent copying. Because the whole reason why we have a statutory license for digital transmission of recorded music is that lawmakers recognized that people could make copies and they wanted to compensate the record companies. So perhaps digital radio could be another source of income for the record companies.

The final subject that I want to get into today is how independent artists can use P2P. In its decision the Grokster court gave an interesting example of substantial non-infringing use: They pointed out that the record company of the band Wilco declined to release one of their albums because the label thought that the album had no commercial potential. The judge wrote, "Wilco repurchased the work from the record company and made the album available for free downloading, both from its own Web site and through the software-user networks' P2P. The result sparked widespread interest, and as a result Wilco received another recording contract." Eric, do you think this is a good example of how a band or an artist can use P2P?

EF: It *is* one example. That's a very specific situation. The broader issue in this case is, can P2P be used by a band to be able to attract a fan base and a following that will attract attention, including attention from people in the industry? For example, we have artists that we're going to be promoting with a customized P2P application, and depending on the artists' decisions we'll be using their MP3s. What P2P does is lower the cost of distribution and lower the cost of promotion and marketing, and allow your fans to be your street team. So from that perspective, any band that has quality music and that is able to generate a fan base will be able to leverage it to get attention from an independent or a major label through P2P. We should still remember that, if you're talking about bands that are looking to make a living from the music that they make, most independent artists are still going to be making most of their sales from live shows. So the question really is, can P2P be effectively used to leverage and increase sales and attendance at shows and therefore sell more CDs. I think that one of the problems that we've had with P2P is that we've been very conditioned in looking at ripping recorded music and putting it onto P2P networks. From an artist's point of view, there are a lot of ancillary products that they could make available on P2P that would excite fans but would not have the detrimental effect on their CD sales. When I buy a DVD today, I get an interview with the director, the actors, etc. Well, what if there was an interview with the artist or producer, to try to generate some noise and excitement?

SG: I'm looking at a New York Times *article from August 16th (2004), "Warner's Trip with Bloggers." It seems that Warner Records experimented with giving free files to bloggers so that they could get the word out, so even big record labels are taking advantage of promotional opportunities on blogs at least, if not P2P.*

What about Heart? That band used P2P to make money from their MP3s, didn't they, Eric?

EF: Well in fact, in the first week they had sold more music through the P2P networks than they had sold through iTunes.

SG: How did that work?

EF: Well, basically, you can trade anything on a P2P network. So the real question is whether what you're trading has some form of DRM [digital right management] that exerts some form of control over the content, or whether you're just putting it in an unprotected file. In the case of Heart they used the Weed format.

SG: Which is a kind of DRM, isn't it?

EF: What's interesting about Weed is, not only do they resolve the transaction issue, but they really attack what I think is the key to P2P, that you're dealing with a network environment. If you buy the Weed file and then send it to a friend you get a piece of the income from the next sale. It's like a pyramid scheme. And it's really interesting because it goes to something DRM companies long ago had imagined called "super distribution." I don't believe that there's ever been any widespread use of that model until Weed.

SG: What about it, Ari? This sounds like a new business model for you. Why don't the labels make at least some of their songs available using Weed DRM and send them out to the P2P services?

AT: I don't know anything about it, but it sounds very interesting.

SG: This could be a way that we could monetize the music on P2P. Eric de Fontenay, do you think that the record companies could take advantage of this?

EF: The problem for the majors is that you're competing already with a whole bunch of music that's already up there. I think that your typical P2P user is less likely to pay for a major-label artist than an independent artist that they want to support

SG: What about this—a closed P2P for legal file-sharing with Weed-encrypted files that you can go to without fearing the RIAA's wrath or being spoofed or getting spyware.

AT: The question that's interesting is when you're talking about revenue. If we look at the ASCAP–BMI model, and we look at the volume of music being traded on P2P file-sharing, if we could find a way to basically use the same type of model we're using for webcasters for P2P—assuming P2P services were willing to pay for it—that could represent a real boom for the industry. What they could collect for each song might not be a lot, but if you look at the mass of songs being traded it would be quite enough possibly to compensate for the loss that there's been in CD sales.

Chapter 11
How to Build a Website & Why

f you build a Web site you can reach a worldwide audience for your music. This chapter is divided into three basic sections:

1. Why Bother?
2. How To
3. Tips

Why Bother?

Create Exposure For Your Music. The primary reason for artists, particularly up-and-coming acts, to invest the time, energy, and a modest amount of money into a quality Web site is that the Internet provides a worldwide audience for your music. In addition, a strong Web site can serve as a cheaper alternative to a traditional "press kit." While virtually all major recording artists now use the Internet as a vehicle to nurture their fan base, a strong Web presence can lend credibility to a new artist's profile—serving as an advertisement, distribution outlet, and information resource all at once. Scott Meldrum, President and founder of Hype Council (www.hypecouncil.com) a leading online marketing firm, advises: "I think it's a good idea to have a Web site if you're an artist because a Web site does a good job of selling your music when you're not around to do it. You can't be everywhere, you can't gig everywhere, you can't put your face everywhere, and the Internet is 24 hours a day 7 days a week, and it doesn't really have any borders in terms of who it reaches. I like that. I like the scope of the Web and how there really aren't any borders." This chapter includes my interview with Scott Meldrum in which we discuss how to create a quality Web site, and common mistakes that should be avoided.

An Example. The following story illustrates why a new artist should have a Web site. In May 2004, the *Washington Post* published an article about how artists and talent finders are using the Internet. The story focused on Joe Berman who searches for new bands.

That used to mean "hanging out in dive bars, enduring hours of unlistenable music by groups whose rock-'n'-roll dreams far exceed their talent, praying for the occasional act that shows promise.[1] The article describes how Berman uses the Net to scout for new talent. One day he decided to check out new rock bands in Australia and New Zealand. So he typed "new zealand rock band" into a search engine. One of the sites that came up was for a band called Steriogram (see www.steriogram.com) whose music is a combination of hip-hop and thrash metal. They only had one song and a video posted, but Berman really liked what he heard and immediately sent the band an e-mail asking for more music. This sparked a swift chain of events. The band mailed a demo CD of about five songs. Berman played the songs for Dan McCarroll, an executive at EMI Publishing. Impressed, McCarroll played the music for another friend—who happened to be the president of Capitol Records. "Two weeks later, Steriogram had a five-album deal with Capitol, home of the Beatles and Garth Brooks."

The point of the article is that the "old" music business is looking at the Internet as a means of finding new talent. The author of the article, Frank Ahrens, explains that the way Steriogram was discovered

> . . . may be a Cinderella story today, but it could be the norm in coming years. Beset by a drop of more than 30% in music sales over the past three years, ongoing piracy, industry consolidation, thousands of layoffs and bottom-line losses in the multimillions of dollars, the music business is searching for novel—and cheaper—ways to find and nurture talent."
>
> For many years bands were discovered in clubs and signed by record labels, with eye-popping advances and massive promotion budgets to plug their singles on radio. But tough times call for tougher deals—the biggest advances are gone and labels are less likely to rubber-stamp the bloated expense accounts of bar-dwelling scouts. Likewise, the record companies no longer spend the thousands they used to invest to get a new song on big radio stations. The stations themselves can no longer afford to turn over their airwaves to acts that are not proven hit-makers."
>
> All of which opens the door to a new breed of scout like Berman, a freelancer who spends his days trolling the Internet for the next Steriogram—"It's actually what the [talent scouts] who make six figures should have been doing all along," he said—"and for new promotion channels, such as satellite radio, to expose new bands to listeners and build the all-important hype."

---

1. *"Technology Repaves Road to Stardom Internet Gives Music Business Cheap New Avenue to Find Talent" by Frank Ahrens,* Washington Post, *May 2, 2004.*

This article illustrates why building a Web site can provide invaluable exposure for your music. Without the Web site Berman would never have found Steriogram. The article also illustrates that music industry professionals such as Berman are actively using the new technologies to discover new talent.

Promote Live Performances and Tours. The most important feature of the Internet is the immediate way it allows artists to connect with their fans. One of the principal reasons for an artist to build a Web site is to announce and share information about upcoming performances and tours. A Web site should include this information in the home page or provide a prominent link in the home page to a separate Web page containing updated information. An artist should learn at least enough computer code to be able to delete old events and add new concerts so the Web site is always up to date. If you're an artist, have your Web designer teach you—once you get the hang of it, it's not difficult to make basic changes.

Sending an e-mail about your upcoming concert to your list of fan e-mail addresses can be accomplished with a few clicks on the computer. This makes the Internet an immensely efficient tool for promoting local gigs as well as tours. The e-mails should provide a link to the artist's Web site where the fan can see the full updated schedule of performances and tour information. Read the section titled "Build and Use an E-mail List" later in this chapter for tips on how to expand a fan e-mail list and use it to promote live concerts.

Sell CDs and/or Downloads. I could have titled this section "How to use your Web site to make money." It is simple to add a shopping cart to your site and start selling your music by mail-order and/or download. See the "Electronic Commerce" section of Chapter 17 for information on setting up an online store and a discussion of how using Micropayments may save you money on transactions for downloads. You can also use your online store to sell anything else you want including concert tickets, T-shirts, etc. You can also link to sites like CD Baby which will create a Web page for you in their Web site from which people can order your CDs. See Chapter 17 for my interview with Derek Sivers of CD Baby for a discussion of how that works.

I could also have titled this chapter "Your Website is Your Record Company." If you are an unsigned artist your Web site can perform most of the basic functions of a record label including promotion, marketing, and distribution. As the head of the legal department at a major label was heard to mutter, "If this thing [that is, the Internet] gets bigger, why the hell will they [the artists] need us?"

Sales of music through the Net, moreover, has become an important source of incremental income for many indie artists. With the advent of online music stores such as CD Baby (Chapter 17) and iTunes (Chapter 13), purchasing music online has become a common practice for consumers under a certain age. Apple iTunes, one of the pioneers of this new business model has itself sold over 150 million copies of singles at the time of the delivery of this manuscript, including those by artists signed to independent labels. Sales of CDs by unsigned artists through CD Baby recently toped 10 million dollars. Perhaps the most exciting thing about the Internet (and the most dangerous for major labels) is that it decentralizes the means of distribution, as well as making marketing and promotional responsibilities far more affordable. Clearly, the Internet is a valuable resource for all artists. The only thing you risk losing by staying off-line are potential fans and potential dollars.

This section explains why selling your music through your Web site is a great idea. Your Web site can become iTunes for your own music, that is, your own record store. You can offer downloads of your singles or albums. You can also offer CDs by mail-order. In my interview with Marci Geller in Chapter 12, we will discuss how one indie artist created her own online record store.

Many new artists build a simple Web site and send e-mails about their next gig. That's great. But some fail to realize they can also sell their music to their fans directly from their sites. Imagine not having to worry about getting a "record deal." Better yet, imagine keeping 100% of each sale rather than 10-15% of retail minus many deductions that may make 15% more like 5%. Perhaps best of all, imagine complete artistic freedom, including control over choice of songs and never being dictated to by a label executive who may demand a more "radio friendly" or "commercial" sound.

Finally, because record companies have much less money to invest in new music these days and are signing fewer and fewer new artists, new musicians may have no choice other than to become their own record company and distributor. The Internet has made this possible.

The Good Old Days Were Never That Good. Even in the heyday of the recording business (the late '90s), a small fraction of records released actually "recouped." That means that the artists rarely received any recording royalties. Under the standard recording agreement, the artist is responsible for recording costs, as well as a large portion of independent marketing, video costs, and tour support. The labels "recoup" these costs at the artist's royalty rate. So if these expenses add up to, for example, $1,000,000, and the artist's royalty is approximately $1 per unit, the record must sell a million units before the record company pays any royalties. An album which sells a million units is called "platinum," and there just aren't a lot of platinum records.

Jacob Slichter spent a decade playing drums for Semisonic, the Minneapolis-based trio that reached its commercial peak in 1998 with the number-one single "Closing Time" from the platinum-selling CD "Feeling Strangely Fine" (MCA). He wrote a book about his experiences in 2004 titled *So You Wanna Be A Rock & Roll Star* (Broadway Books). Slicher reports that under the standard recording contract that the band signed, Semisonic was responsible for all the expenses of recording their albums, and most importantly most of the promotion and marketing costs, from their share of the recording royalties. As a result, although they sold over two million albums, Slicher claims the band never saw a dime of recording royalties. Fortunately, Semisonic wrote their own songs, and as a result they were able to support themselves from mechanicals and performance income.

To be fair, the record companies often advance a great deal of money to pay for the production, marketing and distribution of CDs. But many artists on major labels are quickly discarded if they cannot sell over 250,000 or some other arbitrary number. Big record companies need "hits" to pay for all the misses. So unless you can quickly produce the desired numbers you may not be staying at a major record company for much longer than the time needed for the ink to dry on your contract. The Internet can be a powerful tool in increasing attendance at live gigs and generating revenues from sales of your music without being tethered to a big label.

How To

This section explores the fundamentals of building an effective Web site to promote your career and sell your music. We also discuss how to build and use e-mail addresses to promote your music and live performances.

Construct a Website

What You Need to Bring to the Table. There are three essential forms of content that you, as the artist, need to furnish to create a Web site. They are: a bio, high quality photo, and at least several high quality samples of your music. These items have traditionally constituted a basic press package that managers and agents use for radio promotion, to get club gigs and record deals. They are also the core of any good Web site. Other essential items are tour schedules and an e-mail sign-in for guests. Additional materials, such as digital video files of performances and links to articles in the press add "flavor." Next, it is necessary to consider a visual lay-out of the site and what you would like the site to be able to do.

- Do you want to be able to sell your CDs and/or downloads from your site or just offer samples?
- Do you want to offer "bells and whistles" such as a weblog, a chat room, etc?

These decisions depend to some extent on the commitment you are ready to make to your Web site including (a) your budget, (b) your skill level with computers, and/or (c) your deadlines. However, during the last several years, there has been an explosion of entrepreneurial energy at the intersection of the Internet and the music business including services specifically designed to create and host music-based websites. This has resulted in the emergence of dozens of new and exciting services for artists and musicians that never existed before. In this chapter we will survey the options including services that will register, design, host your site, and provide additional services for a reasonable fee.

Active Links to Resources in CD-ROM. In the resources section in the CD-ROM accompanying this book we will provide additional choices with active links to faciliate your research of the right choice for you.

Basic Elements. There are three elements common to all websites:

Domain Name—The unique ID that points to your Web site, e.g., www.stevegordon-law.com. A good source for information on domain names is www.internic.net which is administered by the U.S. Department of Commerce. Domain names can be registered through certain companies (known as "registrars") that compete with one another. A listing of these companies appears in the Registrar Directory on this Internet site. The price of registrations depends primarily on the duration—I recently paid $109.95 to continue my domain name registration for stevegordonlaw.com for another five years. Domain names include a suffix such as .com, .org, .gov, or .edu. The .com, .net, and .org suffixes are open and unrestricted. Traditionally, however, names in .net have been used by organizations involved in Internet infrastructure activities and .org is frequently used by non-commercial organizations, while .edu is reserved for educational institutions like universities; .gov is used for U.S. government sites; .mil is used for U.S. military sites.

Web Hosting—No matter what you have on your Web site, you'll need a "Web host" to make your site available over the Internet. The physical computer where your Web site exists is called the server. A server is computer or device on a network that manages network resources. There is a great deal of competition from companies small and large for hosting your site. For instance www.DotEasy.com offers free hosting for simple websites in exchange for paying them to register your domain names. I urge you to use the resources section of this book to find the best deal for you.

Web Design—What shows up when people type in your domain name and are transported to your site. The cost can range from nothing—if you do it yourself or your friend does it for you for free, to a few hundred bucks for a bare bones site created by a professional (such as my site, www.stevegordonlaw.com which cost me $500) or a couple of thousand dollars or more for a great looking site designed by a respected commercial service. But bear in mind that the competition for your Web site design and hosting dollars is fierce, with many competitors, so it is really a buyer's market and you can find great deals.

How you go about obtaining and maintaining these elements is up to you, but there is no way around not having all three.

Jargon. The Internet, much like the music business, has its own set of unique jargon that can be intimidating to those who aren't familiar with it. Here are some additional key terms that will likely turn up quite a bit.

- Browser—The software used to view, manage, and access Web pages. The two most common browsers are Netscape and Microsoft Internet Explorer. Web pages often appear differently, depending on the brand and version of the browser intended to view them in.
- Drop-Down Menu—A drop-down menu (also known as a pull-down menu) is used to give the user a choice of options in a form. The CD-ROM accompanying this book uses drop down menus and they often are used on Web sites.
- Digital Rights Management or DRM—Coding computer files including music files to limit portability and/or facilitate payment options such as Weed which allows listening to a music file for free several times and requiring payment for further listening.
- E-commerce—A term that refers to the growing retail, service, and business to business industries on the World Wide Web. E-commerce Web sites facilitate the buying and selling of goods and services over the Internet including music.
- Flash—An animation technology. Flash animations are quick to download, are of high quality, and are browser independent, i.e., they look the same on different browsers.
- HTML—Stands for Hypertext Markup Language; a cross-platform text-formatting system for creating Web pages, including text, images, sounds, frames, animation, and more. A Web site is a collection of electronic pages generally formatted in HTML.
- Hyperlink or Link—An electronic connection between one Web page to either another Web pages on the same Web site, or Web pages located on another Web site.
- Java—Java is a programming language, created by Sun Microsystems, which can be used to create animation as well as more complex applications such as a calculator.
- JPEG—Stands for Joint Photographic Experts Group. File format for full-color and black-and-white graphic images.
- RealPlayer, Quicktime & Windows Media Player—Plug-in applications developed by RealNetworks, Apple and Microsoft respectively that allow users to hear and see audio and video files saved in various file formats. These programs also deliver streaming media, that is, audio or video broadcast live over the Internet. Clicking on certain hyperlinks within a Web site will cause your Web browser to activate these programs.
- URL—URL stands for Uniform Resource Locator and is an address of an individual Web page element or Web document on the Internet.

Two glossaries offering comprehensive definitions of the above terms and many more are: www.red.net/glossary and www.getnetwise.org/glossary.php.

Doing It Yourself. You should conceptualize what you want your site to look like and what you want to accomplish before designing the actual Web page. What is the first thing you want people to see when they log onto the site: flash animation, ad for new release, e-mail list sign-up? What kind of color scheme do you want for the site? What are the visual elements you are going to use to make the site easy to navigate? These questions are very important if you are building your site yourself. If a site has a good "flow" (check out www.ericrevis.com for an example of an independent artist and www.aliciakeys.com as an example of a major artist, for sites that flow well), it can draw a great deal of attention and greatly enhance your image.

The process by which Web pages are created is called "coding" or "scripting." During coding the Web designer creates everything you see on a Web page using one of the programming languages, generally HTML. HTML is rather complex and it is not recommended that you undertake the task of coding your Web site from scratch unless you have a solid background in computers. However, if you do wish to design your own site, there are several programs that can make the process less tedious. Microsoft's FrontPage, Adobe's Creative Suites, and Macromedia's Dreamweaver are software programs that allow the user to create a Web page, not by "coding," but rather by manipulating the graphical interface. In addition, Macromedia's Flash program has become something of a visual necessity for artist Web pages, allowing for an array of stimulating visual designs to be implemented in addition to the regular HTML scripting. Flash is usually seen on the "intros" of many artists' sites.

These programs do not require an actual knowledge of HTML, and all of them come bundled with tutorials that are useful. For those who wish to acquire professional Web development skills, schools of continuing education affiliated with major universities such as the New School or NYU in New York City provide courses in Web design at reasonable prices taught by competent instructors.

Templates. Another available option which requires little time and money is purchasing a pre-made template. Here, you would still need to set up Web hosting and acquire your domain name, but the design of the Web site is already completed for you. All you have to do is make some minor changes to the text of the Web site in order to tailor it to your band, and upload the site to your hosting company. Unlike creating the Web site from scratch, using a pre-made template could generate a fully-functional, professional looking Web site in a very brief period of time. Web sites such as www.freewebtemplates.com, and www.flashtemplates.com offer many free or very inexpensive complete and professional websites; many of them include music-related themes.

Designers and Hosting Services. Web designers with rudimentry skills are currently "a dime a dozen." If you don't know someone who does it, they can be easily solicited at sites such as www.craigslist.org.

Freelance Web designers are always looking to build their resumes by working with highly visible, highly creative people such as artists—some will even do the work pro bono in exchange for a prominent credit in the site.

I found a designer who was a friend of a friend several years ago to build my site. He did a brilliant job for a few hundred bucks and he found a friend to host my site on his server at an extremely reasonable rate. I registered my domain name myself and I was in business. The process took a week and cost less than $750.

If your budget is a bit larger, professional Web designers such as Quabe, Inc (www.quabe.com) can provide a sharp, innovative, and customized design.

Services Offering Domain Name Registration, Web Design, and Hosting. Over the past five years, there has been an explosion of entrepreneurial energy at the intersection of the music business and the Internet. This has resulted in the emergence of dozens of new and exciting services for artists and music professionals. Companies like MyRealTalent.com work personally with artists to not only host their Web sites but give them strategic direction to leverage the power of the Internet. For instance, myrealtalent.com will build your Web site, host it, digitize your music and help you sell MP3s online.

Another good resource for artists and bands is HostBaby, because they tailor their service to musicians. The same people who created CD Baby (see the interview with Derek Sivers, President and founder of CD Baby in Chapter 17) also run HostBaby (www.hostbaby.com). In addition to registering a domain name and providing hosting services, it also helps you digitize, stream and sell your music, construct a weblog and organize your concert calendar and guest book. For example, HostBaby puts at your fingertips an easy-to-update concert calendar that automatically removes listings after the concert dates have passed. It also includes a powerful e-mail list program that lets you keep in touch with fans. Among its many other features are customized e-mail addresses for each band member, a blog, streaming audio, a guest book, and feedback forms.

Build and Use an E-Mail List. As my interview with Scott Meldrum discusses in detail, you can use your Web site to sign up people to your e-mail list. Certain techniques are discussed in detail by Scott including making your e-mail sign-up easy to find, and don't ask for too much information.

To encourage fans to sign up for their e-mail list, some bands offer incentives in their Web sites. For example, the Beastie Boys (www.beastieboys.com) reward their subscribers with early notice of ticket sales, and an indie band called Divahn (www.divahn.com), which plays Jewish music from the Middle East and North Africa, offers perks such as discounts on CDs. Once people have signed up for the list, the goal is to keep them signed up. To this end, a band should be respectful to their subscribers, only sending e-mails related to the band, and not sending too many. The trick is to strike a balance between getting a lot of information to the fans without flooding their in boxes to the point that they decide to unsubscribe.

In addition, you can use live concerts to expand your list. Many artists are playing clubs for exposure without making much money. Even when they are able to make some money from touring, they are usually hoping to increase their record sales either by creating a larger fan base or selling CDs at the venues. If they used their live gigs to collect e-mail addresses they could let those fans know that their music is available 24 hours a day with a click of a computer key. All the band needs to do is have a sign-in sheet for fans to give their e-mail addresses. And don't be shy about asking people to sign it—a simple announcement from the stage can be quite effective.

The beauty of collecting e-mails from people who come to your concert is that if they are interested enough to listen to your music live and actually give you an e-mail address, they are probably also people who would buy your music. The beauty of selling music from your Web site to these people is that they don't have to hunt for your music in record stores.

Use an E-mail List to Promote Live Concerts. In the pre-Internet days, artists, their managers or booking agents promoted shows by pasting billboards on street lamps and brick walls, placing ads in local papers, licking envelopes and mailing flyers, and of course trying to get local radio to plug their concerts. Although all these means of promoting concerts continue to the present day, the Internet allows an artist to reach more people in less time for a lot less money. For instance, an e-mail list with information on the city or town in which the fan lives can help a band develop a virtual "street team" that can help promote a live date in the city or town in which the band is performing. Fans can also be encouraged to visit chat rooms, message boards, music blogs, and generally put the word out about your music.

Build a Virtual Street Team. You can use your Web site to recruit fans to help you promote live gigs. You can ask them to post messages about upcoming shows in message boards and chat rooms (see section below). You can make print-out flyers available to them to put up at locations near the venue. This is a technique employed by Marci Geller (see our interview in Chapter 12). You can also send an e-mail to your fans recruiting them to do all these things. And you'll be able to spend more time on other business tasks such as radio airplay. This is especially useful when touring to a far-away town because you would otherwise be forced to make a trip to that town a month before your scheduled performance or do no promotion at all. For those street team members who help you, you may offer them free CDs or free passes to your gigs.

Use the Internet To Promote Live Performances. In addition to using e-mail addresses to promote live performances, here are some additional ways to use the Web for that purpose.

- Message boards—By visiting the message board of a similar-sounding band's Web site, you can post information about your upcoming show. This works well because if your music and the other band's music are in the same genre, chances are that the other band's fans might enjoy your music as well.
- Web press releases—Nearly all local and regional newspapers, as well as college and commercial radio stations, accept e-mails announcing an upcoming performance which they then publish in their respective papers or Web sites. There are even services such as www.prweb.com that offer free online press release distribution. PR Web claims to send daily e-mail press releases to between 60,000 and 100,000 global contact points including journalists, analysts, freelance writers, media outlets, and newsrooms.
- Electronic online press kits for the media—Once a performance is booked, you can send your press kit to local media for review and radio airplay. But rather than sending a hard copy, you can e-mail an entire press kit in one compressed ZIP file. All recent Windows operating systems allow the user to take the contents of a folder—which would be all the pieces of your press kit—and compress them into a much smaller ZIP file.

Chapter 13 will offer additional ways of using the Internet to promote and sell your music.

Tips: An Interview with Scott Meldrum, Founder and President of Hype Council

This section will give you some practical tips on what to include in your Web site. We are reprinting a portion of an interview that was recorded during summer 2004 with Scott Meldrum, the President and founder of Hype Council, a leading online marketing and public relations firm. The interview was conducted as part of my Internet radio program, which can be seen as well as heard at Myrealbroadcast.com. His recommendations were so brilliant, my producer—Dan Coleman, who is also president of Myrealbroadcast.com—immediately changed some portions of his Web sites to incorporate Scott's suggestions.

Steve Gordon: I'd like to refer back to your remarks during your recent address at the National Association of Record Industry Professionals. Could you share with us some of the insights that you laid out there? For instance, your take on the global audience for music on the Internet, and why, if you are an artist, it is a good idea to have your own Web site?

Scott Meldrum: I think it's a good idea to have a Web site if you're an artist because a Web site does a good job of selling your music when you're not around to do it. You can't be everywhere, you can't gig everywhere, you can't put your face everywhere, and the Internet is 24 hours a day, seven days a week, and it doesn't really have any borders in terms of who it reaches. I like that. I like the scope of the Web and how there really aren't any borders.

SG: Right. If you've got a Web site in Texas it's going to be available in Turkey and around the world.

SM: Yes. You can use that Web site to market your records in Tennessee as well as in Tunisia, and people can buy your music online anywhere else in the world.

SG: How many people are looking at or listening to music on the Web in the United States?

SM: In terms of listening to music online, it's kind of hard to say. I know that in terms of how many people are online in the United States, you're generally looking at roughly 48% of the entire population.

SG: That's a huge number. Reading from your written remarks, "Fully 40% of the USA's 177 million Net users go online for music." So that's like 70 million people. Just by building a little site, you have prospective exposure to all those people.

SM: And those are 2003 figures too, so for 2004 you're probably looking at about a 5% increase.

SG: In building a Web site, what are the fundamentals that the artist needs to create?

SM: They need to have some sort of visual representation of themselves. Regardless of what font you use or what color you use, every artist should make their own creative statement online. But there are certain things that are going to be received more readily and certain things less readily, so you have to make a choice. Do you want your Web site to appeal to the masses or do you want it to appeal to an elite few? Naturally, most of the people that I talk to want to market their music on a mass scale, so their Web site needs to appeal on a mass scale, meaning that the colors and the fonts and everything need to be pleasing to the eye and easy to read.

The navigation needs to be simple and very well understood. They need to be able to get what they want in no more than four clicks. That's a big rule that I have. If you come to my Web site, I've got four clicks to get done what I need to get done. You're here for a reason, I have something that I need to get from you before you go, and there are generally four clicks that I have in order to make that happen. I've told independent artists that those four clicks—you have to put a hierarchy on them, between what you want them to do and what they have to do in order to get you what you want.

SG: Do you want them to listen to a sample of your music within four clicks?

SM: Yes! You need to give them something to listen to that is a fair representation of the music that's on the record that you're selling. That's generally the first thing they will do— they will try to figure out how to listen to your music. If they're there for a reason—now, they may have stumbled upon you—but if they're there for the purpose of experiencing your music or finding out more about you as an artist, the first thing they're going to want to do is listen to the music and you have to let them hear it before four clicks. The second thing they're going to want to do generally is to find out where you're playing. That's just more of a curiosity factor; they generally try to figure out, "Does he play in my area?" If they like what they hear they're going to try to find out if they can experience you live.

Naturally, they don't know that you're from Texas until they click on your links and find out that nine out of ten shows that you're playing are in Austin, which means that you're probably from the Austin area.

The next thing that you want them to do—which is not something that they're going to do very easily—is to register for your e-mail list. That's the first thing that you have to accomplish before they leave the site. That's probably one of the hardest things to do.

SG: Why is it so hard? People don't like to give their name or their e-mail out?

SM: Yes, it's difficult to get people to give information about themselves. On the other hand, many Web sites make it even more uncomfortable for people. Some make it difficult to even find where to register. Some ask for too much information. It's a huge thing, and I tell artists all the time, "You're worried about selling one record, and if you don't get this person to register you're not only going to lose a record sale, you're going to lose five." Because once you have their e-mail address you have a communication channel open, and when that communication channel is open you've got five other items that you can sell to them over the course of a one- or two-year period. You have to keep that channel open.

SG: Do you think that it is worth the effort to offer your CD for sale online?

SM: Yes! I recommend that for almost any independent artist, it is vital to make easily available the purchase of CDs that can be delivered to the buyer's home. I haven't investigated the value of streaming or downloading entire records online. I really feel like there's a value in owning a piece of intellectual property—to *actually physically have* the property.

SG: We just had John Buckman from Magnatune.com on this program [see Chapter 15] and he allows you to buy downloads of entire CDs. This business model is doing well. But he plans on also getting into the mail-order business for precisely the reason you just stated: people do *want something to hold in their hand, read the liner notes, and to own something tangible. Having people pay online is easy, right?*

SM: Yes, mail order is very easy.

SG: Well as you can see from my interview with Marci Geller [Chapter 12], downloading can be easy too. But please go through the steps for setting up a mail order procedure.

SM: Artists can go through PayPal and sell the record on their own, or they can use a retailer like CD Baby [Chapter 17] that handles the shipping and the entire transaction from front to back and charges a commission on the sale. I have opinions about what's more appropriate and less appropriate—I definitely think there's value in offering both, "Buy it from me independently, or you can buy it at this recognized, established 'e-tailer'"—and let the consumer choose what they're more comfortable with.

SG: Now why would you compete with yourself like that? Why would you sell a CD from your site to your fans and then tell them to go to CD Baby where you won't get as much because CD Baby takes a few dollars?

SM: It's the same reason why companies that make the widget don't sell the widget at retail. They use retailers to sell the widget because the retailers are going to do a better job of selling their product than they're going to do. They're going to ship it faster because they've got systems in place to be able to do all of that.

SG: Right. Derek Sivers told me that one of the reasons he moved to Portland, Oregon, was to be near a postal center that does mail order faster than any other comparable facility in the U.S.

SM: Exactly my point—he knows what he's doing. When I was starting out, naturally I thought, "God, wouldn't it be great if I could sell these records on my own." But I know that I'm going to lose a lot of sales due to a lack of confidence on consumers' behalf because they don't know me. They don't know that I'm not going to abscond with their money, I'm not an established e-tailer. Whereas if they buy it at Amazon or if they buy it at CD Baby or they buy it from a name that they know, the chances of converting that sale are a lot higher.

SG: Now that we've talked about what to include in a Web site, can we talk about any common mistakes to avoid?

SM: Yes, I have five common mistakes that I generally try to put out. I call the first one "Where's the beef?" If you've ever been to an artist's Web site and you don't know what you're doing, you don't know where to go, this is a pretty common mistake that artists make. There is too much stuff on one Web site.

They mistake creativity for functionality. So if you're an artist and you have a Web site, that Web site should have as much content and information as you can pack into it, but not all of it should be on the home page. I think organization is the key. You lead your fans to the most important things about you first. Again, you have four clicks—don't make them search to make those clicks happen. They need to be led: *one, two, three, four* and out. Naturally, if they want to click more that's great, but they're clicking things that aren't necessarily going to get you an e-mail address or are a sale.

SG: That's probably a mistake that I make on my Web site too, because on the home page you can keep on scrolling down and down and down.

SM: Right. What I like to see are gated presentations, where you give them one or two clicks, and that leads to another one or two clicks, and that leads to another one or two clicks, and you're taking them down the road. I think that's a much more effective marketing device than to put everything on one page and let the user sort of navigate their way through it. That doesn't give them any priorities, and what happens is that they get frustrated and they bail.

SG: What's the next mistake?

SM: The second mistake I call "Please don't buy my album," because at this stage in an independent artist's career they need to be selling as many albums as they can, and if that's not at the top of the goals list, then you should skip building a Web site in the first place. Many Web sites that I see almost dare the visitor to find the product, let alone buy it. Every time a person visits your Web site, it's an opportunity to sell another CD. Links to buy a CD should be available on almost every page on the Web site. The transaction process should be simple, it should be reliable and secure. As we discussed, are you going to sell more CDs on your own—from a name that they do not know and trust—or are you going to sell more CDs with CD Baby and lose $4 a pop. I'd go with CD Baby every time. Even now, I'd still go with CD Baby.

SG: So the artist can place a link on each page of his Web site to CD Baby?

SM: Correct. CD Baby builds a page in its Web site that includes descriptions and pictures of any CD you want to sell. You want each page of your Web site to link to your Web page in CD Baby. Wherever they are in your site, no matter what page, they need to be able to buy your CD. Again, you've got one click; they're either going to click off or they're going to click to buy, and you want as many of them to click to buy as possible. CD Baby has banners, buttons, icons, and all kinds of stuff that you can put on your Web site that will link directly to your page on CD Baby.

SG: What's the next mistake?

SM: I call the third mistake "Please let me ignore you." It's the same premise as not being able to find where to buy the record in your Web site. I'm talking about not being able to figure out where to register for an e-mail list. It's so difficult sometimes to either find out where to register, or to register. The form is too long or it's too complicated or there's information there that you really don't want to give out. It should be simple, easy to find, easy to navigate, easy to process, and that's it.

SG: No password?

SM: No password.

SG: Which you forget every time.

SM: If you had time-intensive content that was in high demand and you wanted to set aside some of that content for a select group of people that are willing to register, then you can establish some sort of password-driven model, but that generally isn't the case for the independent artist. The independent artist generally is lucky to have that one visitor, and they need to take advantage of that visitor while they're there.

SG: So you've got that guy's name, or that woman's name, and his/her e-mail address. What do you do with it?

SM: Well, you don't sell it, that's the first thing. [Laughs] You don't loan it out. What you do is you take care of it. You treat it like a phone number; it's just like any other communication channel. You don't call it everyday and bug them to buy your record, but you don't also wait a year before you call because they could have moved. You treat it like a viable communication channel. You immediately contact them to say, "Hey, I've got your information. Thank you very much for signing up." You can do this through an auto-response mechanism, which is very easy to program. It automatically sends an e-mail when somebody registers which says, "Hey, thank you for signing up. I really appreciate it. By the way, if you haven't purchased my CD yet, you can do so by clicking here." I did that at the very beginning when I started to sell my CD online, and I measured the results. Over a one-year period 27.8% of the people that registered for my e-mail list and hadn't purchased the CD *purchased* the CD specifically because I sent them a thank-you letter.

SG: That's not a bad percentage—especially for an automated response!

SM: Yes, just because they received it with an invitation to buy the CD, 27% of them did, and that's a huge number. It's something that you don't want to lose.

SG: That also is the power of the Internet, the direct two-way communication it makes possible. Are we ready for the next mistake?

SM: The next mistake is "Cow vs. milk—who cares?" The whole idea of why buy the cow when you can get the milk for free relates to offering only a very brief sample of your music online. I have intellectual property, and I treat that intellectual property very seriously as an artist. I don't want people downloading my music and not compensating me for it. However, I'm in that fragile space in the commercial trade where there's not a huge demand for my product, and if there isn't, I might be able to make more sales by offering some of that music more readily. On my personal Web site I offer three of my songs in streaming format, so you can listen all the way through to three of my songs.

SG: You can't download it, but you can listen to three full songs.

SM: Three full songs, right. Then, if you register for my e-mail list, I will send you a link to where you can download one song for free. You're giving the consumer an opportunity to get deeper, deeper, and deeper into a creative relationship between you and your music.

SG: You're engaging the customer.

SM: Correct. They're more willing to buy, and there's a higher potential for them to buy if you do that. What I see happen a lot is that people offer a 30-second, low-resolution stream of their music, and then they wonder why they're not selling. Well, have you heard stuff online? It sounds like crap, there's only 30 seconds of it. I can't even get the hook before my stream cuts off. I don't think that's a good selling mechanism. If you're going to put your music online, give them the whole song.

SG: Unless you're already famous . . .

SM: Even if you're already famous. If you go to any Web site of any major artist, you'll probably hear one to three songs being streamed in full format. Absolutely.

SG: Okay. Anything else to avoid?

SM: The final and fifth mistake relates to bandwidth. I see this mistake a lot. I think people design their Web sites to look really good, but they put them on such a small bandwidth pipe that it makes it impossible to really experience the Web site. I call that "I shall now attempt to suck this watermelon through a straw." You've got a watermelon-sized amount of content and you're trying to push it through a straw-sized pipe because the Web company that you use to host your Web site, you pay them $19.95 a month. That doesn't allow you to stream all of this content through their bandwidth. It only allows for a certain number of megabytes, and you've got way too much going on with the site. As a result, the retention of people on the site, they just get tired of waiting for a page to load and they get off.

SG: So they have to wait a long time for the page to load and a long time to listen to a stream.

SM: Right. If a stream takes 25 seconds to load and it's a 30-second stream, that's not a good value proposition.

SG: Yes, that sounds very frustrating. Then they remember you by the headache that they got waiting for your Web site, which is not a good way to be remembered.

SM: [Laughs] No. So, the bottom line of all of this is to keep the Web site simple, make it easy for people to purchase, make it easy for people to register for your e-mail list. Don't bother them all the time with correspondence, give them a reason to interact with you again by coming back to the Web site, and don't put too much on the Web site so that people can navigate it with ease.

SG: And if you have a few extra bucks, splurge on the extra bandwidth.

SM: Yes. Even then you still have to be careful because we're still at a point where roughly 60% of the entire country is still on dial-up.

SG: I had forgotten what that's like.

SM: [Laughs] Well, those of us in major metropolitan markets are not, but most of the people that are going to be surfing online are still on dial-up. You don't want to denigrate their user experience with a super-high-resolution Flash site. It's not going to work.

[Note: Some Web sites give you a choice of bandwidths. See the interview with jazz artist Eric Revis in Chapter 12.]

Hot Web Sites by Three Artists: Acoustic & Alternative Rock, Jazz & Hip-Hop

An Interview with Singer/Songwriter Marci Geller

www.marcigeller.com

Independent artist Marci Geller uses her Web site as a marketing and publicity machine, and a record store.

Marci Geller was voted one of the top ten singer-songwriters by *Songwriter Magazine*. She's performed frequently on television, including on *Good Day NY* and *Live with Regis*, and many of her songs have been used in network and cable shows. She has also recorded two albums, *On the Edge* and *Marci Geller*. Her influences include Carly Simon, Sting, Peter Gabriel, and Yes, and she has been compared to Tori Amos, Sarah McLachlan, and Fiona Apple. You can hear her music at www.marcigeller.com.

Steve Gordon: Marci, I'd like to get into some of the interesting things that you're doing online. You have a great Web site. To help us go through some of the interesting elements of your Web site, please welcome to the show James Moeller, Marci's booking agent.

Marci Geller

James, I know that you have a lot of technical expertise, so I'd appreciate hearing your insights as we go through Marci's site, on why the various elements work and how they could work for other people. Marci, when did you first construct this Web site?

Marci Geller: I actually started several years ago, believe it or not. I started with a one-page Web site on Geocities, which was a free Web-hosting company. I got in the game very early because I really saw this amazing tool to get exposure to people that wouldn't necessarily find out about you. The first time I got an e-mail I was so excited I almost had a heart attack! I said, "There's got to be a way to exploit this even further," and I found out about Web sites and started exploring the Internet. I really took note about what I liked and what I didn't like about people's Web sites, and I did a lot of reading. There are a lot of tools that people use like Google and Yahoo to find things, and I really did a lot of investigating to figure out how you get higher rankings on the search engines. So I designed my current Web site precisely with those factors in mind. I wanted something clean and simple that gave all of the important features of me as a product and as an artist right up front so that it was very simple. I wanted something easy to navigate, but I also wanted something that would give me good rankings in Google because there are about 10 million other singer-songwriters on the planet. I really worked on streamlining it and I'm always tweaking, but right now I'm pretty happy with it.

SG: Let's start with the first bit of text, which is titled "What's New." It reads, "Marci has songs being used in seven different episodes on: VH1 (Driven: Jessica Simpson*), A&E* (Biography: Christina Onassis*), ABC Family* (Knock First*) and Food Network* (Dweezil & Lisa*)." By the way Marci, how have you become so successful in selling music to TV? Do you have a special agent for that?*

MG: All these TV licenses happened because of the Internet, so it's a perfect segue. I'm always reading and I'm always investigating, and I always say that it's a good idea to find people that are living the life that you want to live and try to model some of the things that they do. So I started investigating, and I came across these licensing companies that exist only on the Internet, where people and music supervisors who find music for film and television can get music right off the Web. And one of these companies actually found me: Pump Audio [www.pumpaudio.com]. I guess it was three years ago. They had read about me in a magazine or something and they sent me an e-mail asking me to send in some stuff for review to their A&R department. I did, and they requested a nonexclusive agreement for my entire catalog at that point, and I said, "Sure." It's nonexclusive and the deal is fair—why not? And what basically happened is, I just out of the blue got a check and a statement from Pump Audio a few weeks ago telling me that I had seven television placements, and now it's cookin'! Now people call and inquire. I just got a call from a movie producer—I can't remember her name and I'm so sorry—but she's producing an independent film and she used "The Day I Disappeared," so things are rolling now.

SG: That's fantastic. I'm curious, why do you have text about the latest developments in your career rather than a short bio in the home page? I know that you have your bio in the Web site. Is it because you're assuming that most people who come to this Web site already are familiar with your work and you want to give them the latest news?

MG: I did it that way because I think unfortunately the attention span of most Web surfers is very limited. I know for myself, if I don't get grabbed right away I just go to the next site, and I just wanted to bullet-point very recent and important happenings to keep people interested, and then draw them in to find out more about me. What I do is go on this thing called a "webalizer." It's part of my Internet provider, EZ Web Hosting [www.ez-Web-hosting.com], who I love. They host my Web site, and basically I can go in and look at the stats to find out what pages were viewed, how many pages each visitor viewed, how many hits I've had per month, etc., etc. I've noticed that since I changed my Web site to this format, people don't just go to the front page, but there are hits all over the Web site. So they're definitely exploring and they're getting attracted by some of the things that they're reading up front, I guess enough so that they want to hear the music or see what I look like, or read some lyrics, etc.

SG: Now for those who have not seen Marci's site, at the top of the home page is a row of pictures of Marci. The pictures are great. Were they taken by a professional?

MG: I consider her a professional. She's one of my friends; her name is Sirka Louca. I really love working with her because I'm very self-conscious and I don't like having my picture taken. I never like the way I look in pictures, so we just go out and play. She's one of these people who can find art in anything. She can look at a puddle and find beauty, and she'll take the picture and you'll say, "I didn't even see that when I looked at it." I feel like she gets me to be art, and that's a cool thing because it makes me feel better about taking pictures.

SG: I agree the pictures are terrific—they express different moods and elements of your personality. Directly under the photos is "Please sign up for Marci's E-mailing List." Do you get a lot of sign-ups from this?

MG: Constantly, and that's one of the things that I always tell people. Put it right up at the top and make it easy. Always have an entry point for people to get on your mailing list right in the beginning. I decided not to do a pop-up window because most people have the pop-up function blocked on their computers. So I just used a little real estate at the top of the Web site.

SG: I have a pop-up block myself. What I like about your e-mail sign-up is that it's very simple to complete: first name, last name, e-mail address, city, and state, and for "snail mail" please include street address. I've got to ask: what is "snail mail"?

MG: That's what we used to do before the Internet. We used to put things in an envelope and put a stamp on it and take it to the post office. [Laughs]

SG: I like the fact that you don't ask for people's age and serial number and all of the little details. It makes it much more user-friendly.

MG: Right, that's a really simple one. There *is* a more involved one on another page in the site, but I find that almost 90% of my sign-ups come from that first page. So, it's working, and I'm going to keep it that way.

SG: How else do you get people's e-mail addresses? Do you have people sign up at live gigs?

MG: Yes. I'm very assertive about asking people to please sign up for my mailing list, because at this level of my career where I'm not on MTV or VH1 and you can't see where I'm playing all of the time, this is my way of communicating. So I explain that we won't abuse it, we never share it, and I usually get between 30 and 50 mailing-list entries per show—if it's a good show. [Laughs]

SG: How do use these e-mails? Do you stay in steady contact with your e-mail list to let them know new things?

MG: Sure. I do an e-newsletter and I try not to bombard people too many times, but it just depends on what's going on. If I'm doing a bunch of gigs and some fun things have happened in my career, then I'll send out a monthly. But if I've got a really big show that I'm really working on promoting, I'll send more than one e-mail reminder. But I always keep them as brief as possible and very streamlined like the Web site with bullet points, because, like I said, people get bombarded and I don't want to take up people's time. I know how overwhelmed most people are, so I try to keep things very personal and very friendly. They come from me—they don't come from a record label. I invite people's comments back, and I don't think I've ever written an e-newsletter and not gotten back something friendly from a bunch of people saying, "Congratulations" or "We'll be at this show."

James Moeller: I can attest to the fact that Marci's e-mails are sparsely sent and they're sent at the right times. Even if you don't want to read it, at least you're still kept apprised that Marci is still busy and doing stuff.

SG: Marci, if you're going to be, say, in Seattle, will you segregate your e-mail list by city to focus on the people on the e-mail list that actually live in and around Seattle?

MG: I've tried to segregate and I know that that's a good way to do things. At this point, I'll usually send out a general e-mail to everybody, because I'll say, "Look, there are downloadable posters from each gig that I do on my Web site that you can get very easily." And I'll say, "If you've got friends and family in Seattle, I've never played there before, please spread the word." You'd be amazed at how many people will come back and say, "Oh, I've got a cousin" or "My sister lives out there." For this show in Seattle, and I've never been to Seattle before, I sent out flyers to a bunch of people that I've never met before. I've met them through the Internet and they were referred to me and they were really excited about it. They went and heard some music on my Web site and they were like, "Sure, we'll help out." So I sent out a bunch of packages about two weeks ago, and hopefully there'll be a really good showing.

SG: One of the great things about your Web site is that it also functions as a music store. On the left column of your home page, you'll see "Marci's CDs," and right underneath is a link for "Order." If you click on "Order," you can preview practically any song from any CD just by clicking on the song title. And the CDs are also available for purchase by credit card, check, and via PayPal [www.paypal.com], and it says: "Simply click on the item you want to purchase, follow the instructions, and it will be mailed to you." Who does the shipping?

MG: It depends on if I'm in town or not. We're a very small mom-and-pop setup, and I am by no means a diva at this point in my career. [Laughs] So I do a lot of the mailing, my manager John will do a lot of the mailing—it really depends on who's around. But we're always very conscious about getting them out as soon as possible. And when I send out a CD it goes with a welcome letter thanking the person for purchasing it and telling them that we have added them to our mailing list, and that if they ever want to be removed from it for any reason to please let us know and there will be no questions asked. It's all about developing a relationship. I think you have this vast universe available to you through the Internet, and it's a way of making it smaller and more intimate by letting people know that you took the time to write a letter to them and directly thanking them for purchasing your music.

SG: Let me ask you a question about working with PayPal and credit card companies, and then we can get into the download feature of the Web site. What is better for you as an artist: Paypal or credit cards, or does it make a difference?

MG: Well, they both go through PayPal so it makes no difference. When I do my live shows my credit cards are processed through CD Baby, which, if you're just getting started and you're not really savvy about the Internet, it's a great independent music portal. Derek Sivers is president of CD Baby. [See Chapter 17 for an interview with Derek.] He's very supportive and very helpful, and he has great people working with him. So I still have my stuff on CD Baby as well as selling it on my Web site.

SG: So your Web site is your store and you also use Derek. That's one of his pieces of advice to artists, to have your own Web site, and if you have the time, sell your music from your own Web site directly. But people can be introduced to your music through CD Baby. Is there a link on your CD Baby page back to your Web site?

MG: Yes, there sure is. Link, link, link, everywhere you can! [Laughs]

SG: Let's talk about downloads. I'll read from your Web site: "Downloads are available as soon as you complete the checkout process. You should receive a link as soon as you complete the checkout. You will also receive an e-mail that instantly gives you a link to your purchase." So instead of ordering the CD by mail, I can also download your music. Is there a difference in price?

MG: It's a little bit cheaper to download because we don't have to press up CDs and pay for shipping and packaging and all that other kind of stuff. It's a dollar to download each song. [The album] *Here on the Edge* is $15 and the EP *Naked* I believe is $7. If you want us to ship the physical CDs, we add a little bit for shipping and handling.

SG: Are the downloads protected by any sort of digital rights management? Or once I own it, I can use it on any computer or rip it to a CD or MP3 player or anything else I want to do?

MG: Technically, you're supposed to use it only for your own purposes and honor that, but I'm sure that many people share. Look, it's inevitable—as soon as they invented the cassette tape sharing started. The way I look at it is, it's more exposure, and I've found that the people who receive copies of my music from friends—if they like it enough— they'll show up at a concert, or they'll buy the CD.

SG: *So you look at people sharing your music as more exposure?*

MG: Yes.

SG: *How long has the download option been available on your site?*

MG: I've had the downloads probably for the last year; that's pretty recent. I didn't want to go that way for a while. I wanted to find a way to do it that I felt was fair, and when I found a way to do the instant downloads for a very small purchase price, I said, "Okay, I can live with that."

SG: *How would you advise artists to go about doing something like this? Were you able to do it yourself, or did you find outside help?*

MG: I didn't get any outside help. I'm just an explorer. If I want to do something I just start educating myself how to do it. A lot of people don't want to do that, so that's why I also got on the lecture circuit, and I teach a class called "Surviving the Music Industry" for the independent artist. I talk about how to protect yourself and how to get yourself out there and expose your talents and your music in the best possible way to create the life that you want to have. I just educated myself by going on the Internet to see what other people did, and finding out what my options were, and I was led to the downloading source through PayPal.

SG: *They have a tutorial on downloading?*

MG: Yes, they actually have a sister company that works with them that's part of Pay-Pal that does the downloading. And it's protected so that somebody can't just go on your site and get it for free, they have to pay first. The payment is processed through PayPal and you get your money through PayPal in your PayPal account, and it's protected by this company. But all of the music is just on my server. I'm not uploading to a big warehouse per se. I bought a certain amount of real estate on the Internet and I use that for my own server.

SG: *Right. So how much does it cost you to keep the albums on your server and to allow for the downloads? Is it very expensive?*

MG: No. I think EZ Web Hosting is awesome because you can start out really small. They have Internet Web sites that start out as low as $5.95 per month. I have a premium that's $34 per month, and I believe it gives me 500 MB of space on their servers to upload whatever I want to. That's basically it. There are always PayPal fees involved but they're fairly minimal. That's pretty much how it works.

SG: *That's very helpful information. So it seems you've formed strategic partnerships with these honest companies that are really helping you. It's encouraging that there are partners out there that you can do business with and that you can rely on. Now, you also sell the CDs at live events, correct?*

MG: Oh, yes. That's the bread and butter.

SG: *Because when they hear it, they want to take it home. But how are you doing with the sales online, with mail order? And how are you doing with the downloads?*

MG: It's getting there. I'm getting more mail orders than downloads. I think it all depends on your demographic. If your demographic is younger and you're appealing to 13–17-year-olds, you'll probably make more money on downloads. If you're appealing to a demographic that's 21 and older, which I think I'm probably selling more in that area, those people still want to buy a CD. They want to read the cover, read the lyrics, they want to see the pictures. They want something physical that they can carry around and put in their car or whatever, so I'm selling more CDs at this point. But I do think that that's going to change. As the technology progresses, I think we will get to the point that people will be able to download the whole package, and they'll be able to print up the album cover and liner notes and the whole bit exactly the way you intended it to look. That was one of the reasons that I held off doing downloads, especially of individual songs, because I really take a lot of pride in putting together an album.

JM: I agree that one bad thing that MP3s and downloadable music have brought to music is that the album has fallen by the wayside. Singer-songwriters like Marci want to make a complete picture of an episode in their life, and the single-song downloads on iTunes and most other downloadable services are really putting the concept album at risk. I think you're going to see a lot more individual songs—rather than entire albums being released separately—but I agree with Marci that there will be more services where you can download cover art and liner notes. And I think that people will be able to download with one click the entire album—artwork, liner notes, everything.

SG: *You don't offer artwork now or liner notes, but can I download a complete album if I wanted?*

MG: Yes, you could download each individual song, and all of the lyrics are available and that's free. You can instantly get my lyrics for all of the albums on my Web site.

SG: *Do you write all of your own songs? Do you ever do covers?*

MG: Never. [Laughs] No, it's a bone of contention for me. I don't have a problem with cover artists—I made my living that way for years. It's just that it took me a very long time to develop my voice and who I am as an artist and what my vision was, and I'm very adamant about expressing that as fully as possible. I don't say that you shouldn't, this is just where I'm at. I fully believe that there is a listening audience out there that *does* want to hear new things, that *does* want to be exposed to other people's ideas and musical concepts, and it doesn't have to be on Top 40 radio. That's who I attract at my gigs—people who are real listeners, not just to hear a song, but to experience a performance. I always say that the audience is 50% of how well the show is going to go. We're so set in our ways of watching television, staying at home, staying in front of our computers and getting locked into musical boxes. I really encourage people to get out of the house and convene with other humans. It's really good for you. It's good for your spirit and your soul, and there's nothing like being in a room and hearing a live performance, because every live performance is different. You'll never ever have that same performance again.

SG: And by the way, the Web site does *link to your touring schedule, doesn't it?*

MG: Oh, yes. That's a very important factor because I want people to come out to those shows.

SG: Another thing that I wanted to emphasize about your career is that writing your own songs can be very lucrative. If, for example, you license your music to a TV show, they have to pay you extra for the rights to use the song in addition to the master. It's another payment, usually equal to master, and then you get performing rights royalties from the song on top of that. So it's always a great asset if you're a songwriter as well as an artist.

MG: Absolutely. I was at a seminar once and a woman from Mercury Records gave me some very good advice. She said, "Diane Warren makes just as much money as Madonna, and she doesn't have to go to the gym for six hours every day!" And she's right. [Laughs] I still work out every day, but songwriting is a really good income stream, and that's very important for any artist to just have income streams coming in. I really love writing, but I do co-write with some people on occasion. But 99% of my music I write by myself because I'm so enmeshed in me. [Laughs]

SG: If people want to cover your song, they have to pay you the mechanical on the record sales. Have you had any covers yet?

MG: Yes, I've had a couple of covers. I haven't had any covers on an album that's been pressed, but I have had covers in live performances and I've received residuals for that, which is awesome.

SG: Before we go into your label, Sonic Underground, which by the way is a great name, is there anything else that you'd like to tell us about your Web site, anything that you're particularly enamored with?

MG: Boy, I slave over that thing so much, I don't know if I'm enamored with anything! [Laughs] I would say the most important thing is like I said, to keep it really simple for people to get what they want. If they want a picture, make it easy for someone to find a picture. If they want to hear the music, make it really easy. Your navigation tools are really key for that. I like the promotional materials page: If you're looking on my tour page and you see a show that you're interested in, it says, "Posters for the show are available here." And you click here and it brings you to a page where you can download the flyer or the poster. I think that's kind of neat, so I like that one.

SG: How about your journal, Marci?

MG: Oh, the journal's cool too. That's sort of like my diary where I get to complain and whine and be happy and excited and celebrate. Like you said, it's about building a relationship with the people who are going to pay money to see you and listen to you, so you have to give a lot of yourself. So I have this journal that peeks inside my diary and lets people know if I'm having a lousy day or a wonderful day. They feel closer to you, and that kind of draws them into being more interested in your music, I think.

SG: *Do people get into a correspondence with you?*

MG: Oh, yeah. I have friends all over the world at this point, and it's really special. It brings me so much joy to connect with people who appreciate my music.

SG: *Talking about connections to other human beings, one last thing about the Web site: Team MG. Can I become a part of the Marci Geller team?*

MG: Oh, I would love for you to! Can you please become a part of my team? [Laughs]

SG: *What would that entail?*

MG: Well, you have to read the instructions. [Laughs] Basically, Team MG is a street team. It gets people more intimately involved in my career and participating, because I think that if you invest something of yourself it has more value, it means something more. So we ask people if we're coming to their town to do a show to please put up flyers, please play my music for their friends . . .

SG: *And you can print out flyers from the Web site . . .*

MG: So it's very easy. In exchange, depending on what level of a Team MG person you are, you can get free stuff. It's kind of like a "one hand washes the other" situation. I'm not putting myself up on this pedestal where I'm like this great artist and I'm better than you. No. We're all in this together. I want to make music and I want people to hear it, and so I need people to *listen* to my music too. It's very reciprocal.

SG: *No T-shirts yet?*

MG: I'm working on it. T-shirts are coming.

SG: *You have a link to a record label in your site, Sonic Underground. Is that your label?*

MG: Yes, that's the label that I started it with my then manager. We decided to amicably part ways a couple of years ago, and I kept the label.

SG: *Tell us about Sonic Underground. How many artists are on the label?*

MG: At this moment the only other artist besides me is the Deer Head Freaks, which is one of my favorite bands on the whole planet. They're sort of a combination of Smash Mouth meets Frank Zappa meets the Presidents of the United States of America. They're very zany and funny, but extremely intelligent and clever. A lot of the humor will go over some people's heads.

SG: *If you go to the www.sonicunderground.com Web site can you also purchase albums and download songs the same way that you can through www.marcigeller.com?*

MG: Yes, absolutely. And it also has cross-links to my Web site, so that we feed each other. They can get to me through Sonic Underground and you can get to Sonic Underground through me.

SG: *Would you ever consider entering into a deal with a distributor and selling your stuff through a third party, or are you content with the sales that you're making on your own on-line and at your concerts?*

MG: I'm always open to any opportunities, because I don't know everything. If somebody can come to the table with the level of enthusiasm and commitment that I have to my music and help alleviate some of the workload that I have and my manager has, of course I would consider it. I'm very thankful for what is being generated right now. I'm very happy with it, but if I could expand it to the next level, yes, I would absolutely consider it. I guess I just haven't really found the right partner in that area just yet. But if I do . . .

SG: Listen up, A&R guys in the audience. Check the site out—you'll love the music—and give Marci a call. She won't even necessarily say no!

An Interview with Grammy-Winning Jazz Artist Eric Revis

www.ericrevis.com
Eric is an accomplished jazz musician who has one of the most elegant Web sites I have seen.

Eric Revis

A Grammy Award–winning jazz bass player, recording artist, and composer, Eric started his professional career playing with legendary vocalist Betty Carter and for the past seven years has been a member of the Branford Marsalis Quartet. Eric just released his debut album as a leader with *Tales of the Stuttering Mime* on his own label, 11:11 Records.

Steve Gordon: Your album got great reviews from the critics. And I noticed that your site is linked to a page in CD Baby where you can buy the album. How's the record doing on CD Baby?

Eric Revis: It's doing pretty well. CD Baby is a great avenue, because you get all the information of people that buy your record, and I've been able to correspond with them through there. It's really cool.

SG: We'll talk about Web site in a minute, but what I really like is that you're three clicks away from purchasing the record on CD Baby. They also did a nice job of designing a page for your album in their site. Would you recommend CD Baby to artists? [See Chapter 17 for our interview with Derek Sivers of CD Baby.]

ER: Definitely.

SG: One of the reasons that I wanted you to come on the show is that I think the Internet could be very useful to jazz musicians in particular. Let's talk about the economics of jazz music, and whether things have changed because of the Internet. Many successful jazz musicians make their own records but make the bulk of their income through the live performances. And it's because the market for jazz albums has always been a niche market—you don't get sales like Eminem from pure jazz. Is the Internet a good way of supplementing your income?

ER: Without a doubt, yeah. It bypasses a lot of the bullshit that you go through with major labels. It's direct and you're getting your control of your destiny, and it's a direct line to fans and potential fans.

SG: And you're doing a lot better than the normal royalty, which is like, 10% of retail?

ER: Exactly.

SG: So if record sales have always been a supplement to live gigs, what is the role of a record company, whether it's an independent or a major? Do some jazz artists sell more records at live gigs than they do through the label's distribution?

ER: I believe so. I know Branford has started his label up and he started selling records at gigs, and he does very well doing that.

SG: So you sell the records at gigs, and you can supplement that through selling them on the Internet.

ER: Exactly!

SG: Lets talk about the major labels for a minute. If you do have the opportunity to sign with an indie or a major, would you have a preference or a recommendation? An indie who really cares about your music or a major that has worldwide distribution?

ER: For me in particular, I would go with an indie that makes a concerted effort to forward my career and to get my music out there in whatever capacity. The majors almost are like golden bars—they have a lot of resources at their disposal. However, it seems as if you end up getting less of your share, you have less control, and then at the end of the day you have nothing to really show for it. Because as much as they have the power to put your product out there and advertise, they have that power to take it away at any time that they please, and then you're just screwed.

SG: Also since they have the exclusive right to distribute, you might not be able to supplement your income by selling records on the Web.

ER: Exactly.

SG: We all know that the major labels are having a lot of financial difficulties. Whether that's because of file-sharing or something else, sales are down dramatically in recent years—so is income, and thousands of employees at major labels are losing their jobs—Sony/BMG just laid off 2,000 people. So is there less of a shot even if you wanted to get on a major label than there was before? Are they shedding their artists as well as their employees?

ER: Yeah. I know that Warner Brothers basically let go of their jazz department. They kept maybe one or two people.

SG: That is sad. At many major labels jazz was a prestige department. It didn't sell a huge number of records. It didn't make a huge number of dollars, but they kept it going for prestige. Now because of the cutbacks, prestige is often the first thing to go.

ER: Exactly.

SG: Let's talk a little bit about the role of the Internet. Would you say that it's possible you'll sell more records though the Internet than you will at record stores?

ER: I don't know; I would like to think so. I think that because jazz is such a niche market, very few record stores have a jazz section, and if they do, it's negligible at best. So it is my hope, that because most of the people who know of me through the various artists I've played with are somewhat discerning in finding the information, they will find me on the Web hopefully more and more.

SG: Your Web site gives them the opportunity. They know who you are. They might want to purchase the record through your site, and you're giving them the opportunity to do it. And you've got a great Web site, because of its simplicity and its elegance. When you get into the site there's a simple-looking image, a nice piece of eye candy. And then the visitor can choose the HTML version if they are in a dial-up connection, or the Flash version for high-speed users. You give people that choice in order not to alienate the dial-up people who wouldn't be able to get the Flash version?

ER: Exactly. I just got the high-speed within the past month or so.

SG: So you didn't want to alienate yourself? [Laughs]

ER: I wanted to be able to check it out! [Laughs]

SG: It's a useful choice. I like the HTML because it's also very simple. It lays its choices with nice graphics and focuses on the album. But the Flash version is really terrific. I love the initial image: It kind of looks like pieces of a puzzle coming together to depict your brain. And then there's a bit of intrigue: when you roll the cursor over your head, the various links light up. And you can immediately access your bio, photos, tour information, and the new CD, of course. Did you specifically think in terms of simplicity? Because there's so many Internet sites that are all messed up with clutter.

ER: Yeah, I think that was of the few criteria that I had for the Web site, that it wouldn't be complicated at all—something artistic but easy to navigate.

SG: Where did you come up with the image of the brain? It look like you got it from a 19th-century medical textbook.

ER: The phrenology thing! I was doing some photos with the photographer, Lourdes Del-Gado, and she suggested doing the phrenology series. I'm bald, so it worked out well. And the Web designer, Saresh Singaratnam, really liked the phrenology idea, so he just put it together.

SG: I was going to ask who designed your site.

ER: Aestheticize Media is the company. It's listed on the Web site.

SG: I like the fact that you give them credit because they deserve it. Now, how did you find Saresh?

ER: My manager, Rio Sakairi, suggested the guy. Saresh is actually a student at Manhattan School of Music—a trumpet player—and he also does this. He has really, really interesting stuff. We had gone through a couple of people, and it just wasn't happening, so she suggested him. We met, and it really clicked.

SG: That's another rule: there are a lot of talented people out there and they want to do interesting stuff. They're young, they're motivated, and they may be a lot less expensive than established companies.

Another thing that I like about the site is that there is a prominent picture of the album cover on the home page, and if you click on that it brings you to more information on the album and a link to your Web page in CD Baby, where you can listen to tracks in the album and purchase it. There was an Internet music marketing expert on the show, Scott Meldrum, who discussed pointers for creating a great Web site. [See Chapter 11 for the interview with Scott Meldrum.] One of his best points was the "four-click rule." If you can get to purchase the album within four clicks, you're doing something right. Was that part of your plan?

ER: To be honest, no; it was to make it accessible. I didn't know about the "four-click rule." [Laughs]

SG: Did you use a commercial server, or does your Web designer maintain the site on his server?

ER: He stores the site as well.

SG: Who registered the domain name? Did you have him do that?

ER: My manager and I did that.

SG: So the whole site was a collaborative enterprise using various people's expertise and knowledge. Who updates the site with, for example, new tour information? Do you do it yourself, or do you depend on your Web designer?

ER: At this point I depend on my Web designer. We've talked about getting together and him showing me the ABC's of going through it. I tend to be somewhat inept computer-wise, so it's probably going to take a little more than me sitting down once, but I plan on doing that really soon. We're going to open up some more pages on the site as well.

SG: What are your future plans for the site? I noticed one thing that I thought may have been missing, which is a place to sign up with at least a name and e-mail address so you can create an e-mail list. So when people sign up you can do e-mail blasts, keep people informed about the next gig, and have a more interactive relationship with your fans.

ER: Yeah, that's definitely one thing I want to add.

SG: So what's next for Eric Revis?

ER: Branford just released a CD this past week, and I am committed to his band through December, at which point I will be playing a couple of times in New York City with my group at the Jazz Gallery in Soho, on Spring and Hudson Street.

SG: I guess for more information about that, people can check out your Web site.

ER: Go to the Web site, right!

An Interview with Duo Live

www.redemptionmusicgroup.com

Duo Live is an innovative hip-hop act with a kick-ass Web site.

Lyricist Fre and producer Sid V personify Brooklyn's underground rap scene with its street swagger and consciously rebellious music. Their album *First Impressions* sold over 25,000 copies in 10 months, and when I interviewed them they were releasing a new album, *Free Lunch*, on their Redemption Music label.

Steve Gordon: Now, according to your Web site, you used go by the name Duo Die. Where did you get that name, and why did you change it to Duo Live?

Sid: Well, we're both from Bed-Sty [the tough Bedford-Stuyvesant section of Brooklyn], and the slogan for Bed-Sty is "do or die." So we were like, "Yo, let's call ourselves Duo Die."

Fre: We got to a point in our careers where we thought that the word "die"—that whole negative connotation—it didn't fit us, it didn't fit the group, and the music we were making was much more powerful than that. So we said, you know what—forget Duo Die. Lets go Duo Live!

SG: Nobody can doubt it's more positive. I read in your press kit that you started selling your records on the streets, specifically West Eighth Street and Sixth Avenue, my old neighborhood, Greenwich Village. I guess you started doing that before you created a Web site?

Fre: Yeah. Definitely. And we were doing that before we even understood the importance of having a Web site and what a Web site could do for us in terms of promotion and marketing.

Duo Live

Duo Live: Exactly, yeah. It's actually a superstore. And what's funny about it is—I'm gonna tell you the truth, man—we're still in the developmental stages of getting our Web site to where we want it to be and maximizing what it can do it for us. We're still babies in terms of Internet. We're learning as we go along, but every day, every day we're seeing and growing and realizing how important it is.

SG: It looks great now. I know you can add things, and we're going to discuss your future plans. But first, when did you first start building the site and how long did it take to complete it?

Sid: Well, the site we have now was built about a year ago, but prior to what is up there now, we just had a page with our pictures and pictures of a couple covers.

Fre: It was definitely a process to get to where we are now. The site we have up now, we stepped it up. The guy who did it—shout-out to Emerson from Hyper GSP!—he actually helped us. We came to him with the idea. We sketched it out. We got together over the course of a couple months and we just kept coming to him with the ideas, feeding him. He kept showing us samples of what he was going to do. When the site went up, we loved it. It was a process—we were hands-on with it the whole time. We did absolutely no technical work.

SG: I noticed in the credits that you give a credit and link to Hyper GSP. Now, the designer's name is Emerson? How did you find him?

Fre: Emerson lived upstairs from Sid in Bed-Sty. [Laughs] It's such a small world; so many people around us are talented and so many people are really trying to get into technology and broaden their horizons and help other people, so it really just happened that way.

SG: That's how I got to do this radio show. One thing and one person leads to another person. All you gotta know is what you want to do and then ask, and your next-door neighbor might be the guy who can help you.

Fre: Exactly.

SG: One of the nice things about the site is that it's very simply laid out. I like the fact that you go to the home page and you're presented with clear choices of where to go next, including information on the new album. What new album is up there right now?

Fre: The album that's up there is our last album, called *First Impressions.*

SG: Has it been selling well on the Internet?

Fre: I'm going to tell you the honest truth, we actually haven't yet. And it's due to the fact that we've been using the site for promotion. But now with the new site that we're going to launch in November when our album drops, we're gonna push it up a notch, and we're going to be looking to get some sales off the new site. With the site we have now, we were concentrating on our guest book feature to get more people to know Duo Live.

Sid: And read our bio.

Fre: Right, get to really understand what we were about—we really weren't looking for sales. It's funny—we set up the merchant account and then we let it lapse even. But now, this new site, man, I'm so psyched over it; it's going to be hot!

SG: Let's get back to what you've got now: You have the new album, the biography, mission statement, event schedule, contact info, and then you've got the guest book. Are you getting a lot of names from that?

Fre: Oh, man, we've gotten so many hits from the guest book. And the guest book is such a beautiful feature, because what it really keeps us in tune with the pulse of the people and what they're feeling—what songs they like. What songs they don't like. How they like us, personally, you know, when they meet us. And it's such a great way to meet someone and just tell 'em check us out on the Web site. And they can teach you and let you know everything that they're feeling, even if it's a couple sentences.

SG: It's easy to use and it just asks for your e-mail address, so I signed it today. And I also sent a message. And I liked that it didn't ask a lot of questions. I didn't have to give you my age for instance . . . [Laughs]

Sid: Another good thing about the guest list—we have a street team to distribute our CDs. Usually they run into people and they say "We don't have the money, we're not able to buy your CD now." Or we're not familiar—"I'd have to hear the music." So we usually tell them to go to the Web site, and once they go to the Web site and they read the comments that people make on the guest list, that makes them a little more comfortable and they say, "Okay, next time I'll buy their CD because all these people said it was good."

SG: And they can also listen to tracks from the album on the site.

Sid: Exactly.

SG: What do you do with the names that you get from the guest book? You talked about a street team. How does a guest book and a street team work together?

Fre: They feed off each other. The street team will tell someone, go sign in the guest book and let me know what you thought of the album. Then the street team will go look on the Web site, see the guest book, and the guest book has now fed the street team the inspiration they needed because they remember that person and they see that "Oh! He actually went and signed it, I'm so glad." And it makes them feel good about the work that they do. Being out there and getting the good music to the people. Because they it's, like, validation for what they do.

SG: So it builds community—a community of fans. Do you ever use the e-mail addresses in other ways? Do you, for instance, let people know about upcoming concerts?

Fre: Yep, or whenever we go on tour. We went on tour with Angie Stone, and we did a mass e-mail. We sent it out to everyone who hit the guest book and let them know what cities we will be in so hopefully they can come out, and people did come out from different cities. People came out in San Francisco, and a couple people came out here and there, and then they came back to the guest book and be like, "Great show." And let us know they were there. It's beautiful, man.

SG: I notice in the site an event schedule—you're playing Irving Place in New York City?

Duo Live: Right; and we have a new tour that's getting set up right now—it's a college tour. I'm not even sure who we're headlining with or what the dates are, but it will be up soon…

Sid: And the new site will be up soon.

SG: And it will have the same domain name?

Duo Live: Yes, it will.

SG: Let's talk about the new site in the context of what's going on now. If you go to the site's music store, you see three albums and they're all for sale, and it looks like a mail-order operation. They're not downloads, right?

Duo Live: Yeah.

SG: Now, in case you do have some sales, who does mail order for you?

Fre: [Laughs] Yes, we do have sales. We have an administrative assistant, and she takes care of all that. She checks in, and as soon as it comes in it goes right out. People get it as soon as possible. It's a pretty quick operation.

SG: Tell us about the new site. Are you starting to sell the music in a different way, or is it still going to be just mail-order?

Fre: We're going have it available both ways—via mail order or via download.

SG: So you are getting into the download business?

Duo Live: Yeah, we have to. We gotta step it up.

SG: And how are you going to do that? Who do you call to say, "Okay, I want to sell downloads." Is that the same guy who helped to build the site?

Sid: Yeah, Emerson. And he has people that he brings in on the project to help him. That's his whole thing. His whole thing is communication and networking, so he'll be able to put that whole thing together for us, that whole package.

SG: Are you going to let people listen to the music before they buy it? Have you thought about that yet?

Fre: We were actually talking about it, and we're still kind of undecided. It were up to me I'd let people sample an entire album. You know what I'm saying—I'd love to let people hear the entire albums, but it's hard because the music business is suffering so much at retail that to give away so much music—sometimes it's best to give a sample of just a song or two to give them the incentive to buy the album.

SG: Do you have plans for networking with other sites, like CD Baby? iTunes is making deals with independent labels, and there are aggregators, too, like IODA. They will make the connection between you and the commercial services like iTunes. Any plans for networking so your music is available on other sites?

Fre: Yes. We're actually blessed to have a guy like Dexter Wemberly, who's on the team and helping us with our marketing. He's in the process right now, negotiating with iTunes and three others—Sony Connect and at least two other companies, and our music will be available on all of them. We're gonna spread the wealth. We're gonna try and get it to the people any way possible. We believe in getting it out. It's great music. I want it to be available on as many places as possible.

SG: Sounds like Dexter is a real help. By the way, Dexter is a publicist and arranged for this interview. How did you meet him?

Sid: We went to high school with Dexter.

Fre: He was the smart guy we all wanted to be.

Sid: Dexter was about being cool and being in school back then. That was something we didn't do—we were just cool. We had to look up to him and say, "This is the type of guy our parents really want us to be."

SG: Tell me other ways that the Web site's going to be new and improved. How else are you going to enhance it?

Sid: Well, the last Web site was pretty much promoting the last album we had. That CD cover was black and white—everything was black and white—so that's why the Web site is black and white. So, for the next album, there's color in the CD and the layout, so there will be color, among other things.

Fre: And then we have an idea of possibly doing an interactive tour. So once you get onto the site, you'll have the option of going through the site, like I can click on a little image of me and Sid, and we actually lead you to a video feed—we lead you through the site, and the site is actually changing as we're talking about it.

SG: You're making a new video, so are you going to put that on the site?

Sid: Definitely.

SG: Does that take extra money to put it on the server because it's video instead of audio?

Fre: It depends on who you're working with. We do a package situation. We don't like to do too much where everything is an additional cost or whatever. I like to try to work with people who like to work with us, and we get one good fee, something reasonable, and they're willing to work with us knowing that things are going to be coming up and always be changing on the Web site.

SG: It's good to hear that it's not too much of a great headache to put a video as well as audio on, because there's going to be all of these new devices coming up very soon which will feature video.

Sid: There are going to be more Web sites where if a movie is released, you're just going to be able to download the movie—not even have to go to the movie theater anymore.

SG: Any parting shots on the future of the Web site or the importance of the Web site you want to communicate to the audience?

Fre: We're gonna try our best to try and spice up the Web site and keep being creative with it and throw in some different things and have weekly things that pop up—stuff that's just out of the ordinary. The Web site is very important. We recognized the importance of it as a vehicle to promote and market us as a group, us as a label, and just get the good music out to people.

SG: What's the next step for Duo Live? Are you looking for a label deal?

Sid: Well, you know, we have the label. We're going to be looking for a major distribution situation very soon.

Fre: We were talking with Jay Z recently and he was actually very interested. He loves the music, and we have a great working relationship with him now. Whenever he gets in the situation, he's gonna be positioning some labels such as ourselves.

SG: This is the model I wanted to talk about on the show and in my book—you're out there, you're doing your music, and you've got the Web site as your calling card and you use it to increase sales of CDs and also as a presence in the community and in the music business community. So if a major likes your music, they would see you guys already sell records and you know the business, as well.

Chapter 13

Additional Ways to Use the Internet to Promote Your Music & Make a Living

Online Distribution

There are many more ways to distribute your music—and therefore make money—than through traditional brick and mortar record stores. Online distribution is quickly becoming just as popular for indie artists as brick and mortar distribution, if only for the fact that artists no longer need an independent or major label record deal to make money from their recordings. Many online music services such as the companies discussed in the next part of the book allow unsigned artists to sell their music online. What's more, these independent services offer a much more artist-friendly share of the profits than do traditional avenues. Furthermore, these online distributors often have no sign-up fee and offer nonexclusive agreements that allow artists to distribute their music through other channels as well. In fact, many artists utilize numerous online distributors simultaneously which generates greater exposure and additional sales. Online distribution generally breaks down into two categories: digital record companies and online record stores, and we will explore both of these business models in depth in Chapters 14 and 15 (online indie record companies) and 17 (online record stores featuring indie artists and labels).

eMusic is another example of a stand-alone digital music service focused on serving the needs of independent music fans and independent labels. Delivering more than one million downloads each month, eMusic is among the top digital music services, offering a diverse catalog of 400,000 tracks from established independent and emerging artists in every genre from the world's top independent labels. Founded in 1998, eMusic was the first service to sell songs and albums in the MP3 format and one of the first companies to launch a digital music subscription service. A list of other digital delivery services focusing on independent labels and unsigned bands is provided in the resources section of the CD-ROM accompanying this book.

In addition to incremental income, success online for a new artist can also be key in garnering the attention from the traditional record companies, including the majors.

The online music world still does not offer substantial advances for production, and online music companies still do not provide the huge marketing machine that only the majors can supply. Music attorney Paul Unger recently published an article in the online music news magazine, *MusicDish.com*, titled "So You Wanna Be a Rock Star . . . In the New Millennium." Unger represented the "#1 downloaded band on several major Internet 'download' websites for more than two weeks in a row." Due to this success, he received a call from a major label representative who told him that their staff monitors these sites and they "noticed" the band's position, and they were "very, very interested in the band." Unger continues:

> What is the point? The point is that these labels called me—not the other way around. They called me because my clients were able to get their attention by creating real sales—both "brick-and-mortar" units that were recorded by SoundScan (because my clients got a UPC barcode) as well as through digital downloads recorded on major "download" websites—that were monitored by their "in-house" staff. They called me because today the labels are looking more and more to the "outside" for "test market" results (unlike the "old days" when the labels "test marketed" their own products through lots of small deals as described above). And when my clients demonstrate real results—real money generated—the labels call me, and then I'm much more able to parlay the situation into a more favorable result for my clients.

Moderate success online can therefore translate into major label attention, which can still translate into fame and riches.

Using Peer to Peer to Make Money & Gain Exposure

We previously discussed Weed in Chapter 9. Weed is a form of digital rights management available from Shared Media Licensing (www.weedshare.com), which allows you to monetize your MP3s by uploading Weed files to P2P services and letting people listen for free a few times before having to buy them at a price set by the artist.

Simply making your music available on peer-to-peer services, however, could also give your music valuable exposure. This exposure is counted, reviewed, analyzed and communicated to major labels by services such as Big Champagne. I invite you to listen to the interview with Eric Garland, the CEO, and Joe Fleischer, Senior VP of Big Champagne included in the CD-ROM accompanying this book. In the interview they discuss how big labels pay serious attention to information about artists and songs that are popular on P2P services such as eDonkey and Kazaa.

Moby is an example of an artist who gained valuable exposure by using P2P. "I know for a fact that a lot of people heard my music by downloading it from [the original] Napster and Kazaa," he wrote in his online journal last year. "And for this reason I'll always be glad that Napster and Kazaa have existed." In a survey released in December 2004 by the Pew Internet and American Life Project, an arm of the Pew Research Center in Washington, a report titled "Artists, Musicians and the Internet" confirmed that Moby is not unique among artists in his positive view of P2P. The survey recruited 2,755 musicians through e-mail notices, announcements on Web sites, and flyers distributed at musicians' conferences. In answer to the question of whether the Internet and file-sharing have allowed them to reach a wider audience, 65% responded that the Internet has a "big effect" on this ability.

Using the Internet to Promote & Book Live Performances & Tours

The pre-Internet days saw new artists using ancient methods to promote their shows by pasting billboards on street lamps and brick walls, placing ads in local papers, licking envelopes and mailing flyers. The same methods were also used to book gigs. Artists and their booking agents acquired directories of college venues and radio stations not typically available to the public. For out-of-town performances, artists scoured the Yellow Pages for venues. One of the problems with the Yellow Pages was that they offered no indication as to what type of music a particular venue showcased. So a country singer in Nashville who wished to perform in Philadelphia had no idea what type of venue he was sending a press kit to. With the help of the Internet, though, not only is it much faster to find venues, but the large majority of venues have Web sites that describe the music they showcase. Web sites such as Citysearch (www.citysearch.com) and Digital City (www.digitalcity.com) are also wonderful resources for musicians and booking agents, listing venues by location, music genre, and even audience demographic. Often they even have reviews of venues and performance spaces. Additionally, you can find many Web sites that list the venues in a particular city or region. Often these sites are organized by a local musician hoping to help other musicians find gigs. These sites offer a good starting point for finding venues.

Blogs & Weblogs

A weblog, or blog, is a Web site that publishes information or opinions on a specific or wide range of topics. Weblogs are generally focused on the ideas of one or a group of "bloggers," but often will welcome comments and contributions by readers. For instance, I write a blog on a Web site called digitalmusicnews.com about the music business.

Digitalmusicnews.com also hosts blogs by several other commentators, including Tim

Mitchell, V.P. of IODA, whose interview is included on the CD-ROM accompanying this book. Many people use a blog simply to organize their own thoughts, while others command influential and worldwide audiences. Professional and amateur journalists alike use blogs to publish breaking news, while personal journals reveal inner thoughts.

In recent years, music-based blogs have become more popular. Although they have not captured the same national attention as some influential political blogs such as Matt Drudge, music-based blogs are taken seriously by many people who are interested in learning about and listening to new music. For this reason, they can be excellent sources of exposure for independent artists and labels. For instance, talent finders at established labels have been known to regularly check out certain music blogs in search of the next big thing.

Both major and independent labels sign artists based upon what they have already accomplished and what they have the potential to create. A band building a local following and selling out a series of shows in their hometown generally appeals to labels far more than even a brilliant MP3 floating around the Internet. That said, MP3s do circulate around the Internet on MP3 weblogs. Reviews posted on weblogs and various music Web sites expose music lovers to new artists faster than ever before, and as a result, bands who can stand on the quality of their work might be able sell out 200 person, 400 person or even larger venues, certainly winning attention from record labels.

The Arcade Fire, a band from Montreal, is an excellent example of the power of blogging as a tool for music discovery. Prior to September 2004, they released one EP and toured as an opening act for another band. A combination of the promise demonstrated in their recording and the excitement generated in their live show got them signed to the Chapel Hill, NC label Merge Records. Merge manufactured and released 10,000 copies of their album *Funeral* in mid-September. Around that time, several MP3 weblogs that cover rock releases started singing the praises of this album and offered one or more MP3s for download. As a result, at least in part, record stores couldn't keep up with growing demand for the album. In mid-October, the band performed at the Merge Records showcase at New York's Mercury Lounge. Several MP3 bloggers and other journalists were spotted in the front row, watching the band and taking photos. Win Butler, the band's front man, told the crowd "I'd like to thank the Internet." After this showcase, MP3 bloggers got back online and reported how amazing the band's performance was. Even the *New York Times* took notice and quickly informed their readers about this red-hot band that was being touted so heavily on the Internet. A month later they played a show at the Bowery Ballroom, more than twice the capacity of their last New York show, and this time the show sold out weeks beforehand. Less than two months after the CD's initial release, Merge has sold 40,000 copies, making it the fastest selling album in the label's history.

A list of blogs focusing on various areas of music is included in the Resources section of the CD-ROM accompanying this book.

Legal Status of Music Blogs. Generally, indie blogs post music that the webmaster finds intriguing without seeking permission from the artist. Generally though, bloggers shy away from posting material from well-known artists, or even lesser-known artists if they are already signed to major labels. The nature of many music blogs is to spread the word about artists that nobody may have heard of before and provide more exposure to worthwhile music that only a small group already know about. Many weblogs are labors of love, although some rely on banner ads as a way to subsidize their operation. Here is how one blog handles the issue of posting music without permission:

> *Disclaimer and Contact.*
> MP3 files are posted for evaluation purposes only. Through this site, I'm trying to share and promote good music with others, who will also hopefully continue to support these artists. Everyone is encouraged to purchase music and concert tickets for the artists you feel merit your hard earned dollars. If you hold copyright to one of these songs and would like the file removed, please let me know.

Although this disclaimer does not immunize the blog from liability, it is clear that this blog does not intend to hurt the commercial success of any band or artist but to increase exposure for their music.

Creating Your Own Blog. Artists can easily create their own blogs on their Web sites. In fact, a blog can be created with off-the-shelf software. One of the most common uses for such blogs is to allow an artist to connect with their fans directly by allowing the fans to participate in what is essentially an interactive online journal. Not only does a blog allow fans to follow an artist's career, but fans can leave messages for the artist and can pass along the artist's blog to their friends. Of course you can post new messages on your Web site, but blogs have the advantage of allowing fans to read other fans' comments and respond to them. Blogs therefore contribute to fans sharing their thoughts about the artist with each other and help to create a feeling of community for the artist's music. Since blogs are almost always Web-based, the artist can make changes with only an Internet connection and a modest amount of computer know-how. A blog will also help an artist maintain contact with fans while touring. In addition, you can post MP3s on your blog so people can respond to your music. You might also link your music to a download or mail-order buy option in your Web site, or to an online record store such as CD Baby or Amazon.com.

Services That Allow Artists to Create Their Own Blogs. Certain music-based blogging services such as www.blogger.com and www.moveabletype.com help an artist to create and maintain blogs. These services generally allow the artist to use their domain name as the blog's address (for example, www.steve.com/blog) and give them the opportunity to make changes via the service's Web site. See the CD-ROM included in this book for additional resources for creating and maintaining a blog.

Podcasting

A podcast is a radio show that listeners can download online, feed into an MP3 player and listen to any time they wish while away from their computer. They can also "subscribe" to a podcast radio show and every time a new program is posted, it automatically posts to the subscriber's computer.

Adam Curry, the former MTV personality, has been credited as one of the creators of this new medium. He was quoted in December 2004 as stating: "There's a lot of great radio out there that I would love to listen to when I am ready for it." According to Curry, there are about 2,000 podcasts, including everything from talk shows to MP3 bloggers like Roger McGuinn, one of the original members of the Byrds, who podcasts old-timey tunes to his subscribers. Curry himself hosts a show called "Daily Source Code," which he claims has 10,000 subscribers, from his home near London.

Podcasting has the potential to become a very important way of exposing independent music. The reason is that podcasting is cheap. Webcasting music, which requires songs to be constantly streaming, is more expensive because of bandwidth costs. Podcasts are much less expensive to maintain and offer. This allows many music bloggers and weblogs, who could not otherwise afford streaming audio, the opportunity to offer their favorite music as podcast programs. This may help the already influential music blogger community become even more influential.

Further, on-demand interactive transmission of streaming or downloadable audio and video content to portable devices is the exclusive domain of multinational corporations which can afford the multimillion-dollar satellites that circle the earth. Podcasting may help the indies MP3 owners and maintain a presence in the portable device space because of its affordability. This technology may be quaint and kind of "retro," but it gives a shot to the indies to be in your MP3 player.

Check out ipodder.org to download podcasting software and learn more about it.

Digital Music Services and Indie Aggregators

Digital Services Featuring Major Label Content Can Be a Resource for Indie Labels and Artists. There are dozens of online music stores offering streaming music on a subscription basis and/or downloads for sale. But not all of them carry the product of the major labels. It costs a great deal of money to carry the hundreds of thousands of tracks that the majors have made available for online distribution. The costs of digitizing and encoding these tracks is steep, and the majors generally require advances or guarantees against future royalties. But there is no question which service carrying the major labels has received the most attention: iTunes.

There is a great deal of debate whether iTunes is a true success for the music business. It was the first service to persuade the labels to place catalogs *for sale* online. Unlike its competition at the time it started, iTunes allowed downloading and portability. MusicNet and Pressplay, the labels' initial foray into the online commerce, allowed consumers to subscribe to, but not own, music. You could listen to anything you wanted whenever you wanted but if you stopped paying, the music stopped playing. Further, you could only listen to the music in one computer—the one you paid for the music to play on. You could not burn the music or transfer it to any other computer or portable device. Obviously iTunes was a superior product—it allowed consumers to download tracks and transfer them to their computers and, of course, the iPod. Moreover, the iPod is widely recognized as one of the most elegant designs in gadget history.

iTunes has generated much excitement in the business because it has shown that it is possible to sell downloads of authorized music. By July 2004, sales were approximately 100 million tracks, and by December 2004 iTunes had sold more than 200 million tracks. This easily makes it the most successful and most recognized digital music service in this country. But perhaps the most interesting thing about iTunes is that it hardly breaks even. Some speculate that Apple even loses money on every 99 cent download because of what they have to pay the labels, the publishers, transaction fees and marketing and publicity. No one doubts, however, that Apple has made massive amounts of money selling iPods. As of December 2004, the *NY Times* reported that the company sold over 10 million of them, and *Digital Music News* reported in early January 2005 that Apple reported its best quarter ever with revenue of $3.49 billion, up 74% from the year-ago quarter. "Powering the earnings surge were breakneck iPod sales, with unit sales jumping 525% to 4.5 million over the holiday season."

Obviously, Apple is using the music to sell the gadget. This is not the first time in history a technology company has gotten into the entertainment business in order to make money by selling more electronic devices. Think of the acquisition of CBS Records and Columbia Pictures by Sony, one the leading electronics companies of all times. RCA, to cite another example, got into the music business at least in part to sell record players.

This book is written from the perspective of the independent artist and entrepreneur. However, many independent artists see iTunes, which features music from the major labels, as an opportunity for incremental income and exposure. One of the interesting things about iTunes is that it was one of the first services carrying the major labels to reach out to the indie community and bring them into the fold. Now the other major services such as Microsoft's MSN Music are also reaching out to independent labels as well. Every one of them gets basically the same catalog from the majors so that they are all looking to one-up the others with some content that the others don't have. That makes independent music valuable to them. That makes for an opportunity for indie labels.

iTunes catalog is reported to be significantly larger than those of many of its competitors. It announced in August that its catalog consisted of over one million tracks. That came as a surprise to some, with other stores showing more modest totals. Napster, for example, now carries a catalog of 750,000, while Rhapsody offers "over 700,000 songs." Why is Apple outdistancing others in terms of total catalog?

As reported in recent edition of Digital Music News (www.digitalmusicnews.com), a key differentiator for Apple may be its aggressive pursuit of indie artists. The store boasts a catalog of over 600 indie labels, a huge total that is in line with Steve Jobs' pursuit of niche content. Is Apple better able to push the indie licensing process with a cash reserve from iPod sales? It is certainly a possibility, though other stores are also spending cash. But chasing lesser-known or obscure indie content may not make financial sense for other digital music stores, especially if the tracks are not accessed very often. If that is the case, Apple is likely to stay ahead in the race for total licensed tracks.

Here is a list of the leading services carrying content from the major labels:

BuyMusic. Music download site features 500,000 songs mostly from major labels at less than 99 cents. While DRM limitations vary from song to song, those restrictions are easy to find with a "click here for usage rules" for each track.

Musicmatch. Yahoo recently purchased this download and premium subscription service. They claim to have more than 800,000 songs for download at 99 cents. On the subscription side, Musicmatch features automatic playlist with "AutoDJ."

MusicNet. One of the first subscription streaming services originally launched by BMG, EMI, and Warner, MusicNet was one of the first services to offer artists signed to major labels. It now offers downloads as well as subscriptions to streaming audio. It is available through various corporate partners including MusicNet@aol.

MSN Music. Microsoft's new music download store launched in the fall of 2004. The online music cosmos just got bigger with the official release of Microsoft's MSN Music, already a behemoth of a virtual music store, where users will soon be able to browse a library of more than 1 million tracks and purchase them in an à la carte fashion. Launched September '04. Microsoft will go head to head with iTunes and will be compatible with more portable devices than iTunes, which remains exclusive to iPod.

Napster. Not the original P2P service. A subscription-based streaming and downloading service owned by Roxio, with over 300,000 subscribers. This service has nothing to do with the original Napster created by Shawn Fanning, except that Roxio secured rights in the name and logo. Roxio, which built its fortune on creating technology that enabled people to burn CDs, entered the business by buying Pressplay. Universal and Sony Music launched Pressplay as one of the first subscription services.

On Demand Distribution (OD2) is Europe's leading digital distributor of music, founded by music legend Peter Gabriel.

RealRhapsody. Real Networks Rhapsody is primarily a subscription streaming service, with over 250,000 members. Rhapsody offers on-demand streaming.

Sony Connect. Sony's attempt to get into the download business. The creator of the Walkman enters the world of music downloads. Service works well with Sony's new portable music players.

Virgin.net. Offers 300,000 music tracks for 99 cents each.

Wal-Mart. Wal-Mart's clear-cut approach is refreshing for those who fret about keeping track of varying prices and restrictions. All tracks have one fixed price and one set of DRM restrictions. This browser-based service is ideal if you simply want to download music, and aren't looking for a matching media player.

The Resources section of the CD-ROM included in this book provides active links for all these services.

Aggregators. Independent Online Distribution Alliance or IODA (www.iodalliance.com) is a company designed to aggregate content from the independent community for the commercial online music services including iTunes. There are other companies that provide a bridge between independent music and the commercial services. For example, as we discuss Chapter 17, certain digital music stores such as CD Baby and Mperia also help independent artists interface with iTunes. But for IODA, providing a bridge between independent music and commercial digital music services labels is their primary focus.

IODA introduces independent labels and artists to commercial music services, both download and subscription services, including iTunes, Napster, Rhapsody, Musicmatch, etc. IODA also services other online distributors that specialize in niche or indie music. IODA claims that its collective bargaining power enables independent rights holders to receive more favorable terms than would otherwise be possible. IODA is a digital distributor, with the primary goal of making music available to fans via digital "retail stores," and works with the services to ensure that they take full advantage of the IODA catalog. Independent labels send their music to IODA, which then distributes it to the myriad of download services available. IODA receives 15% of the license royalties paid out by the services in exchange for ongoing rate negotiation, catalog encoding and data management services, rendering monthly accounting reports, and the administration and distribution of royalties. IODA enables indie label clients to see exactly how, where, and when their music was accessed. Although most of their clients are small record companies, IODA offers time and cost-saving benefits to both the commercial digital music services and indie labels. The commercial music services do not want to spend time making deals and managing relationships with a myriad of independents who often don't trust or understand them in the first place; indie labels are spared the time-consuming process of reaching out to and negotiating licensing deals with each service.

IODA also claims to keep rights holders educated and informed about the landscape and intricacies of digital music. The CD-ROM accompanying this book contains an interview with Tim Mitchell, a V.P. of IODA, in which we explore IODA in more depth as well as his views of the future of the music business.

Satellite Radio Services

In the period following the enactment of the Telecommunications Act of 1996, which relaxed the rules on radio station ownership, there has been a massive consolidation of radio stations in the hands of a few corporations, and a corresponding reduction in local ownership. Many complain that as a result there are many more commercials, and much less new music on the air than ever before. Critics also point to a dearth of courageous DJs who could champion new artists. Enter satellite radio.

As we reported in Chapter 3, XM and Sirius, the leading satellite radio services, may play any musical recording they wish pursuant to a statutory license under the Digital Millennium Copyright Act (DMCA). As of the date of this manuscript, Sirius, which began in 2002, offers 65 commercial-free music channels as well 55 additional channels of sports, news and talk. The non-music channels carry a modest level of ads (approximately 5 minutes per hour) compared to much heavier advertising on commercial broadcast radio. XM offers over 100 digital channels including over 65 ad-free music channels. A nearly unlimited selection of different kinds of music are offered by both services— from underground garage bands to rock classics from each decade, hip-hop, soul, R&B,

classical, world, dance, electronica, bluegrass, jazz, Broadway show tunes, etc. In addition, as we discuss in a sub-section below and in my interview with Lee Abrams of XM, satellite radio also plays a significant amount of indie music, including unsigned bands.

The radio signal is sent from satellites to special radio receivers that primarily reside in new automobiles for now, but increasingly are becoming portable. Both XM and Sirius are available with a satellite radio receiver for about $150, although many auto companies, including GM, Ford, Honda, and Chrysler, offer either Sirius or XM radios in their option packages to buyers. As of the end of December 2004 Sirius increased the number of its subscribers from approximately 600,000 in fall of 2004 (before the Howard Stern deal was announced) to over 1 million. Sirius subscribers pay $12.95 per month. XM reached the 3 million subscriber mark by the end of 2004. XM subscribers pay $9.99 per month. XM launched nationwide in Nov. 2001, a year ahead of Sirius.

Tremendous Growth Predicted. Satellite radio may be on the verge of tremendous growth. On October 7, 2004, Howard Stern and Sirius announced that he was leaving broadcast radio altogether and would start his own channel on Sirius. Although he will be paid more money than he earned from conventional broadcast radio, Stern said he made the decision because of the freedom satellite radio would give him. Unlike conventional broadcast stations, satellite radio is not fettered by the "indecency provisions" set forth by the FCC.

Mr. Stern's act, which he himself describes as "bathroom humor," has long been under attack by the FCC. Since 1990 the stations carrying his show have been fined more than $2 million dollars. The FCC regulates the broadcast of profane content. The FCC has been even more rigorous in enforcing these standards after Janet Jackson's breast baring incident at the 2004 Super Bowl half-time show. Earlier in 2004 Clear Channel, in a separate incident involving Stern, dropped his show from its stations after it was fined $450,000 by the FCC. By contrast, content on satellite radio is not regulated. Stern lamented: "When we do best-of shows and replay some of the material we've done in years past, there is sometimes 50% to 60% of it that we can't use—bits are hacked—interviews are cut off."

Stern knows that his audience will initially sink from more than 10 million on broadcast stations to approximately 10% of that number, but the attention that his presence will bring to satellite radio and Sirius in particular has many analysts predicting that satellite radio will reach larger and larger audiences and may soon compete with traditional radio much like the growth of cable, which now rivals network television. *The Wall Street Journal* reported that Stern is promising to lure other high-profile personalities to satellite, and if that happens "terrestrial radio eventually could find itself falling behind satellite in ratings and buzz, just as broadcast television is struggling with cable." [*WSJ* October 7, 2004, p 8, Sarah McBrise and Joe Flint]

In an article published in fall 2004 in the Wharton Business School newsletter "Satellite Radio: Wave of the Future or Niche Play?" experts at Wharton and elsewhere say there's little doubt that satellite radio will eventually become big business. The question, though, is when.

Sirius plans to pay Stern $100 million a year for five years and share revenues as the company grows its subscriber rolls. Sirius CEO Joe Clayton announced that Stern, whose audience is estimated to be around 10 million listeners, "is capable of changing the face of satellite radio and generating huge numbers of subscribers for Sirius." The company also notes that if Stern were to attract 1 million more subscribers, the deal would pay for itself. Sirius has also paid heavily to broadcast all National Football League games, and has hired former Viacom president, Mel Karmazin, to oversee its projected rapid growth.

XM has been working on striking its own massive deals to retain its competitive lead over Sirius. In October 2004, XM announced an 11-year, $650 million deal with Major League Baseball. The company said this agreement would enable XM to broadcast every Major League Baseball game starting with the 2005 season.

According to Wharton professor Kevin Werbach, signing such blockbuster content deals makes sense since each additional subscriber will cost both companies less as they expand. "The issue is whether satellite radio is a niche play or the future of radio."

Wall Street analysts have voted that satellite radio is the future, especially since Stern jumped onto the bandwagon. The Stern deal "reinforces our belief that satellite radio will become ubiquitous, and that investors should start to think of the duopoly of XM Radio and Sirius as Coke and Pepsi," wrote Bear Stearns analyst Robert Peck in a research report.

Opportunities for Unsigned Artists. In May 2004 the *Seattle Times* ran an article titled "Technology Helps Bands Hit It Big" by Frank Aherns. The article reported on one independent artist who had a very good experience with XM. New York–based artist stellastarr* was signed to a five-album deal in May 2003 by RCA Records. But five months earlier, deejay Billy Zero broke the band on XM after he got hold of stellastarr*'s sole CD, "recorded on the cheap in New York." Zero runs XM's "Unsigned Bands" channel, which exclusively plays bands that do not have record contracts. He left Washington's WHFS (99.1 FM) for XM in February 2000, after growing frustrated that the Infinity Radio station would not play enough unsigned bands.

Commercial radio is now notorious for playing only established artists and failing to try anything new. When the XM Unsigned Bands channel launched, Zero had to solicit CDs from unsigned bands. Now, he receives many CDs from hopeful bands, beseeching him to play their songs. One of those artists was stellastarr*. Zero added them to his playlist and soon thereafter they were signed to a deal with RCA Records. According to the lead singer and songwriter for that group, the XM exposure combined with play on college radio stations and articles in the alternative music press generated the buzz, "which is ultimately the foundation for a band getting signed." And RCA President

Richard Sanders said although XM did not play a direct role in stellastarr*'s signing, XM and its rival, Sirius, "are vital to building recognition for new bands and, more important, album sales." After stellastarr* signed to RCA, XM moved the band's songs to the XMU channel, which has a college-radio sound. Zero is also starting a new show called "Inked," which will play songs from bands that landed a major label deal but either got dropped or never had their record released, the fate of many signed bands.

Satellite Radio Goes Internet. XM offers a stand-alone PC-based streaming service, which mirrors its satellite offering, for an incremental fee of $3.99. Online only customers will pay a monthly charge of $7.99—less than a satellite subscription. The stand-alone Internet offering is at listen.xmradio.com. XM also offers the service as a free 30-day trial to new Dell Inspiron notebook and Dimension desktop computer owners. The advantage of the Internet service is that you don't have to buy a satellite radio.

Transition to Smaller Devices? Both Sirius and XM have already launched their satellites, built networks and signed deals with leading content providers. In addition, satellite radio will gain subscribers as consumers buy new cars. "By installing the receivers in automobiles, it takes much of the decision out of the consumer's hands," says Wharton professor Werbach. "All the consumer has to do is decide whether to subscribe or not." The automobile strategy should give satellite radio a captive audience and grab new customers. XM has projected that it could reach 20 million subscribers by 2010, largely because of its deals with GM and Honda, which churn out millions cars each year. Sirius has deals with Ford and Chrysler.

But ultimately, some experts contend that XM and Sirius will have to get by without depending on automakers to market their receivers. "Right now the model depends on people buying new cars, but ultimately the businesses will have to stand on their own. In a couple of years, I see satellite radio growth divorced from the auto market," states Professor Peter Fader from Wharton. Selling satellite radio services in the absence of collaboration with automakers will require the industry to transition to new, smaller devices. A few weeks after Fader expressed this opinion, speculation became reality as XM announced in November 2004 that it would sell a portable device about the size of a cell phone which would provide the same content that XM provides to subscribers who possess XM automobile or home receivers. This device will initially bear a suggested retail list price of approximately $350. The rechargeable battery will provide for 5 hours of service. According to Professor Fader: "As technology improves, it won't be surprising to see MP3 players in the future function also as satellite radio receivers."

Target: iPod? The potential success of satellite radio may have even bigger implications than whether it will attract more listeners than free radio. Professors Fader and Werbach say both types of radio, free broadcast and pay satellite, will coexist much like skis and snowboards. Satellite radio could also wind up being a major competitor to Apple's iPod as services and devices converge, suggests Fader. For now, consumers choose to download music and carry it around via devices like the iPod. Satellite radio, however, can in theory carry more songs. With technology improvements, devices will be able to sort songs played over satellite. It could be the ultimate subscription music service, says Fader, who believes that subscription music services will ultimately win out over downloading. Toss in real-time data and local information, and satellite radio could be a big rival to downloading devices. Werbach says the iPod vs. satellite radio will offer an interesting contrast. Apple's business model revolves around its iPod players; iTunes is used to boost hardware sales. XM and Sirius, in contrast, aim to sell their satellite radio content as a service and the hardware devices are secondary. Are XM and Sirius gearing up for a battle with iPod? "I doubt they are thinking that far ahead, but they need to think that way," says Fader. "It's important if they want to bridge the chasm between early adopters and the mass market."

An Interview with Lee Abrams, XM Radio's Senior Vice President and Chief Programming Officer

Satellite radio is a relatively new technology of great significance for the music business, and XM is the largest satellite radio service in the world. Lee Abrams, XM Satellite Radio's

Lee Abrams

Senior Vice President and Chief Programming Officer, has been shaping the American radio industry for over three decades. In 1993, *Newsweek* listed Lee as one of America's 100 Cultural Elite for his contributions creating modern radio, and *Radio Inc.* listed Lee as one of the 75 most important radio figures of all time. Lee joined XM in June '98 and helped to create the next generation of radio. You can find out more about XM Radio at www.xmradio.com.

Steve Gordon: Lee, let me read from the XM Web site and ask you to comment. "XM is 68 commercial-free music channels; 33 channels of news, sports, talk, and entertainment; 21 dedicated channels of XM Instant Traffic and Weather, and the deepest playlist in the industry with access to over 2 million titles, all for just $9.99 a month." Let's get into the music. Can you tell us a little about your various music channels?

Lee Abrams: There's a channel pretty much for every imaginable genre of music. In the super-popular genres, such as country and rock, there are numerous channels—several channels for alternative, for example. And if you feel like listening to oldies instead of one oldies station that you might have on an FM band where Buddy Holly might collide into Abba, we have the luxury of having dedicated '40s, '50s, '60s, '70s, '80s, and '90s channels, so we can go deep and create kind of a complete listening experience without compromising fans of other decades. It's all about diversity and depth and the fact that we're not driven by the gods of research and advertising when it comes to deciding our playlist.

SG: *And it's all commercial free?*

LA: That is correct, yes.

SG: *That's a blessing. Do you know which music channels are the most popular?*

LA: We do a lot of surveys and it varies quite a bit, but generally speaking, as you'd expect, the more traditional channels are the most popular. For instance, our country channel Hank's Place, which is traditional, kind of modeled after the way a country station sounded in Lubbock, Texas, in about 1957. Then there are the classic rock stations, which are more about careers and not just the same hit songs over and over again. We have something called the "enough already" factor. If you asked somebody do they like "Born To Run," they might say, "I like 'Born to Run' but enough already! Play some other tracks." So these channels drill deeper into the artist's career. But to answer your question: the country channels, some of our rock channels, certainly '70s, '80s, '90s are real popular, and it's not only music but our two comedy channels, a filthy one and a clean one, and the filthy one is incredibly popular.

SG: *I know there's an entire channel for unsigned artists, and with my show I'd like to think I have a lot of indie labels and unsigned artists listening. So let me read to you what your Web site has to say about this channel, and then I'll ask you about it: "Serving local bands nationwide, it's Radio Unsigned, the first and only national audio platform dedicated to unsigned, independent, and emerging artists. Unsigned plays music across all genres." How would an unsigned artist go about trying to get his music or her music on this channel?*

LA: Just submit it to XM Unsigned or directly to Billy Zero, the Program Director. Billy listens to everything. Some of them are really unplayable—some guy singing into his cassette player in his bedroom—but the vast majority are really good bands. It might be a really talented band from Dayton, Ohio that has no clue on how to get a record deal or how to hire a lawyer, but they perform great music and take a lot of care in putting their demo together, and that's what we're looking for. Those get played. We even have a countdown at the end of the week of the most-requested unsigned bands, which I know a lot of the A&R guys at record companies listen to.

SG: *There's an article in the* Seattle Times *about Billy Zero that focuses on an unsigned artist who actually got a deal. You know for a fact that record companies are listening?*

LA: Oh, absolutely! We visit the record companies constantly just to talk about ways to introduce and work with our artists, and you walk through the halls and see a lot of XM radios. I talk to these guys, particularly the A&R guys. The talent scouts are constantly listening to that channel to hopefully find the next big thing.

SG: Do you have any idea how many listeners you have for the channel?

LA: No, not really. It's not one of most popular channels because the nature of the music is unfamiliar—it's unsigned new bands—but among the musicians and record-company communities I'd say it's probably one of our most-listened-to channels.

SG: That's certainly a very important audience for unsigned artists. Are there any other opportunities in your vast network of music channels that unsigned artists or independent labels should know about?

LA: Yes—there's XMU, primarily indie artists and some unsigned artists, kind of like a college station but a little more disciplined and the staff doesn't turn around every semester. A song goes on there, kind of develops there, and if it becomes a hit it's actually dropped by that channel and goes to another channel, because that channel's for discovery. We also encourage unsigned artists in many other genres. Our Lost channel will play some more of the singer-songwriters. Fine Tuning is very eclectic—you'll hear Peter Gabriel mixed with a Bulgarian women's choir next to a lost Beatles track, but if there's something very unusual that is unsigned or not available in this country, Fine Tuning plays it. But almost all the channels—except for the ones that are designated to be hit machines—will welcome unsigned artists.

SG: You have a Web site. Would it be possible to send an MP3 version of a demo via the Internet?

LA: Right now, no, and I'd need a physics degree to figure out why, but it's because we're digital—there's some compatibility problems. We would prefer a CD by mail. That will change, but as of this moment the CD is the way to go.

SG: Now going to my favorite subject, the law: I had John Simson from SoundExchange on the show. SoundExchange administers the statutory license under the Digital Millennium Copyright Act (DMCA) for non-interactive digital transmission of music recordings. My understanding is that you can play any record you want under your DMCA license. Is that right?

LA: We can play anything we want, but we're subject to some restrictions under the DMCA as far as how many songs we can play, for example—a maximum three cuts an hour from an album within a three-hour period. However, if we go to the record company and get a waiver—which happens daily—then we can play almost as freely as anybody. So when we do artist specials—coming up we're doing every song Elton John ever did over a two-day period, from Universal—they're giving us a waiver. It's a little more of a pain to do that, but we do.

SG: Do you have good relationships with the labels?

LA: Excellent. I think they look at us as a savior because traditional radio has gone so research driven, so tight, so much focus on rocket science, where XM is like radio back in the '60s—it's wide open. We actually listen to everything that comes through.

SG: And commercial radio is infested with commercials. I find it almost unlistenable.

LA: Personally I find it unlistenable. There are just too many. I think a big advantage of XM is there aren't any on our music channels.

SG: How many minutes of commercials per hour do you have in your talk channels?

LA: It averages about 12 minutes, less on some, rarely more than that.

SG: And commercial radio, what would the average be there?

LA: Anywhere from 18 to 30 minutes an hour.

SG: Do you think satellite radio may one day overcome terrestrial?

LA: Yes, I think we will follow the same pattern that FM followed. And we'll do to FM what FM did to AM 35 years ago.

SG: Another analogy is that some people say that satellite radio is like cable is to traditional broadcasts.

LA: Yes, both of those are pretty accurate.

SG: For someone like me who makes his living working with producers of music-based TV programs, do you ever see the day that you'll transmit video as well as audio?

LA: Oh, absolutely—but again, I don't know when. I don't think it will happen within the next couple of months, but I know it's being considered and looked at.

SG: MP3 players are going to go visual soon with a new generation coming out soon. They will have little windows, and you'll be able to see music videos and other programming. All you have to do is just add a little screen to your XM device, no?

LA: Yeah, but there's a bandwidth issue. We're governed by the FCC and have a certain amount of bandwidth. We could have 500 video channels, but they'd be walkie-talkie quality. And I believe that one of the problems that's being worked on is that video eats up a lot of bandwidth.

SG: I hope you can overcome that hurdle; I'd love to see some video programs on XM.

LA: Well, before we launched, the limit was 50 channels, and now we're up to well over 100, so it gets better and better as technology improves.

Chapter 14

How to Build an Independent Digital Record Label

This chapter explores how artists and entrepreneurs can use the Internet to build a successful record company by telling the stories of two indie record companies, Tay Music and CU Records.

An Interview with Kirk Casey and Tim Gorman of Tay Music

http://www.taymusic.net/

TayMusic.net is an example of online record company created by and for independent artists. Indie recording artists Kirk Casey and Tim Gorman are pursuing their dream of

artistic freedom with TayMusic.net, an Emeryville, California-based online record company. Guitarist Casey, TayMusic.net's founder, boasts credits on ten Sims video and computer games and has released two albums, *Rocktronica* and *Ten Soundscapes*. Classically trained keyboardist Gorman has played on sessions with the likes of the Rolling Stones, Elton John, and the Who, with whom he has toured. He has also toured with Jefferson Starship, worked on the Sims games, and has released an album called *Classical Daydreams*.

Tim Gorman and Kirk Casey

Steve Gordon: Kirk, when did Tay Music get started?

Kirk Casey: This is our first year out—we got started in the summer of 2003.

SG: What inspired you to come up with the idea of an online record company? You physically exist, but your record company is virtual.

KC: Several things, though it actually didn't start out that way. The initial concept was just seeing that the Internet was becoming a bigger and bigger medium, and the chances of my music being purchased and distributed by a major label didn't seem like something that was going to happen, because the types of music that I was working on weren't very mainstream.

I was talking to a friend of mine, and he said, "Look, we've got to get your music out there." So that's where we started. I was working on a Sims project—Sims 2 actually, which was released recently—and recording hip-hop tunes for that particular game and was at the studio where I now currently have a room, and Tim was there also. I met Tim and we just hit it off. I came to him several weeks later after we'd had lunch a couple of times and talked about music and things, and I said, "Hey, do you have any music sitting on the shelf? Because I'm going to put some of my music on this site." And as we talked we decided we would get a couple more artists. I originally thought of the idea of Tay Music, but after I met Tim it really progressed into something bigger, and that's where we are now.

SG: So you guys are working musicians who have done just about everything, and you found a niche in video games. But you also wanted to continue your careers as recording artists, and the Internet gave you that chance.

Tim Gorman: Oh, absolutely. All of the record companies that I had been with in the past were major labels, and I was then with a boutique label, a classical label over in Marin. When I met Kirk he explained this idea of putting my music out on the Internet, which I'd done with MP3, but this was a chance to actually be a bit more pro-active and own a piece of it myself and control it a bit more myself. That was very entertaining to me, and so after we talked a couple of times it seemed like a good thing to do, and it's worked out very well.

SG: I think that the idea is so intriguing after working at major record labels for a dozen years and every week seeing the lists of artists who were dropped from the label—out of 100 new artists dozens were dropped over the course of a year. For artists to get control of their own destinies like this is terrific. How did you guys come up with the name Tay Music?

KC: That was on my end. My wife and I went to Scotland in 1995 and got married there in a little town north of Dundee where my grandmother was from—her house was still there. She had a little ticket on the pew there at the little church and everything. We decided to do something a little bit different, so we went back to what my roots were, and we were married near the banks of the River Tay. I had some time to think about what I was going to do in the future, and so a few years later we were thinking about what to name my company, and Tay Music sounded cool.

SG: You guys have a lot of different music on the site including Celtic music, so I guess that represents Scotland pretty well.

KC: Yes, and we plan to have quite a bit more of that as well. Our goal is eventually to have enough music, enough of a variety from different artists in each genre for the label to catch on.

SG: How many artists do you have currently?

KC: Right now we only have about four.

SG: Including you and Tim?

KC: Yes.

SG: Can you tell us about your music and the two other artists? What kind of music we can look forward to when we go to TayMusic.net?

KC: We have five, actually. We have a new artist we signed recently called Scraping for Change—they're more of a rock act. Young guys, a great band, Tim and I produced the record and it came out real nice. They're just starting their big push around the Bay Area. And we do have several other artists in the wings. But for now, with Tim's music we have the *Celtic Loop* CD, which is a great contemporary Celtic album with some incredibly talented players on it. We've been marketing it on the Internet radio, Live365, and several other stations that are affiliated with those people that have Celtic sites or Celtic radio sites. *Celtic Loop* is real popular. The next artist we have is Kenneth Nash. He's a master jazz percussionist and world music percussionist. His roots go to the Herbie Hancock and Weather Report bands that he was in. He currently is a producer in Oakland and does his own music as well. He along with Tim and I had some music sitting on the shelf and wanted to get it out there. It's really interesting stuff—it goes between world music and some spoken word. Tim has a couple of albums on the site, including *Music for Visuals*, which is a collection of film-score music that he'd done in the past.

KC: Then we have an artist named Art Hirarara. He's kind of a young-lion jazz pianist, a very talented guy. His album is his second. His original release, *Edge of This Earth*, is a great piece of work. Then we have Scraping for Change, so there's something there for a little younger demographic.

SG: How have you been able to use Live 365 to get the word out about Tay Music and your artists? [See Chapter 19 for an interview with Rags Gupta of Live365.]

KC: Originally I went to Billboard.com to see what kind of music was getting played and see the visibility of music over the Internet and what's really happening, who's selling music. Maybe people are listening to music, but is anybody selling music? Are any artists flourishing? And so Live365, along with CD Baby and several other companies, are listed in that section of their site. And just by going to check out each one of those I found out more about it. I learned about Live365 and started a dialogue to see if we could get our artists in that flow and on their stations. I think they have about 5,000 stations right now.

SG: So you have your own Tay Music station at his Web site?

KC: No we don't. We did send them three cuts of each CD to distribute to radio stations in their network that provide music that's suited to each one of those genres, whether it's jazz or Celtic music, or whatever.

SG: So it's like a network.

KC: Yes. I guess you could have a Live365 Celtic radio or a hard rock or hip-hop station or whatever. I think it's a subcategory within their network, but it's really interesting, and through them I found a Celtic radio station. There are probably over 2 million people a year that are streaming just this one radio station's music all the time when they're on their computers.

SG: On Live365 is there a way that people can associate the music with your names or Tay Music?

KC: I believe that there is a search engine involved, and you can probably type in our names and it would take you to the station that's playing that.

SG: And when the music plays would your name appear on the Web page?

TG: Yes, it does.

SG: I also had Derek Sivers from CD Baby on the radio show. Would you ever consider using CD Baby as a partner?

KC: We do. Both Tim and myself have releases on CD Baby as well as Tay Music, and the reason for that is if you did really well on the Internet and you sold a lot of CDs, he has a way to track that, and that information then goes to NARAS and you're then part of that community. Whereas right now, artists like myself who have their music solely distributed on the Internet can't vote or be a part of that musical community because they don't have a way yet to track the sales.

SG: Your Web site says, "Tay encompasses techno and electronica-based pop, urban hip-hop, contemporary and smooth jazz, folk, progressive rock and R&B, new age, world beat, Celtic, Latin, Middle-Eastern and Indian music. Is there anything that you wouldn't play?

TG: Probably not. There might be something lyrically that we might object to in terms of content, but in terms of musical genres we're pretty much open to anything because Kirk and I as composers embrace so many different styles of music. To say that we wouldn't listen to someone else trying to do the same thing would be somewhat hypocritical. So we've been very open-minded about the artists that pitch things to us and the things we're looking for. We'd like to expand each genre by about 10 artists each—that's our goal right now. We're both out looking for Celtic acts, hip-hop acts, all kinds of things.

SG: How would people get in touch with you?

KC: They can go to *www.TayMusic.net*, and under Support they can e-mail us, tell us about themselves, and we'll get back to them. So we can open up a dialogue that way.

SG: And I guess people can send their MP3s that way.

KC: We can do that. We do have an FTP site that we would probably guide them to at that point, but the first place to begin would be by contacting us and opening up a dialogue.

SG: I want to talk a little bit about the mechanics. First of all, who built the site? It looks good. Are you guys computer nerds as well as musicians?

KC: No. I still have to have the guy down the hall come and help format my computer if it crashes or something. But we use a company called Neko Media Inc. out of Pleasant Hill, California. We feel that they've really helped us along. We use their main guy, Bob Peacock, as a liaison for our account, and he's really done quite well for us.

SG: For people who are considering doing this themselves, how expensive is it? What are we talking about in terms of a very approximate range to start an operation like this?

KC: If you have a company build your site, just as in music production, there are several different levels of how good an Internet site can look. And you have to weigh the pros and cons. Do you want something that looks one way but doesn't have the ability to do something else? We're not only a record company, we're also a record store, so we have to have this retail thing going on where all of our products have codes. There are other things going on behind the site that have to be figured out in content, and that's where the money comes in because that stuff needs to be developed. And as you go you find that things change. The site as it looks now will be changing its look in another four weeks. We will morph into another way that we want to present ourselves, because as you go along you certainly want to improve on the things that maybe are stopping someone from staying on the site and downloading more music or whatever. It needs to be easy, it needs to be straightforward.

SG: Is bandwidth a big expense?

KC: I've heard that it can be if you have high traffic, but that would be a good thing. You know, is filling up your gas tank to drive to a gig an expense? Yeah, but there's a gig at the end of the line. It can cost you anywhere from $1,000 all the way up to . . . we're still working on things, but I would imagine that before we're done we will have spent many more thousands.

SG: But to start up it sounds like the original costs can be modest. I've got to ask you, why .net instead of .com? Is there any reason for that?

KC: Well, .com was taken, and we decided that since we were dealing with a water feature, the River Tay, the ".net" went well! [Laughs]

SG: Do you offer downloads and mail order, or one or the other?

KC: We do both, definitely.

SG: Do you handle mail order yourself?

KC: Yes. We actually manufacture *and* ship.

SG: That sounds like a lot of work.

KC: Well, when it becomes a lot of work we'll just deal with it. [Laughs]

SG: Are you ever going to do traditional retail, or are you content selling over the Internet?

KC: I think I speak for Tim as well as myself when I say that we're really in it for the long haul on the Internet. I don't see anything on the Internet getting any worse than it is— it's only getting better. There are many other driving factors that are going to make the Internet a place where people are going to do most of their shopping in the future. So if you can find places that you like their style or their flavor of music, that's what we want to be.

SG: When I got to Sony, they originally took me out to the Pitman plant in New Jersey where they made all of these CDs, and people were walking around in astronaut uniforms and the plant must have cost tens of millions of dollars. And to think of all the other stuff they had: Factories all over the world, warehouses all over the world, sales agents throughout the world—all of these to create and distribute these shiny discs to stores all over the planet. But for a few bucks you can create a Web site that can reach potentially everybody in the world. It's breathtaking.

TG: It is! And there are a lot of pluses to being an online record company in terms of operating the company, we have no warehousing to speak of, there's no free goods clause, and there are no returns because when they buy it they own it, and they only buy the things that they stream and probably listen to. So we don't have to worry about that. And because we're running the company with very little overhead, it really makes it look that much more attractive, especially if we're turning a profit, of course.

SG: The words "free goods" and "returns" bring up the issue of contracts. What kind of arrangements do you have with new artists? Are you looking for one-off deals for any album that you like, or do you want long-term relationships with new artists that come to your label?

TG: Well, my deal with Tay, like with most of the artists, is nonexclusive. So if you get something else, say, in the more traditional end of the record business going, you can stay with Tay and enhance your career by going with the traditional thing as well. But I consider myself exclusively with Tay now because I'm just doing so much work that way. With Scraping for Change, I think they're of the same mind that I am. It's different for each artist, but most of us have signed on for a nonexclusive, but in my case I've changed. But many of my friends in the business, like Peter Townshend, Peter Gabriel, David Bowie, have all gone online. They're all running their own record labels this way. It has nothing to do with the fact that they're older, it's just that many of the younger musicians and bands are doing it this way as well, like Bad Haggis who I worked with on *Titanic* and *Braveheart*. They're a modern Celtic act who do everything online; they actually started online before Kirk and I did.

SG: There's another feature of your record company that intrigued me—the educational element. Let me read the relevant passage and then ask you to comment: "For Kirk Casey, TayMusic.net is also about teaching younger players. Along with his artists, he hopes to forge partnerships with computer and music equipment companies to grow the label and ultimately form a music education foundation." Kirk, can you tell us more about this dream to create a music foundation?

KC: We both have been educators, and my premise is that if we can succeed with our label and reach a point where we can put things back into the community, we would like to have a curriculum where you would be able to use downloads in teaching different aspects. The musical foundation is something that Tim is more involved in. Tim, why don't you talk about that?

TG: I've been affiliated with a company called Korg USA for 25 years now. They build my keyboards, they build the synthesizers that I play. About a year ago they asked me to give a speech for Apple Computers to a group of educators from all over the world at Camp Apple. It went quite well and it got me into the education side of Korg, which is called Sound Tree, and the education department at Apple, which are the two fastest-growing divisions at both of those companies. My idea is to produce online music lessons given by different members of the music community. For instance, you could have somebody like Jimmy Page giving you an acoustic guitar lesson. I'm not just speaking off the top of my head—I actually contacted the people who work for Jimmy and they said that he was very much into the idea. There were several artists that lined up to help me do this, like the Tubes, Journey—everybody was in. The idea would be to create an educational database of people giving everything from one-on-one first-day-of-school-type lessons on different instruments all the way up to graduation day if they get that far. I thought how nice it would be if people could learn that way online, because the budgets aren't there to put the money back into the schools. My dream is that maybe 25 or 50 years from now, somebody that learned to play guitar that way will show their kid the same lesson and it will be there. And they can say, "I learned to play acoustic guitar from Jimmy Page; here's the lesson." And they can recall the database and these things could be bought or downloaded and stored. It would be like buying an electronic encyclopedia for your family.

SG: And could this dream be a part of the Tay Music site?

KC: Yes it could. It's out in the future, but companies like Cablevision—and I got the idea from Sound Tree at Korg—the educational director, Lee Whitmore, said that they might be interested because they've already got the pipe laid to broadcast these things. So I'm talking to different people like that right now.

SG: It's fantastic how one thing leads to another. But keep me in mind if you want to add music law to your curriculum.

KC: [Laughs] We would love to have you!

SG: On the home page there is a list of different kinds of music, and when you click on any one of these categories, such as "ambient music" or "hip-hop" or "hard rock," you get a rather detailed description of the music and you can play samples of each. Is this a part of the educational mission of Tay Music?

KC: Yes and no. I'm glad that you saw it that way. There is another reason for it, which also has to do with search engines and being an Internet store. Having the content of each musical style with some examples from our catalog helps a search engine find us. And when people are looking for ambient music we want to come up as #1 in their search. This is a game that we're playing very, very seriously. We work on the text continuously; it changes every few weeks to a month or so. But we always want to keep working that as part of our marketing plan. With the Internet as your market, you have to think outside the box, and by doing that we're just trying to be as creative with it as we can.

SG: So the more times you use the word "electronica," the more likely it is that you will come up first in a Google search?

KC: Exactly. It's a frequency-based search engine. And what we'll do is we'll Google ourselves every once in a while and find out what comes up before what we want to come up, and then we'll take that data back to the webmaster, and he'll look it over and go back and work on the text, on the bios and stuff. It's kind of fun, actually.

SG: Guys, how do you measure success? What primary goals are you looking to achieve from Tay Music?

TG: For me, success as a composer is hearing somebody whistle something I've just played after I've played it. But certainly as an artist recognition is a part of why we do this. It's not everything that drives us and I can't speak for the whole artistic community, but I know why I do it. Basically I'm just trying to make things a little bit more beautiful than I found them. It is that simple for me, because that's the way I see the world as an artist. If I play a certain melody one morning, to me the morning seems a bit better. If I can convey that to people, that's a real mark of success for me.

SG: Well, Kirk, now that we know that Tim is a true artist, are you looking to be the next Berry Gordy or Ahmet Ertegun of the Internet?

KC: [Laughs] Well, success for me would be to see Tay in a place where we would be respected in the music community as well as the international community of music listeners—a single place that you could count on having fantastic quality independent—not Britney Spears—music, from world music to all different kinds of genres. That would be success for me. Knowing that we were the coolest on the block.

SG: What's happening at the moment with your site?

We are changing things a bit. We will have a streaming radio station of our own on the site in the very near future. You'll be able to go there and stream just about anything you want with instant access, instant gratification. And we'll be adding the DVDs and Quicktime movies and interviews.

SG: Is the site is going to look a little snappier?

KC: We're going to add some more eye candy and more things to just play around with. We're going to take some of the text off the front to try and get less wordy. It will all remain on the site but it will just look a little different. We felt it was time to change things a bit.

SG: On the webcast are you going to play exclusively Tay Music or will there be other music as well?

KC: We're going to play exclusively our music. And as we add artists, that's going to be one of the things that we provide for them. We'll be able to get some more exposure for them.

SG: So I guess you won't need a license from SoundExchange, which licenses masters. You'll have the rights in all of your own masters.

KC: We own our own inventory—or we license our own inventory; let's put it that way. And what we don't have agreements for, we've composed and recorded ourselves.

SG: You guys are working musicians, you founded an online record company, you've got a whole load of experience to share with independent musicians. What advice would you like to give to musicians?

TG: I just think being as proactive as you can about your career is the best thing. Go to places like CD Baby, Live365—there are several radar screen–type sites that you can go to as artists to get your name out there, and I would embrace that as much as possible. For example, I try to spend one day a week just going through my phone calls and contacts and making sure that people got the information I was sending to them. Making sure you make your calls to your manager, your agent—any of those people that represent you and support you—so that everybody's on the same page. All those little details really add up and bring your career along.

KC: I would ditto that and add that I think for any up-and-coming artist, if you want to get your music out there it's really important to play out live. If you can create a live experience, then people will have a reason to go to the Internet and buy your music.

TG: Even if you don't have it down in the CD shop next door to the nightclub you're playing, that doesn't matter. There's a way that you can get them to get onto the Internet and either download a song or buy a CD. It could be as easy as, for the price of admission they get a ticket that has a four-number code on the back. Then they can go to the site and type in the code for the next couple of weeks and download those two songs from you. And while they're there—gee, there are CDs there as well. You still need the traditional exposure to some degree, and that in my viewpoint is playing out live.

SG: So you're attracting your live listeners and your fans who really like your music to come to your Web site. And since your Web site is your music store, you're inviting them to your store. That's really valuable advice.

TG: Also, high-speed burning at the concerts has become very popular as well to enhance the ticket sales, so that people can take home the concert right at the end of the gig.

SG: That's a controversial area since Clear Channel developed some sort of a patent on their technology to do that and they don't want to share it with other people. But if you didn't use the Clear Channel technology, how would that work, Tim?

TG: Last summer I did a live webcast with the Jefferson Starship at the old Avalon Ballroom here in San Francisco, which is where a lot of the psychedelic music got started in the old days. They had a lot of high-speed dupers, people came in and got an extra ticket when they entered the foyer of the building, and then there's a kiosk at the end of the show that they go up to and present the ticket, and the CD for their order is done. They just paid a little extra money for a CD of the show. It's all being done with high-speed burners, and it's being streamed as the band is playing live.

SG: And the band gets a piece of it?

TG: Yes. They're actually selling quite a few copies that way. It's a way for an act that doesn't have a record deal to get CDs to their fans. It's much like the Deadheads did, but they're bypassing the label part of it and just going direct to the listener right there in the audience.

SG: So if a band plays a particular venue with this technology installed at the location, they can use this to make some sales.

KC: Exactly. Other bands that are doing this would be Phish, String Cheese Incident, and the Sting/Annie Lennox tour last summer.

SG: Phish used to produce their own recordings at the event and then put them up for sale the next day on their Web site.

KC: Right. That's what's really taking place. I don't think there are any record companies behind that kind of a thing or big corporations like Clear Channel. I'm pretty sure that Phish and all of those other guys were just doing it on their own, getting their own forces together and putting the computer nerds in one room to figure it out.

SG: Do you guys have non-music day gigs?

TG: No. I start in the studio, believe it or not, at seven o'clock in the morning.

KC: I'm in at nine o'clock.

TG: And our day usually ends around five, but it can go later. When we were working on Sims we would often have many 18-hour days, but that's usually at crunch time only. Our day starts out with a little bit of running the business, and then we go into recording mode for the majority of the day. We're creating content, and the biggest part of the day-to-day of running a label is creating the catalog.

SG: Has this given you the financial independence to work full-time on your dreams?

TG: Not at the moment. I'm still playing concerts for the Starship and the Who and for Clear Channel and many other recording sessions, films, and stuff. So that's how I supplement my income with the Tay thing.

SG: Do you see the day coming when you guys can devote yourselves full-time to the record company?

TG: Absolutely. For me and for Kirk I would say that it's definitely full-time. But my other employment comes usually at nighttime, so usually I'm done in the studio and I have plenty of time. But I can see doing Tay full-time really soon, all of the time.

Alphonzo Terrell and the CU Records Story

http://www.curecords.com

CU Records is an indie record company with a strong online component, created by students at Columbia University.

This section tells the story of Alphonzo Terrell, the founder of CU Records, an artist and a student at Columbia University. We explore how he set up an indie online record company to support his career as an artist and those of other new talents. We start with Alphonzo's history of CU Records and then present an e-mail exchange on how he took advantage of the Internet to achieve his dream.

Throughout its history, Columbia University has been a steppingstone for some of

Alphonzo Terrell

the biggest names in music. Reaching back as far as Paul Robeson all the way to stars of today like Alicia Keys and Lauryn Hill, the school has continually attracted talented students who had gifts both in the classroom and on the stage. Home to the widely respected radio station WKCR, the school would eventually offer a strong player in the digital music scene. CU Records, an online-based record company, was founded in the spring of 2002 by six university freshmen headed by a young hip-hop producer/performer named Alphonzo "Phonz" Terrell. Having produced and distributed three full-length albums of music before graduating high school, Terrell's initial vision for CU Records was to use the Web to promote and distribute the numerous talented artists he kept on meeting who, like himself, had full-length projects.

"I came up playing basketball," Terrell recounts, "and if you want to make it to the pros in basketball, you usually go to college first to get your skills up, and then go on to the pros afterwards. I had the same idea in mind when I started CU Records. I wanted to create a very communal yet ambitious atmosphere for artists and business people alike who wanted to go on to careers in the industry. Columbia, where everyone was using the Internet all the time, was the perfect place to start cultivating a farm system for industry talent using the Web."

Joining Terrell in this pioneering effort was economics major Zach Silverzweig, who secured the label's non-university start-up budget, and graphic designer Pepin Gelardi, who created the entire look of the label from the logos to the flyers to the chic appearance of the label's initial Web site. From the outset, it was clear that the label's presence on the

Internet was going to be a key factor to its success. Operations manager Akinwale Ogundipe found Robert Kayinamura, a graduate student in the computer science program. Kayinamura, already a proven entrepreneurial success with the half-million-dollar tech service company Etanoia to his credit, gave the label a huge break on Web developing and hosting. He instantly recognized the power of using the Internet to promote and distribute music and was impressed with Terrell's talent as an artist and the talent that Terrell was attracting to the label.

"We felt like, hey, the whole industry is on its knees in a large part due to college students trading music on the Web, so who better to come up with the solution than the college students themselves?" says Terrell. "Zach, Rob, and I managed to get meetings with label executives at Arista, where I had been an intern, and Universal. They essentially asked us what to do—so, naturally, our egos were through the roof, and we thought we were going to make a good chunk of change selling student artists back to the students through the Web. We had some dreamy flow charts, a lot of confidence, but we learned real quick that it's pretty hard to fly without a plane ticket."

Their first official release was a compilation record entitled *Baby Blue Vol. I*, a record that featured everything from hip-hop, rock, and R&B to classical, jazz, and new music not adhering to any standard category. The label initially promoted the release of the record in September 2003 at the Soundz Lounge a few blocks uptown from Columbia's campus. CU Records sold the record on their Web site, fulfilling orders from e-mail requests by mail and sometimes sending staffers to deliver the records to students on-campus. Designed to satisfy the eclectic tastes of students at Columbia, the record was released with very high expectations. Sadly, it flopped, failing to sell more than 100 of the 1,000 copies that were initially pressed.

"Yeah, we learned a lot of painful truths from *Baby Blue*, the first of which is that most people do not buy records because of the record label or a flashy Web site; they buy it because they like the music," Terrell notes. "Second, compilations of multiple genres are generally a bad idea, especially when your label has not yet carved out its own niche in the market. We were far too gassed up over the novelty of our existence; we simply assumed that because we were college students doing this somewhat remarkable thing with no formal support from the university, people would naturally want to 'support' us. Well, support does not recoup costs, and we found out what 800 CDs tasted like."

Discouraged but far from defeated, Terrell took it upon himself to prove that CU Records' implementation of the Internet plus the talent of students as both artists and staffers was a viable business model. He started working on a new album, *Connexion Romantic*. Unfortunately, *Baby Blue*'s failure had dried up the patience of nearly half of the staff members of CU Records. For many of them, the idea had failed—the school had refused to officially recognize the group, so meetings had to be held in public cafes and dorm basements. The start-up funds had all but dried up behind the failure of *Baby Blue*, and none of the artists on the label's roster, except for Terrell, had any projects pending for the near future. There were also nasty rumors, as there often are when a record label or executive suffers a setback. Word was that Terrell alienated people because of "cut-throat ambition" and that he was the Ivy League's answer to Sean "Puffy" Combs.

"I heard the rumors, but I knew what CU Records had to do." Terrell says. "The result was a near overhaul in the business model of CU Records. I sat down with Rob, Zach, and Pepin to discuss the most potent way for us to reach their fans without spending a whole gang of money on production, manufacturing, and promotion for every single project. That's how the 'hybri-digital' distribution idea evolved."

According to Terrell, the "hybri-digital" distribution model was designed specifically to exploit the low-cost benefits of the Internet and the ever-dropping price of professional studio gear while focusing more on live performance and word-of-mouth promotion to build the fan base. In the model, the Web site is the epicenter of the label, with new songs being released for digital purchase every month, with an option for fans to purchase a physical copy of the record should the artist provide them. The front page of the site shows a top-10 list of downloads for each month, as well as rotating showcase profiles for the top three artists each month.

"The point of the move to (almost) all digital was to play to the strengths of the university community," Terrell explains. "Internet is everywhere and high-speed access is free in college, as are computers, and a lot of kids own all sorts of portable digital devices like iPods. Spending a whole lot on a video or traditional promotional items doesn't make much sense when the artist is literally in the same building as the fans—it's a different kind of sell. What people respect is when they experience something live—the live performance has never been more valuable. You can't bootleg it or even fake it at this level. And knowing that the number of people with home studios like myself is only going to continue to grow, I felt it was better to let the artists produce their own music, and for us to help them once they had projects to move. So, essentially, there are only three jobs at CU Records—artist, promoter, and webmaster. In this way, we can have as many artists as we want, giving the smaller projects to our trainees while supporting our 'stars' with the more experienced members of the organization. It's a pretty new and rather different way of experiencing the music industry, but for our niche, I feel like it is really going to work."

CU Records currently has eight artists on its roster, with three new full-length projects set to be released in 2005. Their hybri-digital distribution model was set to be launched in spring 2005.

E-mail Interview with Alphonzo Terrell

Steve Gordon: What inspired you to use the Internet in creating CU Records?

Alphonzo Terrell: It was less an "inspiration" to use the Internet than a cost-efficient necessity that played to our strengths being at a major university. In addition, the concept of distributing our product digitally appealed to us more and more as the proliferation of iPods and other portable media players intensified on campus.

SG: Any favorite business model or Web sites?

AT: Naturally, iTunes was an early inspiration, if only for its sleek design and total integration with Mac computers. As we progressed, however, the subtle marketing tactics of Google as well as the articles in MusicDish.com gave us a vision of kind of Web site we could eventually expand to beyond the music.

SG: How did you actually use the Web site?

AT: The Web site was used on several levels, but primarily in two ways. First, we have an innovative back end that allows us to add e-mail addresses for promotion and post files on a server that only the executive board has access to. The front end is primarily used as an online distribution method, in addition to serving as an online press kit for artists looking to book shows both locally and nationally.

SG: What were the benefits of using the Internet?

AG: The primary benefits of using the Internet were, quite simply, people believed that the label was legit due to the quality of our site. It provided a centralized distribution mechanism as well as an information outlet for all our showcases, releases, and artist background info. Finally, it was incredibly cheap, and most of our initial efforts were merely labors of love, with little overhead.

SG: The greatest success from using the Internet?

AT: The greatest success, again, is that people believed the label was real. From artists, to fans, to industry professionals, the quality of the Web site allowed us to be taken seriously.

SG: What were the biggest frustrations or disappointments?

AT: The biggest frustration is, naturally, selling records. You can have a captive audience, tons of hits on your site, all the promotions perfectly timed, yet if you do not have a product that people want, it is useless. Despite our rather unique entry point, we still had to face a lot of the same problems that major labels have to face. Our first record, *Baby Blue*, attested to that fact.

SG: Do you plan to offer downloads?

AT: Certainly. Our new model makes this a central feature and will be fully implemented by the time this book is released.

SG: Is that expensive?

AT: If you are lucky enough to pull a few favors, not at all. However, set next to the regular manufacturing and distribution model, it is a much better deal assuming you have the same amount of orders coming in.

Chapter 15

Artists Who Create Their Own Record Companies

An Interview with John Buckman, CEO and Founder of Magnatune

Magnatune (http://magnatune.com) is a small but innovative Internet-based independent record company. Based in Berkeley, California, Magnatune incorporates dynamic means of gaining exposure as well as income for its artists. Its motto is, "We're a record label. But we are not evil."

Magnatune is interesting for at least three reasons: (1) it offers free MP3 streams of all of its music, although it offers downloads for payment, (2) it distributes its entire catalog without using digital rights management (DRM) or copy protection, and (3) it incorporates Creative Commons licenses as part of its business model. [The next chapter explores Creative Commons in more detail.] Magnatune was founded in 2003 by John Buckman, the company's CEO and President. The following interview was conducted with John in summer 2004.

John Buckman

Steve Gordon: John, what inspired you to create Magnatune?

John Buckman: A few different things. One was that a number of my friends who were musicians and who I thought were really talented were venturing into obscure music areas and were having a hard time making a living. For example, in classical music most of the labels are either going under or the major labels have pulled out. And everyone says that the future of the music business is the Internet, but no one is really trying it. So if not me, who?

SG: When did Magnatune go online?

JB: About 14 months ago.

SG: What kinds of music are featured in Magnatune?

JB: There are seven different genres that span the variety of tastes that I have. It goes from classical and new age to world music, heavy metal, rock, and electronica.

SG: How long did it take from conception to launch, and what kind of obstacles did you face?

JB: It was about four months, and unfortunately because it's the music business probably a good two-thirds of that was legalese.

SG: Do you have a legal or technical background?

JB: I have a technical and a business background, and I've also founded other software companies that have done well.

SG: What kind of legal problems did you face?

JB: The biggest issue was: Is what I'm doing even legal on the Internet?

SG: What kind of contractual relationship do you have with the artists?

JB: I'm much like a record label, so I am recruiting individual artists. I have about 170 of them right now, and there are about 300 releases from those artists. We sign a record contract that's nonexclusive with our artists, which allows us to try and find money however we can with their music, and we do that a few different ways. We sell downloads on the Internet, and we also do a lot of music licensing, so the music shows up in films and compilations.

SG: I'm interested in the relationship with the artist being nonexclusive. For many years I worked for or with various major record companies, and the paradigm is an exclusive relationship, so that once an artist signs with a record label, generally he can't sign with another label. But if your contracts are nonexclusive, if the artist gets the opportunity to sign with a major, say, because of the exposure on Magnatune, does he still have that right to go with the major label even after he signs your contract?

JB: Absolutely. The gift I get is a five-year right to try and make money from that recording. So that gives me enough time to invest and advertise and get that music out there, and for five years I have the right to sell it—nonexclusively—but I still have the right to sell it. If Sony is willing to sign the artist and still have another company selling the music out there, which is usually the case when they're coming from indie labels anyway, then that's fine by me.

SG: Let's talk about distribution—online distribution, and then we can talk about your plans for selling CDs. How does it work? You said that I can listen to an entire album for free?

JB: Right. If you go to the Web site you can go to any of the 300 albums and say, "Play in hifi" and it will give you an MP3 stream of the entire album. Most people will then go back to whatever they're doing, work for a while until the album ends in an hour, and then try something else.

SG: Then what incentive will I have to purchase the album?

JB: Well, most people want to listen to music on a hi-fi [system], in the car, or at home. I'm not giving them anything that you can easily burn to a CD. I'm giving you something that you can easily listen to on your computer, but only the stream. So that's the obvious incentive.

SG: So, to download the music I have to pay?

JB: Right. Also, I'm giving you what's called a 128K MP3 stream, which sounds quite good, but it's not CD quality. When you purchase it, you do a get a full CD-quality WAV file from me, so you get an absolute mirror of the original CD.

SG: I guess the standard is to be able to sample 30 seconds, and then if you like it you can download the singles straight from, for example, iTunes. But you let people sample the entire album, and then if they like it, they can download the album. How much do you charge for downloads?

JB: It's a little strange and there are a number of experiments I'm trying with Magnatune. One of them is the idea of paying what you think the album is worth. So when you go to buy an album, I ask you to pay between $5 and $18, and you get to choose how much you want to pay. On average people pay just over $8.50, and I ask for $8. So people pay a little more than I ask for, even though they don't get anything more for paying anything over $5.

SG: So the consumer makes the judgment of how much to pay, but the minimum is $5 and the average is $8.50.

JB: But half goes to the artist, and that's absolutely crucial about Magnatune, that 50–50 split of the actual purchase price. So when you pay $8 for the album, $4 goes to the artist. So people are motivated to do good, and they do.

SG: Are you selling CDs by mail-order yet?

JB: We sell music through all sorts of different channels. The short answer is no, but in about two weeks we're going to start selling CDs, and it will be like MP3.com was— they'll be burned on demand with artwork. We also sell music through iTunes, we sell through eMusic, and you can also hear our songs through radio stations on AOL and iTunes.

SG: Why did you decide to sell CDs? Do people like to have something in their hand—the artwork and the jewel case and all of that good stuff?

JB: Well, there are a few different reasons. One, yes, people like to have artwork. We *do* give you a .pdf file of the artwork, so that when you buy a download you get a .pdf that you can then print and cut it with scissors to put into a jewel box. But that's a fair amount of work and people tire of that after a few albums. Also, just like Visa purchases over the Internet were scary for a long time—and I think that people have finally gotten over that—I think that music downloads are still scary in that same way that online purchasing was. What we see is both good and scary: when four people come to the Web site, one of those four people clicks the "Buy" button—which has got to be the highest "Buy" button conversion rate on the Internet. But the turnaround is that only one of 10 people that hits the "Buy" button actually buys, which is a terrible rate. So it looks like people are really motivated today to buy, but they aren't buying because something isn't quite right for them, and I think that's the lack of a CD.

SG: How is your collaboration with the other major services like iTunes going? Have you been satisfied with your relationship so far?

JB: We're just starting that, and, honestly, on most of the major services we're not making much money. iTunes completely dominates that market, and initially they were not interested in working with indie labels. And we were looking at working with one of these so-called "aggregator services" where they work with record labels and then they submit all of the record label's records to all of the online services. But the buzz we got when we started checking references was that none of these people actually pay their bills. They don't pay the labels and it's just kind of a scam right now.

SG: So you decided to go direct to Apple?

JB: We held off on it completely, until just by chance, I was speaking on the same panel with someone from Apple who was extremely excited by Magnatune and really wanted to work with me. So that was pretty exciting.

SG: I have heard Apple is interested in working with independent labels, and since you have over 170 artists I guess that was a major inducement for them to get a lot more content and diversity on their service.

JB: The key for them is that they have something differentiating, so if you send your music to Rhapsody and other services as well as iTunes, then they aren't going to treat you as specially—and why should they? But if you work directly with them, and especially if you give them releases a few months before everybody else, then they *do* treat you better. It also turns out—and this is just completely crazy, I think—that most of the record labels are treating iTunes really badly. They require them to either increase the price, or if you go to iTunes you'll see that there are two songs missing from a variety of albums, because the record labels won't let the whole album be online, or the bit rate is not very good. Most of the things on iTunes are 128K downloads, and this is because a number of labels are very ambivalent about online sales and are okay with crippling it for now.

SG: Yes, I remember when I was clearing music for MusicNet at one of the major labels, some of the executives were ambivalent because they thought that online sales might cannibalize their CD sales.

JB: Well, they're absolutely right, but the margin is better, so what's the problem?

SG: Let's talk about the Creative Commons license. We had Professor Larry Lessig on our show, and he discussed it a little bit. Can you recap what a Creative Commons license is?

JB: A Creative Commons license means, if you are an artist and you create a creative work, you have a copyright on your work, and everyone has to contact you to do anything with it. If you put a Creative Commons license on it, you're saying that noncommercial use of this work can occur without contacting you, but for commercial use of your work, they need to contact you.

SG: So people can make noncommercial use of the music on Magnatune, like making a remix of a song or sampling from a song for private use, but if they want to sell or license the new work for money, they would have to get permission from the artist. Can you tell us about the licensing part of Magnatune?

JB: All of the music on Magnatune is available for licensing. So if you want music "on-hold" for your telephone, or you've got a film or a commercial, then you can go to Magnatune, choose some music, and license it online.

SG: I do a lot of licensing, and the prices for a commercial film can be very steep. For instance, a well-known song can cost $100,000 or more for a commercial movie. What kind of fees do you charge for licensing music for a movie? First of all, can I get a festival license?

JB: The festival license starts at $44, and that means that you can play your film with my music in any film festival you go to, which is naturally the first step to getting your film sold. Then the prices go up. I think that the most expensive we have is $18,000 for a license, but that would include extremely broad rights to get up to that level.

SG: Including home video?

JB: Yes, home video and television advertising, maybe even some sort of video game tie-in to get that far up. Most of the film licenses are in the $2,000 to $6,000 range. The reason is that I'm mostly dealing with artists who aren't well-known, and films are really free advertising for us. While it's great to get paid and we *want* to get paid—it's how we pay the rent—at the same time we want to be overly competitive in our price so that we get our music in films and get heard.

SG: Beginning filmmakers: you should be warned that if you want to use a Rolling Stones or a Bee Gees tune it could cost a fortune. This could be a very good alternative for getting quality music at a reasonable price. Do all of your artists consent to your licensing of their music?

JB: Yes. A requirement in order to get on Magnatune is that you allow Magnatune to go out there and find deals for you. Magnatune actually sets the price, and then we split the revenue 50–50.

SG: Are there any production costs that the artist has to wait for you to recoup in order to get his 50–50? In the traditional record business, an artist generally has to wait until the record company recoups the cost of production and certain marketing costs. Do your artists get 50% off the top?

JB: Everything at Magnatune is 50% off the top, so when someone pays $2,000 for a music license for a film, $1,000 will go immediately to the artist.

SG: How do you find new artists?

JB: Every month we get about 300 submissions, which come in by e-mail, CD submissions, and people uploading music, largely because we've gotten so much press from NPR, *Wired*, *USA Today*, and *Newsweek*. So we have a high visibility. If you go to our Web site and you hit "Info," there's a link to click that has all of the previous articles that have been written about us. Obviously if you search for Magnatune on Google, a number of them, like the *USA Today* article, will show up on the first page.

SG: We talked about the kinds of music that are included in Magnatune, including techno, rock, and classical; is there any kind of music or any particular artist that you're excited about now?

JB: I'm obviously very excited about my wife's music since that was a big motivating force for getting Magnatune together. She signed with an independent record label—it was a UK label and we're Americans—and we were very excited about getting the CD out there. But then when we saw what it was like to get a CD distributed and in the stores, we became quite unhappy with the way CDs are sold today. So about a year ago we got the rights back to my wife's CDs and they're now on Magnatune. You can find them either from her name, Jan Hanford, in the new age section, or under Human Response, which is her electronica project, in electronica. The radio mix plays a mix of every song there, and that's something that you might listen to while you were working. After that you'll see a list of each artist alphabetized, probably starting with ABA Structure and down to Human Response under H.

SG: John, how do you measure success?

JB: Success obviously is the possibility of getting money in the bank, but my real goal with Magnatune was to get about $3,000–$5,000 per year to at least half of my artists. That was my goal, and we've done that for about one-quarter of the artists. The reason I picked that number was, when I was interviewing artists I asked them what they were looking for, and what they were looking for was not sinking every year. It was paying off the cost of the recording and not losing a little money. It turns out that $3,000 to $5,000 is about what it costs for a few days in the studio and to master and produce their CDs.

SG: The cost of recording an album have gone way down with the new technologies, so Magnatune gives artists an opportunity to pay for their production costs and hopefully supplement their income.

JB: Musicians make a living, at least those that *do*, by getting money in many different ways. That means session work, making CDs, playing live, playing weddings, and that's just the way it is. If I can give you a few thousand dollars more, that's great, but the truth is that record labels generally don't support their artists. It's only the top that make enough money; otherwise you've got to find work in a number of other fields in order to supplement your income.

SG: So you gives artists an opportunity to supplement their income. What advice would you give to artists starting out?

JB: The number-one piece of advice is, don't be starry-eyed. In other words, have some sort of realistic idea of what you're going to do with your career. If you want to be a rock 'n' roller and get all of the chicks you can, that's fine, but that's going to be hard going. More realistically, it's going to take years and years of hard work to make it happen, and in order to make it happen you're going to need to keep the rights to your music. So my advice is, don't give up the rights to your music. Keep them and try to find as many nonexclusive deals that you can, people who will find you gigs, for example. Agents are a great thing—they find you gigs and they take some money off the top. They only make money when *you* make money, and it's the same thing with Magnatune.

Postscript: In fall 2004 Magnatune started a mail-order operation.

Chapter 16

Creative Commons: A New Way to Encourage Creativity Online

Introduction to Creative Commons

During the interview with John Buckman, we discussed the fact that Magnatune utilizes the "Creative Commons" license. Creative Commons is mechanism for faciliating new expression online.

As we discussed in Chapter 1, one of the exclusive rights enjoyed by a copyright owner—incuding composers and creators of musical recordings—is the right to make "derivative works." Generally, no one may use a work protected by copyright to create a new work without consent, and the copyright owner's consent is often conditioned upon financial compension.[1] On the other hand, copyright infringement only occurs where the copied work and the allegedly infringing work are "substantially similar," and generally a work will not be considered substantially similar where the portion of the copied work is too small and insignificant. This standard has allowed for a great deal of creativity in the development of new music, especially hip-hop, where sampling small excerpts of other songs is very common. But in a recent and very controversial decision by the U.S. Court of Appeals for the Sixth Circuit, the court ruled that *any* sampling of prerecorded sounds is an infringement of the sound recording copyright in the original master, no matter how little was used or whether the material used is even recognizable. The court stated in its decision, "[I]f you cannot pirate the whole sound recording, can you 'lift' or 'sample' something less than the whole? Our answer to that question is in the negative." The court declared: "Get a license or do not sample. We do not see this as stifling creativity in any significant way." *Bridgeport Music, Inc. vs. Dimension Films*, 2004 U.S. App. LEXIS 18810 (6th Cir. 2004). This decision was the subject of a pending motion for reconsideration as

---

1. *The law does, however, permit certain exceptions to this exlusive right. For instance, the "Fair Use" doctrine, discusssed in Chapter 1, may in certain circumstances permit a creator to use a copyrighted work to create a new work. But the Fair Use doctrine is highly complex and often cannot be relied upon in specific cases.*

this book went to press. For updates check the Web pages accessible from the link in the included CD-ROM.

Creative Commons is designed as an antidote to cases like *Bridgeport*. It seeks to foster a more permissive atmosphere in which creators will not be afraid of being sued each time they use portions of existing works to create something new and original. This is especially important now that new technologies such as the Internet have made it so easy to sample and build on existing works. Creative Commons makes it possible for creators—including composers and recording artists—to allow others to take and build upon their work while retaining financial control. Here's how it works: Creative Commons developed a free set of licenses that artists can attach to their content online. Content is marked with a "CC" linked to a license. The creator can choose a license that permits any use, so long as attribution is given. The creator can also choose a license that permits only noncommercial use, thus retaining financial control over their work. Creators can also choose a license that permits any use as long as the same freedoms are given to other users ("share and share alike"). Other choices include: any use at all within developing nations; any sampling use so long as full copies are not made; or any educational use. These licenses expand the freedom of new creators while recognizing the rights of the copyright owners.

All the music in Magnatune is available under the "Attribution–Non-Commercial–ShareAlike" license from Creative Commons. Under this license you can make any non-commercial use of the music you like provided that if you do make money ("commercial use") from the use of music by Magnatune's artists, you'll have to "share the wealth" and give Magnatune's artists a share. Derivative works (for example, remixes, cover songs, sampling) are explicitly allowed. Some of Magnatune's artists even publish the "source code" to their music so you can rework and improve it. This includes scores, lyrics, MIDI files, samples, and track-by-track audio files. Magnatune's Web site enthuses: "If you make a great new version of our music, we'd love to know so that we can promote it!"

Creative Commons was founded in 2001. It is led by a Board of Directors that includes cyberlaw and intellectual property experts such as Professor Lawrence Lessig , MIT computer science professor Hal Abelson, lawyer-turned-documentary filmmaker-turned-cyberlaw expert Eric Saltzman, and public domain Web publisher Eric Eldred.

Fellows and students at the Berkman Center for Internet & Society at Harvard Law School helped get the project off the ground. Creative Commons is now housed at and receives support from Stanford Law School, where Creative Commons shares space, staff, and inspiration with the Stanford Law School Center for Internet and Society.

Professor Lessig, in *Free Culture* (Penguin 2004), says of the project,

> "Creative Commons is just one example of voluntary efforts by individuals and creators to change the mix of rights that now govern the creative field. The project does not compete with copyright; it complements it. Its

aim is not to defeat the rights of authors, but to make it easier for authors and creators to exercise their rights more flexibly and cheaply. The difference, we believe, will enable creativity to spread more easily. (p 286)

One obstacle to the rapid adoption of Creative Commons licenses is the fact that artists frequently do not own their publishing and/or master rights for commercially released work. They are therefore not always in a position to grant a Creative Commons license or any other license without the consent of their label or publisher.

To find out more about Creative Commons or secure a license to use in conjunction with your work, go to www.creativecommons.org. You can also listen to an interview with Professor Lessig in the CD-ROM accompanying this book. In the interview we explore Creative Commons in more detail, as well as other issues raised by his latest book, *Free Culture: How Big Media Uses Technology and the Law to Lock Down Culture and Control Creativity*.

An Interview with Thomas Goetz, Articles Editor of *Wired* Magazine — Creative Commons in Action

In this interview we discuss the November 2004 issue of *Wired* magazine, which included a free CD featuring tracks by Chuck D, the Beastie Boys, David Byrne, Paul Westerburg and other artists. In addition to the music, there was another interesting thing about this disc. Each track was subject to a Creative Commons license, which gives listeners more than the right to just listen or make copies for their private use. The interview explores how *Wired* put the Creative Commons license into action for the benefit of both new creators and those who would like others to expand on their work. After the interview I will discuss how Creative Commons can be used to create a new business model for recording artists and producers.

Thomas Goetz

Steve Gordon: November's edition of Wired *featured a free CD including 16 tracks from Chuck D, the Beastie Boys, David Byrne, and others. All tracks on this CD may be used for additional purposes other than just listening. What was the genesis of the CD and how did you pull it off?*

Thomas Goetz: The CD came about because we knew about Creative Commons, which is a great group that's out there trying to reform or take a new approach to copyright with the backdrop of an extremely restrictive model. The intellectual property industries—the entertainment industries principally—have taken a maximalist approach towards intellectual property. They want to lock down all their rights, and in the music business it's coming against the otherwise wonderful opportunities that technology offers. Digital technology allows something like file-sharing, which is a great way to learn about new music and a great way to sample music. Digital technology also allows people to be much more creative with their music—look at a GarageBand with Apple computers—with a few clicks, users can write and compose whole new songs and have it be available for fleshed-out compositions. So there's this polemical difference between what the music industry is doing on one hand and the opportunities digital technology offers on the other. Creative Commons is trying to present the third way; find a middle ground where the rights holders are able to grant certain specific permissions and let people use the music in certain specific ways. And as a correlative, hopefully they get more exposure, more promotion, and more people interacting with and using the music. The Creative Commons idea was out there in theory, so we thought we'd try and take the muscle of *Wired* magazine, which has some pretty good cred, and see if we could talk people into actually using the licenses; see if we could talk major artists into putting these licenses to the test.

SG: Are there any new tracks or are these all cuts from existing albums?

TG: We tried to put together a CD that not only has this cool, big, high-concept idea behind it—the Creative Commons licenses—we also wanted to put together a CD that people could just listen to and get good songs, so we tried to get exclusive songs. The Beastie Boys is an exclusive track—it's an outtake from their new album; David Byrne is an exclusive track; they're mostly kind of rare B-sides. A couple of them are tracks off of new or upcoming albums.

SG: It's ironic that tracks that may never have gotten a lot of exposure are now available to be used to create even more new music.

TG: Absolutely. The CD was a way to start the experiment and hopefully open up the floodgates to what Creative Commons could accomplish.

SG: Did you work with any of the artists directly?

TG: We were talking to managers, we were talking with bands—we largely avoided trying to go through labels because the labels hear you messing around with masters and copyright and they run screaming the other way. So we tried to go to people who might be aware of this issue, aware of how the copyright model in this industry is kind of broken, and people who might have an open ear towards that idea. It took us 10 months to a year.

SG: All of the tracks on the CD are subject to a Creative Commons license, but if we look at the playlist, which is printed inside the magazine, some of the songs were licensed under one kind of Creative Commons License and other songs are subject to another kind. David Byrne's track, "My Fair Lady," is subject to a license that states: "Sampling Plus: Songs under this license allow noncommercial sharing and commercial sampling, but advertising uses are restricted." But the license for the Beasties' "Now Get Busy" states: "Noncommercial Sampling Plus: Songs under this license allow noncommercial sharing and noncommercial sampling." What rights would these two different licenses give you?

TG: Let me give you a little background: Creative Commons has about a dozen licenses or a dozen kinds of licenses on their Web site; they are all fully valid licenses that have been drawn up by their lawyers, and they apply to circumstances for different reasons. So if you want to create something and you want to give it away and have somebody do whatever the hell they want to do with it, then you can use a certain kind of license. If you want somebody to be able to use something but you want them to give you credit, than that's a slightly different kind of license. There's this whole armada of licenses and it's a little confusing, but it's actually a great virtue of the Creative Commons models because it allows people to make a choice to give up specific and precise rights that otherwise they wouldn't be able to sacrifice based on the All Rights Reserved model. Creative Commons has this good phrase called "Some Rights Reserved," and the idea is that you're giving up specific things in a specific context and that's all. Any other use is covered by the whole well-tested body of copyright law.

In the case of our CD, Creative Commons came up with something called the sampling license. This would allow people to sample songs, take a little cut from a song and use it in another song, and you wouldn't have to call a lawyer first. You're giving before-the-fact permission for that.

Then they have something called the Sampling Plus license, which not only allows the samples but also allows commercial sampling. When talking with Creative Commons it became clear that there might actually be a use for another kind of license—a noncommercial sampling license—so what we use on our CD is both a Sampling Plus, which allows file-sharing and then commercial sampling, and then there's the Noncommercial Sampling Plus license, which is what the Beastie Boys, My Morning Jacket, and Chuck D chose, and that license allows file-sharing and noncommercial sampling. With one of the Sampling Plus licenses, somebody could come along—say Eminem finds a little loop on the Rapture song that he really loves, and he puts it into a song and the song goes number-one. The Rapture isn't going to get a penny out of it. That's kind of the whole point of the license. They've opened the doors to some wider creativity, and they aren't looking for commercial gain.

SG: But Eminem would have to give them credit?

TG: Yes, absolutely.

SG: So that's the quid pro quo. The artist gets credit and theoretically more people get interested in his work, knowing that they used his work in their song.

TG: Exactly. The idea was that basically the whole heritage of music was a sharing, creative process. It was something where one musician heard something based on what a predecessor had done; somebody else came along, built on that, used a line, tweaked a riff.

And there was a great history in the '50s of these rock 'n' roll "answer" songs, and all that's gone away now because people are so conscious of the rights.

SG: If you look back before the advent of digital technology—prior to digital sampling—there was a lot of sharing of style. People would try to sound like Sinatra or they would try to imitate Little Richard's wailing. Jimi Hendrix was famous for borrowing from a lot of different styles in his presentation and the way he looked. But digital sampling made it possible to do more than borrow style—it made it possible to borrow actual sounds and pieces of the original master recordings. Copyright law was not written to deal with that. The law said simply if you take a piece of a song and make it an important part of your new song, that is infringement, period. The law didn't recognize how sampling could contribute to creativity. Creative Commons is a way out of that dilemma, allowing people to sample, without violating someone's rights and also helping promote the original by assuring that it gets credit.

TG: Right—look at the history of hip-hop just as an art form. It started with people taking whole sections of songs and resectioning, playing them, and lo and behold, you have a new thing. The Beastie Boys are a great example of this in something like *Paul's Boutique*. That album had something like 200 or 300 samples, and it was before the lawyers caught up to the phenomenon. So they did it with abandon, basically. Many people would say *Paul's Boutique* is the best hip-hop album. What they did is create something new, and they didn't have a full legal apparatus telling them they couldn't do it. And now that legal apparatus is there, and it's overly restrictive. Creative Commons is a way of opening up the creativity again.

SG: I was going to ask about the Beastie Boys because they actually opted for the more restrictive license. You can sample, but for noncommercial use only. Is that because of their record company?

TG: The whole point of the licenses is that different people have different choices. Different licenses let people tailor their choices according to what they're comfortable with. I think that when the Beastie Boys chose the commercial license, it probably has something to do with the fact that they're more aware or have more experience than other bands. They sample for a living, so they know what you gain and what you lose. But the fact that the Beastie Boys were willing and eager to put a song out there—allowing file-sharing to go on and allowing people to chop up the song and put it on their Web site and share it with other people, and they get full permission for that—I think they've done an amazing thing.

SG: I think you're right, but as a lawyer who worked for a record company, I do want to make a point: If the artist is with a record company there may be a limit on what the effect or usefulness of Creative Commons may be, because the artist gives up both commercial and promotional rights in the distribution of his music. In effect, under the standard recording agreement, an artist can't grant a Creative Commons license without the permission of his record company, and some record companies are going to be less liberal than others.

TG: Absolutely—we walked into uncharted territory with this.

SG: That's why it took a year?

TG: Right—no one had gone to artists of this caliber and said, use this license, give up your rights. We asked a lot more people than we got, and lots of people were terrified by that idea and rightfully so. The record industry has sued over 7,000 people for file-sharing, and here we were asking these artists to say file-sharing is okay for the song, so it's a seriously gutsy move on these guys' parts.

SG: And a seriously gutsy move on your part. I wouldn't have wanted to be the one to try to get the record companies to give permission to use the Creative Commons license! But congratulations on getting a fine piece of work out there.

In that edition of Wired *you wrote an article titled "Sample the Future." The first line reads, "by nature, musicians are thieves." What did you mean by that?*

TG: I meant what we were talking about earlier. You look at something like the Sex Pistols. They were hailed as this breakthrough group who pioneered punk rock. Well every step of the way they were borrowing and cribbing from other people—look at a song like "Holiday to a Sun," in which the guitar lick is a direct rip of the Jam's "In the City." That's how the Sex Pistols made themselves. They took the best of what other people were doing, the New York Dolls, the Ramones, the Jam, and created a new and unique sound.

SG: Some people says it goes back to composers like Bach and Beethoven using themes from other people's music.

TG: Absolutely—it's part of the creative process no matter what art form you're in.

SG: In "Sample the Future" you wrote, "at root, sharing and stealing music start from the same impulse. Cribbing is creation. Building on what other musicians have done, with or without their blessing or collaboration, is what it takes to make new music, music that will delight and sustain people." That said, don't you think that the original artist should have a choice as to whether or not his music should be sampled?

TG: Absolutely. I think they should have a choice. That's the purpose of Creative Commons—right now the traditional copyright regime allows no choice. It is the fact of All Rights Reserved. You want to do anything with this, you have to call a lawyer. Creative Commons is offering that choice. It's saying, if you want to give up right X you use this license. If you want to give up X and Y, use this license. It's specifically laying out very precise guidelines where artists are now given the choice to let other artists build on their work, and that didn't exist before.

SG: A recent federal court ruling said that taking any sample from a master, no matter how brief—or even if the sample is unrecognizable because you changed it—cannot be done without permission, and if you do it, you've violated the copyright in the original master. That's as severe as you can get.

TG: If that case was upheld, it would do away any right to sample. It would be a stunning landmark.

SG: It was so disturbing and one-sided that even the record labels have filed a brief in support of overturning the decision, maybe because it means their artists couldn't produce their records if they had to get permission for every sample they use no matter how small. But that gives us an example of the usefulness of the Creative Commons license, because if the artist gave such permission, you wouldn't need to ask for it.

You state in your article that "The music industry has become a business on the brink of collapse, waging an unwinnable war against technology. Every day, millions of people, fans, take songs they know at record labels and exploit digital technology for all it's worth. Willfully swapping and stealing music. In response, the RIAA has employed an army of lawyers, initiating copyright infringement suits against [thousands] of file sharers. Now, we're not here to argue what party is at fault. We simply realize that there is no long-term solution to this scenario. There's just a slow decline. Creative Commons is trying to find a middle ground." What kind of middle ground would Creative Commons find if it merely authorizes file-sharing but without paying the artist? How would that help the record companies and artists get back on their feet?

TG: We don't think Creative Commons is the solution to the record industry's problem. We think that it is potentially part of the solution. And I think the problem the record industry is having is one where their business model is not flexible enough to deal with digital distribution and a digital environment. They've exploited the CD and lived off the whip of CD sales of the last 15 years. They have nothing in its wake to offer another push. What you have is a business model built around physical distribution of records, and there's a huge amount of money and labor that goes into putting plastic discs into stores, and you have to give the stores a cut, and you have to give the labels a cut, and somewhere down the line eventually the artists get a cut. That is a model fraught with problems, and what we're seeing in terms of file-sharing is the coming dissolution of that model because digital distribution is infinitely cheap and infinitely possible.

SG: I remember going out to Pitman, New Jersey, when I was at Sony, to the factory where they manufacture CDs. It looked like the Kennedy Space Center! An incredibly huge plant, and people walking around in astronaut suits, cranking out millions of shiny little discs. I can't imagine how much that factory must have cost, and in addition to that, you've got inventory and warehousing and trucks delivering all of these CDs all over the world. It's hugely expensive undertaking.

TG: I think file-sharing is showing that digital distribution is possible whether labels get behind it or not—because it's happening to the tune of something like 5 billion songs a year.

SG: Eric Garland at Big Champagne estimates at least 12 billion files being shared each year.

TG: It's climbing every day. There's been no definitive argument that file-sharing actually has a negative impact on record sales. There's anecdotal evidence, but there's a fair amount of research that says that file-sharing helps record sales. It exposes people to new artists, to new kinds of music, and helps create demand. I think the problem is that the record labels haven't figured out how to contain file-sharing—how they can leverage it in an immediate way. And this is a phenomenon that lots of industries are facing when it comes to digital distribution in an Internet universe, where you can't control the message and it's a confounding thing. So many businesses are frustrated and have campaigns and have fought against this kind of new technology—a movement that is, in fact, millions of people strong and goes against everything they've learned in business school. It's confounding to a traditional industry like the music business.

SG: There's news that certain labels are at least going to get their toes wet embracing peer-to-peer. Let's hope that the industry will learn from the last few years and embrace these new technologies instead of continuing to battle against them, because you're right—it's a losing battle unless they learn how to embrace the new technologies.

In the article, you wrote "The artists of the CD have boldly decided to put their work at risk, to offer it up at free of charge to give blanket permission ahead of the fact for anyone who wants to build on it. As far as we can tell, this is the first time that so many major artists have actively encouraged their audience to make something of their music." Was that your goal for the CD, for the project?

TG: I think the goal was pretty open-ended. We wanted to get the idea out there. We wanted to get the idea of Creative Commons—the idea that there's another way to approach copyright—out there. I think it's an abstraction until you get something like a physical piece of plastic that's a song. We could have put the songs on our Web site and it probably would have been a lot cheaper for us and it would have been a more efficient way to get the tracks out there, but we wanted to have a physical piece to show the idea. We're hoping to see what happens to that idea, what happens to the song, what kind of uses the songs are put to, and what kind of freedoms and new opportunities the artists are given.

SG: Larry Lessig put out his book Free Culture *under a Creative Commons license, and some people put music to it, other people did all kinds of things. Have you gotten any feedback from the CD or new music out of it after a few weeks?*

TG: Yeah, it's amazing. There have been a few Web sites where people have started to post remixes of the songs—and they're all noncommercial remixes—and the songs are being file-traded like you wouldn't believe. They're all over the networks, so I think so far it's everything we've hoped for and more.

Creative Commons as a Business Model

Clearly, Creative Commons is a great new way for forward-thinking artists and copyright owners to allow others to use their work to create new art without the fear of reprisal or lawsuits. But Creative Commons can be used as a business model as well.

As Thomas Goetz said during our interview, there are a range of Creative Commons licenses. Under the least-restrictive license, which was used in connection with a few of the tracks in the CD that was bundled with November's *Wired* magazine, anyone may sample the music for any purpose including commercial use, provided that they give appropriate credit. But the majority of creators of the tracks included in the CD selected the Creative Commons license that would allow the user to sample the track for noncommercial purposes only. Commercial sampling or commercial remixing would require permission. This license could be the basis of an effective new type of business model for recording artists, producers, and labels. Suppose the new user is very talented and samples the original track to create a commercially viable new work. If that artist has a deal with a record label and they want to release the track, at that point he or his record company will have to contact and negotiate with the original copyright owners, including the artist, for the use of the original music. In this way the original artist can open the door to others to create something new and at the same time reserve the opportunity of earning money from the new track. Without Creative Commons, the new work may never have come into existence.

This could be an especially effective business model in areas such as hip-hop and dance music where use of others' work to create new work happens frequently. Creative Commons can be used to ease anxiety and indeed encourage borrowing from an original work. The Creative Commons license, even if it permits noncommercial use only, signals that the creator is empathetic and does not have a negative attitude. Then, if there is a commercial opportunity, as we discussed, the original creator can be rewarded for his progressive attitude.

That being stated, there are also certain practical limitations on Creative Commons as a business model. If a licensee uses the *master* under the Creative Commons license, he must be aware that the license may not cover the underlying *song*. This is because, as we discussed in Chapter 1, the owner of the copyright in the master (created by the artist) may be different than the owner of the music (created by the songwriter). Just because the owner of the copyright in the master employs the Creative Commons license does not mean that the owner of the underlying music has also agreed. The owner of the copyright in the master should be careful to indicate to the user that the license does not apply to the song, if they do not control that copyright in the song, and the licensee should be careful that he has acquired rights in both the master and the song. Similarly, the original owner of the copyright in the song may have transferred his rights to authorize the exploitation of the song to his publisher. The publisher may be the only party that can authorized a Creative Commons license. Furthermore, if the song was written by more than one person, even if the rights in the song were not transferred, an agreement between the writers may curtail any one writer from authorizing the use of the song under a Creative Commons license.

For discussion of another way Creative Commons may be incorporated in a new business model, see the interview with John Buckman of Magnatune Records in the prior chapter.

Chapter 17
Online Record Stores

This chapter features:

- An interview with Derek Sivers, founder and president of CD Baby, an online record store.
- A discussion of micropayments, a means for facilitating payments for online music.
- An interview with Rachel Gravengaard, the general manager of Mperia, a music store incorporating micropayments.

An Interview with Derek Sivers, Founder and President of CD Baby

www.cdbaby.com

CD Baby is the largest online retailer of music by independent artists. The store deals directly with musicians, avoiding any middlemen. That keeps the pie less divided and offers a better alternative for smaller artists. The Portland, Oregon-based company was established in March 1998 by Derek Sivers. This interview with Derek was recorded in summer 2004.

Steve Gordon: Derek, didn't you start off as a musician?

Derek Sivers: Yes, and that's actually how CD Baby started too. I've been a musician since the age of 15, went to Berklee College of Music in Boston, and straight out of college I moved to New York City. Sometime around '96 or '97 I put

Derek Sivers

213

out my own CD and sold about 1,500 copies of it on my own, and I started to do a national radio campaign. Getting those little pockets of interest from college radio in places like central California and Alaska and Maine had hyped my CD, and I wanted ways for people to be able to buy it. So I called the big online music stores at the time—this was before Amazon sold CDs; they were just a bookstore—the big online music stores were CDNow, MusicBoulevard, and Tunes.com. I said "Hey, I've sold 1,500 copies of this CD on my own. Would you guys like to sell it?" They said, "Well, sure, who's your distributor?" [Laughs] So I said, "I don't have a distributor, and I don't really want one because I don't want it to sit in shopping malls in St. Louis; I just want to get it to the people that want it. There aren't that many people that want it, but there are some. Can't you help me get it to them?" And they laughed and said, "Sorry, kid, it doesn't work that way." Then I said, "Wait, can't I just send you a box of CDs for you to put up on your Web site, and when somebody buys it you ship it to them and you pay me. What's so hard about that?" But they said, "Sorry, it doesn't work that way." So I said "Screw it, I'll set up my own Web site." I'd already had my own Web site, but I decided to put up a shopping cart on it. This was the end of 1997.

SG: Right before Napster.

DS: Yes. It turned out to be much harder than I'd ever expected to get a credit-card merchant account and all of the red tape and fees and paperwork. Then to build a shopping cart was harder than I'd imagined. So when I was done, I told some of my friends that were in bands, "Hey, I already built this thing. I'll sell your CD too if you want. I can just put it up on my band's Web site." So then my band's Web page became a place where you could buy my CD *and* those of five of my friends. Then I started getting calls that were like, "Hey, dude, my friend David said that you can sell my CD." So, pretty soon it was 20 of my friends, and that's when I decided to just push it onto its own Web site and call it CD Baby.

SG: You had the right idea at the right time. But to clarify one thing, when MusicBoulevard was starting they didn't sell like you do now or like Amazon does now. How did they sell stuff, if not directly to customers?

DS: I believe that all of the big online record stores were just dealing directly with the distributor—they would do a bulk import of the catalog and put it up on the Web site, sending the shipping reports back to those warehouses. So, literally the only way to get into their system was to get into that distributor.

SG: So you were ahead of your time.

DS: Yes, but the interesting thing to keep in mind to understand the spirit of CD Baby is that this wasn't meant to be a business. I was a full-time musician making my living touring and producing people's records, and I was having a blast. It was a great feeling of pride, you know. I'm a musician! The last time I had a job was 1992! I was really happy making my living making music, and CD Baby was never meant to be anything more than a hobby. In a weird way I think that was part of its benefit, because during the dot-com craziness, I was desperately trying to keep CD Baby down to being only a hobby with me in my bedroom. Meanwhile, all of these investors were trying to toss money at me, and I was saying, "No, you don't understand. This is my hobby. I don't want your money and I don't want to answer to investors." That would make it no fun. By avoiding all of the investors and just carrying on like I'd been carrying on and reluctantly growing only when necessary, CD Baby is still really fun. It still feels like a hobby, like a little rock 'n' roll record store. It's absolutely not like a typical dot-com.

SG: Yes, and I love the little baby logo. [Laughs] What kind of music did you play, by the way?

DS: I was doing a cross between James Brown and the Beatles. [Laughs]

SG: I would have loved to have seen your wardrobe!

DS: Anyone who's interested in the music can go to www.dereksivers.com. I just put up all my music as MP3s that anyone can download for the fun of it.

SG: How does CD Baby work? Does the artist deliver copies and then you put the CDs in a warehouse until somebody buys them?

DS: Yes. We tell everyone that we're just a consignment mail-order record store.

SG: A record store—not a record label?

DS: Oh, god, no! [Laughs] We're just a record store. That's really the mantra inside the company whenever people call us confused about what we do. Again, because of the dot-com era, a lot of companies had these very vague and broad descriptions of what they were all about, and the whole time CD Baby was just saying, "Look, we're a record store. That's it." So somebody who's made their own CD and wants to get it out to the world can go to cdbaby.com and sign up and then mail us a box of CDs . . .

SG: They don't even have to sign a contract? They just do a form?

DS: Yes, there's no contract. You just go onto our Web site and say what the name of your record is, how much you want to sell it for, and how you want it described. After you answer those basic questions it says, "Great, here's our address. Mail it in." We do ask for a $35 setup fee because we give about a half an hour of attention to every single record that comes in.

SG: You build a Web page for each artist?

DS: Yes. We scan the album cover, we make the audio clips, we run the cover through PhotoShop to make it look just perfect. We make a Web page for it and we listen to it to make sure everything's correct, and then we publish a Web page dedicated just to that CD, full of clips, reviews, links back to the musician's Web site—everything to do with that CD. The cool thing is that it's all under that musician's control. We just keep a $4 cut per CD sold.

SG: I went on the site today, and I did a search for people that sounded like Sinatra. [Laughs] I found several different artists, and I checked out the Web page of one guy who looked as well as sounded like Sinatra. So your search engine works pretty well.

There is one very cool thing that you say on the site. In a regular record deal the musician is only making $1 per CD, if that—if they ever get paid at all, because they have to recoup production costs and marketing costs, and so many musicians never do recoup. You say that when selling through CD Baby, musicians make $6–$12 per CD and get paid weekly. How does that work? What accounts for whether an artist gets $6, $7 or the full $12?

DS: They do. The musicians set the selling price at whatever they want. Some punk bands want to make an $8 CD, but some people who have spent three years of their lives making a record don't want to sell it for less than $18. That's their creative decision, and we don't touch any of that. We just keep a flat $4 price per CD sold, because no matter what the selling price and no matter how many tracks are on the CD, it's the same amount of work for us to take that piece of plastic off the shelf and get it to the customer and do all the customer support for it. We pay every Monday night.

SG: You pay by check?

DS: By anything—bank transfer, PayPal, whatever.

SG: So I can price my CD up to $16, and that accounts for the $12 cap?

DS: Well, I just picked a range. Honestly, we have people selling CDs for $5, and I think we have a CD selling for $250! [Laughs] I forget who this guy is, but he has said that his music is precious and that nobody is allowed to have it for less than $250. So check this out: every time he sells a CD, he gets $246 per CD sold—I think he's sold two. You know, relatives, friends, family.

SG: I notice that there is a discount—$5 specials. Buy three of these and they become $5 each. Does the artist give special consent for the discount?

DS: Yes, we made that an option for the musicians. I realized that now that CD Baby has been around for six years there are quite a few artists that have pressed a CD in 1999, and it's pretty much done—they've moved on. But they've got 400 of them sitting in their garage and they'd rather just dish them out to the public for basically free. I was about to make it free, but then I thought, "Let's get some kind of a price on this thing." But it would hurt our business if we just sold a single $5 CD, because we'd actually lose money on that order. So we created this optional $5 bin where musicians can put their CDs, but the customers have to buy a minimum of three if they're going to get the discount. It encourages people to browse around and keep looking and discovering new music, which is what this is all supposed to be about anyway.

SG: There is no contract—just a submission form. So the artist is granting no rights to you other than the right to sell the CDs he/she/they actually give you. That means that the artist can continue to sell these CDs through an old brick-and-mortar store or through another online mail-order service, or even through their own Web site, right?

DS: The artist can do whatever the hell they want. We don't even know what they're doing. Think of it like any old record store on Route 17 in New Jersey somewhere, like "Jim's CD Shop." You bring in a box of CDs and you say, "Hey, could you sell these for me, and if they sell pay me?" He says, "Okay" and you leave your contact info and you walk out. There's no rights, there's no ownership or signing of contracts or anything—it's just another record store.

SG: One of the really nice things about CD Baby is that when you go to the Web page that you've created for the artist, you give them an opportunity to link to their Web site. Today I was going to the pages in CD Baby, and once I found the artist I'd link to his Web site for more stuff. Here is my question: If he can sell his record by mail-order on his Web site as well as on CD Baby, why doesn't the artist just encourage people to buy the CD from his Web site to save money?

DS: Some do. I just think that CD Baby's priced at the point that for people who are selling more than one every few months, it's worth it to them for the $4 to have us take care of it all. Because sometimes CDs arrive with broken jewel boxes, sometimes they don't arrive, and you get customer service phone calls. Anytime you're selling to more than just immediate friends and family, you're going to get customer service complaints and double-billed credit cards by mistake, so we take care of all of that stuff, plus shipping—everything. It saves the musician from having to run down to the post office every time somebody orders a CD. If somebody's only selling one CD a year, then it might not be worth their time to get on CD Baby except for the exposure. The artists who seem to appreciate us the most are the ones who are selling five, ten, 20 CDs a week. They're not spending two hours of their day every single day running down to the post office.

SG: Why do you recommend that the artist have his own site?

DS: Every musician should have their own Web site. It's like when LP record art went away, something had to fill the gap. CD booklets did it for a while, but now a lot of people aren't even buying CD booklets. I think the Web site is the home base for every musician for their creative vision to come out, whether it's the look and design of the site matching their vision, or for them to give their news and updates and writings and lyrics and tour schedules. Every musician definitely needs to have their own Web site, and I really believe that—especially now—there's no reason for a musician *not* to have their own dot-com or their real domain name. Not just have a page on MP3.com. I think that the dying dot-coms of the late '90s showed that you can't depend too much on any dot-com—you've got to have your own domain name where all of your stuff happens.

SG: Have you known of any instances where music business professionals or record companies or publishing companies or what have you have gotten to know or have first recognized an artist through CD Baby?

DS: Oh, yes. We did get these really cute e-mails, I'd say about once every week or two. We'd hear some little success story from an artist that will write in and say, "I've just got to thank you guys. I was in your new-arrivals page and somebody from the WB Network (who probably goes through CD Baby every week to check out the new arrivals) called, and now my music is being played on *Buffy* or . . ."

SG: [Laughs]

DS: I think a lot of the film- and TV-music types in LA browse through the new arrivals every week and the editor's picks and stuff like that.

SG: *That's of special interest to me because that's what I do for a living—music on television. So you get those buyers for shows like* Sex and the City, *or* The Sopranos, *or* Queer Eye for the Straight Guy, *looking for music from CD Baby?*

DS: Oh, yes. I think it's another way that our two-minute clips have come in handy. A lot of our biggest customers—and by customers I mean the people that buy the CDs—have really thanked us for having the two-minute clips because they say that this is the place that they choose to come to buy CDs now, because we honor them enough to let them listen to a full two minutes and not give them just 30 seconds of the hook and then shut it off. It lets them really get into a song and decide if they're going to like it.

SG: *So CD Baby, in addition to being a place to make a few bucks and to sell your CDs, is also a place to expose your music—not only to the public, but to music buyers, be they record companies or TV producers.*

DS: Yes. We've had a funny avenue that I never expected. We sell to retailers in Japan that pay us full retail price and then mark it up over in Japan. Especially in the R&B and soul genres, we've got a couple of different customers in Japan that come to our new-arrivals list every week and buy about one of everything in the R&B/soul category.

SG: *[Laughs] So you're guaranteed one sale.*

DS: Actually there are quite a few people that do this. They buy one of everything in R&B, and we ship that box off. Then a week or so later we get an order for 20 copies of this, ten of these, 30 of these, and they pay full retail price because retail at CD Baby is often $12–$14. And in Japan they sell it for $18 or $20 because it's a rare special CD that you can only get at this one shop in Tokyo. It's amazing. Somebody in Atlanta makes an R&B record, puts it up on CD Baby, and sells 150 copies in Japan.

SG: *That's the beauty of the Internet—it potentially reaches all the way around the globe.*

DS: Here's an interesting fact: 30% of our orders go overseas.

SG: *I noticed that you have a submission form for people in the U.S. and then one for people outside the U.S. But it looks like you're asking for the same basic information.*

DS: There are some slightly different questions if you're overseas, dealing with bank transfers, stuff like that.

SG: *So you are available to artists throughout the world and you have a global audience, which is amazing because in the old world—the real world—you'd have to have a huge record company to have global distribution. You have global distribution from a box in your office and your server. That's really amazing!*

DS: Yes. I don't know if you know this, but I started the company when I was living in Woodstock, N.Y. I moved it to Portland, Oregon, four years ago, partly because I couldn't handle the upstate New York winters anymore, but I also chose Portland strategically because they've got a postal hub where all the mail from the entire Northwest comes to this one hub post office that's right at the airport, and we're just about a half mile down the road from that office. So when a customer buys a CD on a Tuesday afternoon, two hours later it's on an airplane. People around the world usually get our CDs from CD Baby within three or four days of ordering.

SG: You mean the post office in Woodstock wasn't as good?

DS: [Laughs] Almost as good, because they brought it down to JFK right away. But we've definitely found that being right there at the post office hub really gets packages there surprisingly fast.

SG: So back to that "Sinatra" guy—if I buy one of his albums today, when can I expect to get my Sinatra sound-alike?

DS: Three or four days.

SG: Not bad. I notice from your site that you only sell CDs that come directly from the musicians—no distributors. "Musicians," it says, "send us CDs, we warehouse them and sell them to you." What's the philosophy behind that? Are you trying to give artists a shot to make a living without signing with a record label?

DS: It wasn't so much a decision as it was just saying, "This is how it generally works." You're on the "about" page, which is written more to our customers' point of view. We just want to let them know that everything that they buy on CD Baby is generally coming directly from the musician. Record labels have a really bad reputation, because they're seen as the evil guys behind the RIAA that are suing their customers. So we find that a lot of our customers love the fact that when they buy a Regina Spector CD from CD Baby, it's not going from her to a label to a distributor to us to the customer. It's Regina pressing a CD and sending it to us. And on the back end, we put the musicians in direct contact with the customers. So that every time somebody buys your CD, we e-mail you to tell you who bought your CD today, and here's their name and address, here's their e-mail address, and here are their comments at the end of their order.

SG: And that's voluntary on the part of the customer?

DS: Yes. We frame it in a nice way, saying, "Please send your comments directly to the musician's ear."

SG: And then the artist can communicate with the customer directly?

DS: Exactly. What's kind of nice is that we've had some artists that used to be on a big record label, and now we're doing a direct for them. And for the first time in their career they're seeing the actual name and address of everybody that buys their CD. It's amazing to them! And they love getting paid every week instead of never. [Laughs]

SG: Scott Meldrum from Hype Council gave some great advice. He says that when he was an indie musician before he started Hype Council, when he got customers' or fans' names and e-mail addresses and he sent them news about his latest record, his sales shot up because of the direct communication. People like the attention.

DS: Of course. It didn't used to be that you could buy a CD by an artist, the CD arrives in the mail, and the artist himself, the person that's on the cover of that record sends you a thank-you note. The customers love our policy of putting the musicians in touch with them. I'm sure if you were running Amazon or whatever you'd worry about the privacy policy and you'd keep that stuff locked tight where nobody's allowed to see it. But we've found that the customers love hearing directly from the musicians. A few opt out, but that's fine.

SG: What if I am an indie musician, but not completely indie because I have a deal with a little label. The little label, which, say, has half a dozen artists, has the right to sell my music exclusively. What do I do to get my music up on CD Baby? Get consent from the president of my little label?

DS: Usually if it's a little label that doesn't have traditional distribution and isn't already in every damn online music store in the world, they just come to us directly and we hook them up. If it's a guy who has four artists signed to his label out of his living room, I mean . . .

SG: Alfonzo Terrell is a student at Columbia who started an online record company called CU Records. He has six artists up and he actually services people on campus who buy the records. They have little messengers that bring a CD directly over to the dorm room. Could you deal with that kind of record label and put their artists up on CD Baby?

DS: Yes, if he had the rights to be selling it. There have been a couple of times where we've found that somebody contacted us, or just kind of anonymously put something up on CD Baby that looked legit to us, but we heard from the musician one day saying, "Hey, this guy's not paying me. I didn't give him the right to do this." We immediately yank it down, and we always err on the side of the musician. When in doubt, even if there's a contract, we'll take the musician's side. There have even been a few times where, legally, the guy running the label *did* have the right to be selling that record, but once we found out that the musician wasn't cool with him doing that, we just weren't comfortable selling it anymore and we'd say, "Well, we'd rather you just not sell it here."

SG: Which is your right. Your Web site has some interesting numbers. About 68,000 artists are now selling CDs on CD Baby—that's quite a number!—1,112,000 CDs sold online to customers. Is that an accurate amount?

DS: Yes, and it's updated every day. Just go to cdbaby.com and click the little link at the top of the page that says "About." The numbers you see there every day are updated to the day, including how much we've paid to the musicians and how many CDs we've sold.

SG: Which is over $9 million that you've paid to artists. How many new artists would you say you put up each month? There is a button that you can click to see new releases. How many are you getting, say, a week or a month?

DS: We add about 80–100 new albums a day.

SG: Anybody can put their albums up?

DS: I decided that long ago, when this guy who was a friend of a friend sent me this godawful record on a Maxell CDR with a piece of notebook paper as an album cover. I'm thinking, "Do I put this up?" And I said, "Well, it's true to my original mission for doing this." Maybe there's somebody somewhere who wants to buy this, and I'll be glad to provide that service to make it available. We just don't judge.

SG: *I've read that they don't have to shrink-wrap the CDs, but do they need to give you album artwork?*

DS: We tell people that we're a record store, and to send us something that you're proud to sell to the world. If the only thing that you're proud to sell to the world is a Maxell CDR with a piece of notebook paper as a cover, well, then, "Hey, good luck to you kid! We'll sell it for you if you want."

SG: *Is anyone sending you DVDs these days?*

DS: Just a few. We've got some music DVDs on there. Selling a film would be a different thing—a Film Baby or something. Right now we try to stick with the music. People have often asked us if we sell T-shirts, hats, posters, stickers, but if it's not music I don't get excited about it. I'm not that into clothing, and I never really wanted to start a clothing store.

SG: *Other people have started licensing services and then they put up these laundry lists of what you want to use the music in—you know, your corporate package or your film festival, your studio blockbuster, your commercial, your radio commercial, and it gets a little corporate-looking.*

DS: I have this really deep-set philosophy that the most beautiful designs are always very simplistic, when you're talking about any kind of product. Look at the iPod. How nice and simple. It doesn't have 125 buttons—it has that wheel and two buttons. Anything that's designed nice stays simple and focused, and I really think that applies to running a business. Once you start saying "yes" to everything and adding in dozens of different avenues and options to what you do, you're making the design of your business uglier.

SG: *Did I see any ads on CD Baby?*

DS: Never, never, never.

SG: *That's amazing. You must have been tempted.*

DS: No! God, no! I'd be repulsed. Remember that I started this thing before the dot-com boom, and when I started seeing those stupid rectangles at the top of Web pages I was disgusted. It was just ugly. Why would you just make your site uglier in return for a few pennies?

SG: *I was at a seminar when Napster first came out, and they said, "Well, this is what we're up against. Every song ever recorded any time you want to listen." And then they put up the label's site, and you had to go hunting through a slew of banner ads to find a Mariah Carey single priced at $3.98. [Laughs]*

DS: I still think there are so many other things in terms of design. You've got to ask yourself, "What's the beautiful thing to do?" And if it doesn't meet that criterion, just toss it out. You've got to do whatever the right thing is and then not worry about the money up front—make that a secondary concern.

SG: Your statement of purposes says: "We use our middle-man position to hook up indie musicians with helpful tips, advice, and opportunities to promote their music. Then we hook up magazines, reviewers, and other industry folk with great music." Can you give me some examples of how this policy works?

DS: It's nothing that's systematized on the site, but it happens every day. We've got a team of people that are answering e-mails and phone calls all day, and we constantly get calls from people saying, "Hey, I'm doing this extreme sports show. Can you recommend some artists that are in the vein of Linkin Park?" So we say, "Sure, no problem. Hang on." And we pull up our database and listen to every single CD before we sell it. So we know what our favorites are, so when a person like that calls up, we say, "Sure."

SG: But they can do it themselves, right? That's how I found this Sinatra sound-alike—I used the search engine in the site.

DS: Yeah, but you know how it goes. Some people just like to talk to someone.

SG: Of course. Especially if they're important music industry executives. So you do take those calls and you can help the artists out like that.

DS: To me it's also just a nice service. We're doing well, we're profitable. I don't need to charge a percentage for doing that. Sometimes people say, "Hey, you should start a License Baby.com!" But I figure that we're doing fine. People pay us $35 to be here, so we can recommend them without asking for a cut.

SG: Yes, I think there's something to be said for staying pure, for the reputation and the image. It must attract more artists and quality music.

DS: It also keeps you focused. If your business hangs on being the best record store you can be—and you're not distracted from that—you're going to focus all of your energy on being the best record store you can be. If you all of a sudden start trying to do 25 other things, they're all going to hurt because you're not focused anymore. So we keep the whole business focused on being the best little sales and distribution outlet for your CD that we can be.

SG: Here's another little factoid on the site that I found interesting. You say, "No Microsoft products were used in the creation of this Web site."

DS: [Laughs] People love that! Look, Microsoft makes a great . . . Windows XP or whatever. It's a great thing to use on your desktop. But there's this long history of Web sites that are being run by Microsoft servers always getting hacked. So I was kind of making that joke for the Linux snobs too. I've had quite a few Linux and Mac snobs see that and go, "Right on!" It's funny, if you take that exact phrase and put quotes around it and Google it, you find quite a few fans that have put that in their blogs, saying, "Check out why I love this store." But it's just kind of a joke, which is funny because—

I'll feed you a little transition here—in our digital distribution program we're feeding plenty of Windows Media files to places—even the new up-and-coming Microsoft music store.

SG: And you're already up on iTunes, I understand. Tell me a little about how this works. I've got a CD, suppose I'm the Sinatra guy, my name is Tony. I give you my CD and do the submission form to sell mail-order. How could you help me sell it by download?

DS: The most important thing to know is that it's a totally optional thing, because there are plenty of musicians who just aren't interested in selling their stuff on iTunes or whatever. Once you're a CD Baby member, as a free service inside your "members" area you can choose this optional thing saying, "Would you like us to get your music up and selling through all of these digital distribution outlets?"

SG: And there are a lot. How many are up now in terms of partnerships?

DS: There are 29 signed up, and there are at least five new ones coming up.

SG: I know the usual suspects: MusicNet, Napster 2.0, and iTunes, of course. But there are dozens that I've never heard of before.

DS: And there are more on the way with some of the biggest companies in the world also starting online music download stores. You've got to hand it to iTunes. Because of the success of this music store there are lots of other companies doing it, which I think is great because every single one has something they're doing differently, something they're doing better. I think it's awesome for all this music to be getting out there.

SG: And you interface with all of them. So I give you my CD, I give you the right to sell it digitally, and zoom, *it goes out to over two dozen digital Internet music stores.*

DS: I call them digital retailers, because they're really taking the place of the retail store but selling downloads instead of selling physical product.

SG: If I give you consent to do this does it automatically go into iTunes, or does iTunes filter some out?

DS: To date none of the services has filtered anything out. All of the companies have taken everything we've sent them. We're sending them like 30,000 albums, so they'd have to hire three employees just to sit there and decide what not to put up.

SG: And they love the extra content too.

DS: Yes, they get to brag about the numbers. But that being said, it does say in the fine print of their contracts that they reserve the right to . . .

SG: Right, if you're the musical version of Michael Moore, they might not like that! [Laughs]

DS: It's funny because I wanted to put that disclaimer in there when announcing that to the musicians, saying, "Look, just so you know, the contracts with these companies *do* say that they don't have to do this." And it's funny, a lot of people love to just focus on the negatives. Some people were saying, "I can't believe you want to do this and you're not even promising you'll get anywhere." Of course, you can't even promise that the sun will come up tomorrow.

SG: That does breed conspiracy theories. But the economics look pretty simple. Your cut is how much?

DS: We keep a 9% cut and pay the artist 91% of all income generated. The reason we've left it vague and don't name specific dollar amounts is because this thing is brand new and most of the stores that are out there now—the iTunes-type model—sell the download for about 99 cents and pay the label about 65 cents, which I think is a pretty fair split. So we just keep a 9% cut, which means that most people are getting about 59 cents.

SG: That's pretty good considering that one of the major complaints of artists about what the record companies are doing in terms of licensing their tracks for digital delivery—and one of the reasons why certain artists haven't consented to putting their tracks up—is because the labels are recouping their unrecouped balances from digital income, and few artists are getting anything. And some managers are really very upset.

DS: There was this whole Internet campaign called Downhill Battle [www.downhill-battle.org]. They mean well, but they were kind of attacking the wrong place. They were saying, "Apple iTunes sucks because the musicians aren't getting paid." But the truth is that Apple *has* been paying *the labels* every single month $0.65 per download; it's just that the labels aren't paying the musicians. I thought that it was a little unfair to attack Apple because the labels aren't paying the musicians.

SG: That's absolutely correct. The labels gave Apple the opportunity to do this because they get just as much or more than when they sell single CDs in record stores, and they thought, "Oh, we're going to take Steve Jobs for a ride here." What they may not have foreseen is that he would be selling iPods hand over fist. So it worked out well for Steve Jobs. Now everybody's picking up that model, so we'll have to see if it continues to work for his competitors.

DS: It's going well so far. I was also pessimistic about doing this, but I just thought that it was inevitable. I realized that we were already providing 90% of what was needed here. We were already digitizing everything that came through the door, we were already paying the musicians every week, we already had all of the data on every single CD, all of the song titles and descriptions—everything. So all that was left was just getting the musicians' permission to encode it, send it to Apple, and distribute the money from Apple back to them.

SG: It's so obvious. The technology makes it possible, so you have to do it.

DS: It *was* kind of a no-brainer. But I went into it thinking there wouldn't be many sales.

SG: So how's it going?

DS: I'll just say that it's about five times higher than what I thought it would be. Every time we get a check from Apple—which has been every month—the eyebrows go up and we're like, "Damn!" It's been a lot higher than I thought it would be, and it's still just getting started.

SG: It really is great that the artists are getting the bulk of the money.

DS: Yeah, and it feels nice too. We figured out that because we were already doing most of this that we could make it profitable for only a 9% cut. We didn't get greedy with it and we didn't take any more than that.

SG: Is there anything in CD Baby that you want to fix? Anything that you plan on doing to make it better? Or is it perfect the way it is?

DS: [Laughs] I'm still the guy that does all of the programming, and I spend about four to eight hours a day programming, constantly.

SG: So you're constantly making it better?

DS: A lot of it's the back end, believe it or not. As the company's grown, the only way to keep doing this and be profitable is to constantly find ways to get things more efficient on the back end—more efficient ways to ship out 1,500–5,000 orders a day with a crew of only four people. To do that you have to leverage the technology, to use a corporate-sounding phrase. But I'm also constantly adding new stuff on the Web site that can help the musicians to get their music out there better. Things like the $5 sale—that took about 20 hours to write something like that. I'm constantly trying to think of any new ways to get more exposure, get more sales for these musicians, because that's what it's really all about.

SG: I'd like to hear your thoughts on the future of the music business. My old employer, Sony Music, just merged with BMG. It's all approved now, and they're facing the threat of major layoffs. Warner Records was already sold. Do the big record companies have a future?

DS: I think all predictions are crap.

SG: [Laughs] Okay, so what would you like *to happen then?*

DS: I think that nobody knows, and you've just got to be strong enough and flexible enough to react to what the market needs. As long as you're making the music fans happy and you're making the musicians happy, everybody else needs to understand that they're just an in-between. And there are plenty of roads for the in-betweens, but when it comes down to it you've got to do what the music fans want and what the musicians want. Who knows? There might not be any CDs two years from now, and if that happens, I'm fine with CD Baby just . . . I always tell everyone that our plan for the future is to ride off into the sunset, just getting smaller and smaller.

SG: Smaller and smaller? What do you mean? Because of the digital music landscape getting bigger and bigger?

DS: I just mean that I would like CD Baby to stay pure and sell CDs. And people say, "Yes, but what about the days when there are no more CDs? Don't you want to be selling T-shirts?" And I say, "No." Maybe I might want to start another business someday that would do that, but if it does come to the day where we're only selling two CDs a day and CDs are like LP records are right now, just these obscure little things that some people want, I'd be totally happy with CD Baby just being a little two-person operation and just riding off into the sunset like that. Staying pure to your original motives.

Postscript: According to an October 2004 article in Digitalmedianews.com, CD Baby sur-

passed the $10 million artist-compensation level. That accomplishment is based on over 1.2 million units sold, with a roster of 75,000 artists. CEO Sivers pointed to a "sales boost for the less-famous but more-talented musicians of the world," with CD Baby sales doubling every year since 1998. That sharply contrasts with major declines in major-label CD sales.

Electronic Commerce & Micropayments: Making Money Bit by Bit

A major factor in the evolution of the Internet is electronic commerce: the ability to buy, sell, and advertise goods and services to customers and consumers. Many online music sites accept payment by credit card and payment networks such as PayPal. PayPal basically enables one person with an e-mail account to send money to another person with an e-mail account. If a merchant wants to take payments with PayPal (along with or instead of credit cards), then a "shopping cart" and some Web site development is in order although they can download a shopping cart from PayPal for free. However, both credit card companies and PayPal charge a set minimum fee (the range is 20 to 30 cents) for each transaction as well as a small percentage. For purchases of small-ticket items such as music downloads of individual songs, this could cost the merchant a significant part of his profits. Micropayment systems are designed to facilitate the purchase of such small items, including single-song downloads, by reducing the transaction costs for the vender. Also, Micropayment companies will work with the vendor to set up their store, monetize all their content and create unique payment options such as bundling various content and selling at discounts. Micropayment systems also offer prepaid options to the consumer (similar to prepaid calling or laundry cards) and the ability to reload credit for additional purchases.

Micropayment Overview. Before the dot-com bubble burst, micropayment companies such as Beenz, Flooz, and Digicash rushed in to take advantage of the projected rise in the distribution of fee-based content on the Internet. Although these business models had potential, most failed when the bubble fizzled. Some experts believe that too few people had high-speed Internet connections for online shopping to be practical. Pictures of merchandise, for example, took too long to load on dial-up connections. Now that more and more people have high-speed Internet connections, and there is more content available for purchase including digital music, there is a great revival of commerce online.

New players are now entering the business of providing micropayments, including BitPass. According to company co-founder Kurt Huang, too many variables were at work against the early players. In recent comments to the *San Francisco Chronicle*, Huang noted that "the early firms struggled because most content was free, consumers were not yet comfortable with e-commerce, Internet browser software was cumbersome, and few people had broadband connections." But as the technology evolves, so have the opportunities. "Now," Huang continues, "people are at ease buying online, publishers are charging, the browsers work well, and broadband is widespread enough to enable many people to download music, video and games."

BitPass isn't the only player making serious moves in the micropayments space. Leading micropayment providers Peppercoin and Moneris Solutions recently announced an alliance to better meet the small payments processing needs of merchants. Other players in the micropayments game include Firstgate, PaymentOne, bcgi, Qpass, and E-Gold.

Significant sales from digital music services like iTunes and the RealNetworks' Rhapsody have helped attract renewed interest in micropayment systems. But the digital music business is part of a much larger picture, with other Internet growth areas commanding attention. According to TowerGroup, in 2003 the total value of Internet micropayment transactions in the U.S. was $1.9 billion—driven primarily by media and Internet publishing services, and digital music (e.g., iTunes), and other audio services. By 2009, TowerGroup predicts that the total market for digital micropayments will grow to $11.5 billion, with Internet micropayments accounting for $6.7 billion and mobile micropayments reaching $4.8 billion.

Consumer behavior is validating growth predictions. A 2004 survey from Peppercoin revealed that more than 10 million Americans bought digital content for less than $2 in the past year. That's a 150% increase over 2003. While companies such as RealNetworks charge on a subscription basis, they also offer à la carte download purchase options. Although subscription services could gain substantial traction, download options continue to proliferate. New downloadable elements like games and ringtones as well as music downloads are showing major consumer appeal, with ownership as a reward for purchase. That traction could power a resurgence for micropayment companies.

An Interview Rachel Gravengaard, General Manager of Mperia

www.mperia.com

In the interview below, conducted in September 2004, we discuss micropayments with the general manager of BitPass's new online music store, Mperia. BitPass specializes in setting up micropayment systems and Mperia, an independent online record store, integrates micropayments.

BitPass allows online sellers to place a point-of-sale "button" on their Web sites. That button is generated by BitPass after content is registered through a vendor account. When a sale is made, money is then transferred to the vendor's BitPass account and then paid out to the vendor. BitPass then takes 15% of each transaction on lower price-point items without any minimum payments. So even if the transaction is a dollar or less, the vender can still make a profit. As mentioned earlier, credit-card companies and PayPal usually re-

Rachel Gravengaard

quire a minimum fee as well as a small percentage that could deeply cut into the vendor's margin. BitPass has a tiered pricing structure—on items over $5 they currently take a 5% plus a 50-cent transaction fee rather than the 15% that they charge on lower price points. BitPass's payment system is geared towards a wide range of online content such as music and games, and it offers secure anonymous payment. For the consumer, no special software is required—just a recent browser.

If you are considering setting up an online store, however, you should explore all the payment options available.

Rachel Gravengaard is the general manager of Mperia and oversees marketing and business development. She has over a decade of experience in technology management, focusing largely on product management and marketing. Prior to joining BitPass, Rachel was the product marketing manager for I-D-E, an enterprise software company focusing on product development.

Steve Gordon: Rachel, your overview of Mperia reads, "Mperia is an online music store owned and operated by BitPass that focuses on creating communities of independent artists and their fans. Now, what is BitPass?

Rachel Gravengaard: BitPass is a micropayments company that owns and operates Mperia. The reason we launched Mperia is because one of the biggest markets for paying small amounts for digital downloads on the Web is obviously the music space. So we thought that that was the best showcase for the need for micropayments. That's how Mperia got associated with a payments platform.

SG: What is a micropayment?

RG: A micropayment is any small amount that anybody's not going to want to whip out their credit card and spend ten minutes to purchase an item. For example, a 99-cent download.

SG: When did Mperia start operating?

RG: February 2004, so we've been up about seven months now.

SG: I understand you're already making a big impression in the indie music scene.

RG: We've got about 1,200 artists, all who've found us on their own. And those 1,200 artists have uploaded about 4000 songs, so we've got quite a large database already. We're working on some digital distribution agreements to enhance that database quite dramatically in the coming months.

SG: Do you know how many people are actually using the service?

RG: There are a variety of measures we use. We have listener profiles and we have over 1,000 listeners who have signed up for profiles, but we don't require people to have a listener profile in order to buy the music. And because BitPass is somewhat anonymous in terms of payment, we don't track specifically how many people have bought at Mperia.

SG: Is Mperia a music store primarily?

RG: It is from the consumer standpoint. From the artist's standpoint we really see ourselves as a platform to enable them to sell directly to their fans worldwide.

SG: What kind of music do you include in the site?

RG: Basically anything that is independent. Meaning, the artist owns all the rights to the music. Anyone can come in and upload. We have everything from Christian rap to spoken word to Christmas music. We've got a great classical harpist on the site—it's a real variety. Two segments that have really found Mperia to date—we have a lot of electronic artists from France, Sweden, from all over the U.S., and early on we got hooked up with the U.K. and the industrial goth crew.

SG: How did people all over the world find out about you?

RG: It's really been very word of mouth. We have not done too much paid promotion. We do a few Google ad words here and there, and we have a few banners here and there on a few sites. But we got in with the blogger community, and of course they share anything that they find that's interesting.

SG: I heard your president on National Public Radio the other day, so you're doing a great job of marketing yourself.

Let's talk about the "how." Do you offer a mail-order service or just downloads?

RG: Just downloads. We're not in the physical-distribution phase at all.

SG: Do you offer samples or full songs for free before people decide to buy?

RG: Yeah; we have two-minute previews and full-length previews. The artists can decide whether to allow you to listen to two minutes of their song or the full thing. And the [preview] downloads are at discounted bit rates—so it's not the quality that you would get when you download.

SG: About the relationship with the artists, the overview says: "We believe that the Web provides a new and exciting distribution and promotional model that gives musicians a unique opportunity to sell and promote their work without resorting to the traditional and often exploited mainstream music industry. Artists can reach their audience directly without compromising either their work or their ability to profit from it. With Mperia, artists set their own prices and keep the majority of their own profits." Does that mean the artists can set any rate they want to sell their music?

RG: We have a range for tracks and albums. For tracks it's anywhere from 25 cents to

$1.50. Clearly it's not profitable to sell music for 2 cents, and, equally, we don't think that anyone is going to buy a track if it's $3.00. There are some long jazz tracks that are probably worth more than the $1.00 you would find on iTunes. So many jazz artists who are doing long improvisational pieces won't sell their work on other outlets.

SG: Right, a jazz album that I recently worked on included a track by Dizzy Gillespie that went 12 minutes. Tell us about some of the special features. For instance, the overview states that Mperia offers tools for artists to connect to listeners about gigs, listenings, reminders, forums, and broker-direct communication. What does that all mean?

RG: We've provided a variety of ways for people to interact with each other on the sites. Artists can list all their gigs, and listeners can sign up for them, and they will get reminded of those gigs before they happen. There are forums on those listener profiles and artist profiles. Artists now have blogs on their artist accounts where they can keep in touch and keep people updated about what's going on. And if you're a listener on the site, you can click the "connect" or "contact" link and send an e-mail through us to any of the artists.

SG: Scott Meldrum, a marketing expert, says that one of the most efficient ways of establishing a fan base is to be able to actively communicate with your fans. I assume that some artists are better at responding to their fans than others.

RG: Yeah, there's a wide range of kind of marketing and business sense among the artists.

SG: The overview also mentions that Mperia offers free set-up and song hosting. Does that mean it's free to an artist to join Mperia?

RG: Yes, it is.

SG: And you'll host the artist's music for free?

RG: Yes.

SG: Can he or she or the band put up as much music on Mperia as they wish?

RG: Yup. Right now we have an artist with 60-plus tracks.

SG: Can the artists sell an entire album?

RG: Yes, but it's going to be virtually delivered through Mperia. The buyer will get a Zip file with from three to however many tracks the artist wants to put on that album. It changes the dynamic of what an album is, too. The artist can put one song on three different albums—basically three different playlists that they've made for their customers.

SG: If the artist wanted to sell tracks separately they could, but if they wanted to sell the tracks as an album, they could offer that as well for a cheaper price?

RG: Well, the album costs anywhere from $3 to $10.

SG: What are your requirements for artists? Can anyone sell their album on Mperia? If I recorded "Santa Claus Is Coming to Town," and I'm not a very good singer, would you accept that?

RG: We would, and we're thinking of adding a category called "programs," for shows like yours—an Internet radio program can be sold via Mperia, too.

SG: Has anybody taken advantage of that so far?

RG: We have a couple of people who are interested in doing something like that. Because we don't have content yet, we haven't put the category up, but I think it's a very interesting opportunity. One of the people that we've been talking to had a show on terrestrial radio for a long time—she has a bunch of archived material that she would love to make available.

SG: According to the Web site, 70% of the revenues go to the artist, and Mperia keeps 30%. That's 70% of gross? Are there any other costs that the artists have to worry about?

RG: Nope, the transactions are the only cost.

SG: Do you offer the artists contracts or do they merely register with you?

RG: There's a use policy that they have to sign, an agreement, basically.

SG: Can they offer their music on other sites? Is it nonexclusive?

RG: It's nonexclusive. We have no contracts for them to only sell through Mperia. And they can take down their music at any time as well. We're trying to do everything that we can to enhance rather than restrict commerce, because there's a number of settings that get in the way of an independent musician trying to sell music. We're trying to knock down as many of those barriers as possible, and nonexclusive agreements are one of the things that we're committed to keeping.

SG: It seems like a no-loss deal for the artists. They can continue reaching out to their fans, selling music on their Web sites and selling CDs at their gigs, and Mperia offers an additional outlet.

RG: And we give them more revenue than I think any site I've run into so far, so why wouldn't they have a preference for selling their music on Mperia?

SG: How does it work from the listener's point of view? Do you have to become a member of Mperia in order to hear the music or download the songs?

RG: No, absolutely not. You can preview or purchase without a membership. You do need a BitPass prepaid account.

SG: How does that work?

RG: It's kind of like a phone card that you buy in a drugstore. They start at $3.00, so it's not a huge investment. And you can put in as much money as you like and spend it at any site that uses that text. And you're not restricted to buying music on Mperia. If you find two songs that you like, you can then go to the other BitPass-enabled sites and find records or photos or what have you.

SG: If you're not using a credit card, how does the money actually change hands? Do you send me an invoice at the end of the month, or something like this?

RG: There's actually a reporting feature at BitPass where you can go in and see all of things that you've purchased.

SG: Right, but how do I get the money to you? Do I send you a check?

RG: No, you can load it with a credit card or a PayPal account.

SG: So the money is coming out of the PayPal account or the credit card. But you avoid those transaction costs? How do you do that?

RG: The reason that we have the prepaid card at BitPass is because the transaction costs are too high to sell a 25-cent item. So we bundle that transaction fee on a $3 or $5 card, which spreads that fee out across ten items.

SG: And how much would a credit card cost you if I did a credit-card purchase of 25 cents on my Master Card or Visa, and I paid that way? How much does the credit card company keep?

RG: It could cost you as much as 25 to 30 cents.

SG: Okay, so it wiped out the total paid. That fee is paid by the vendor or Mperia. You avoid that payment to the credit card companies by using the micropayments system.

RG: And customers are clearly willing to pay if they believe there is a fair price for these small-priced items and it's easy for them to do so. One example is all of the mp3.coms, which are very popular. People are still buying music. But they don't feel like they're getting a fair price for it. There is a willingness on the part of the consumer to buy at various price points.

SG: I think that if they had to go to individual sites to set up separate accounts, that might be somewhat irritating. But if I love the music on Mperia and I only have to set up one account and then add to it from time to time, it seems fairly easy.

Let's discuss your possible deal with CD Baby.

RG: I've actually been trying to contract with them to digitally distribute their music.

SG: How will that work? They have a huge number of songs and a huge number of artists. Will everything on CD Baby be available through Mperia?

RG: We would ideally like that. We're still doing the technical evaluation on the integration, but we would like to bring that whole database into Mperia.

SG: They may already have that kind of deal with iTunes, correct?

RG: Yeah, absolutely. This actually brings up a good differentiator for us. People need to discover you before buying your music and so what we try to do with Mperia is add a lot of social networking functionality to the site so people can share and discover music and link to their friends, and have profiles with playlists so people can find the new music; find the little independent guy that doesn't have the big promotions budget. It's harder to do that in iTunes. We think for that reason we're really complementary to iTunes. I love iTunes—I think it's great for mainstream, big-label music. But it's less valuable if you don't know exactly what you want.

SG: How do you foster the networking? Do you have an instant messenger service between customers?

RG: We have a profile for every listener where they can bookmark their favorite artist, their favorite songs, their playlists, and forums. And then we have a "connections" feature where they can connect to a number of different people—whoever they want to—who also have profiles on their site. Or they can send out invites to friends that aren't on the site. So they are creating a community of people who all like the same music. And they usually link around to those other profiles to see what people are listening to!

SG: If I like somebody else's playlist and I want to download it, can I sample that playlist without paying?

RG: You can preview all of the music without paying. And then you can download and buy it.

SG: Can you download it directly from the other person; how does that work?

RG: Yeah, we actually have snippets on the listener profile, so if you see something you like on somebody's profile, you can buy it right there. You don't have to jump to the artist's page; there's a song page.

SG: Lets talk about restrictions and DRM [digital rights management]. Once I download a song from Mperia, are there any restrictions in using the music after I buy it? For instance, can I burn it to as many blank discs as I want?

RG: There are no DRM restrictions, and again it gets back to our philosophy of enhancing commerce rather than restricting it. Right now there are no standards on DRM. And for the independents, it's less important. They're trying to get their music out there so the music gets shared, and that's actually good for them in the long run.

Because we're dealing with the independent labels, it's less of a problem, and we want to again make sure that we're compatible with everybody. MP3 is a good way to do that.

SG: It's less of a greed factor. When they put out a new Eminem album, the label is looking to sell 10 million units based on a brand, if you will, so every unit that is downloaded but not purchased, they feel it's a loss. But for an indie artist, it's actually a good way of getting increased exposure.

RG: Exactly. I hear all the time from the artists, "I'm just happy people are listening to it." I think the vast majority of independent artists have day jobs, or they get the majority of their revenue from live shows. So digital distribution revenue is something on top of that, and without any costs to the artists.

SG: Can you give us an idea of the success of the site, in terms of income?

RG: I would say that it's not "interesting" yet. Part of that is because we haven't made a concerted marketing effort yet. We're planning on doing some of that—we just received a new round of financing, so we actually have some money to do some increased exposure. The other issue is that people are coming to us because they are finding it very interesting and there is a lot of music, but I can still, in my favorite genres, get through it in a couple of days myself. I think once we get the CD Baby material integrated and we start doing some marketing, the revenue numbers will get interesting.

Look for exciting things in the coming months—we've got a few interesting plans going on. So come back, check things out!

Chapter 18
Online Financing

An Interview with Brian Camelio, Founder and President of ArtistShare

www.artistshare.net

ArtistShare uses the Internet in an innovative way to finance music and other cultural projects. Brian Camelio, founder and president, is a 38-year-old guitarist and computer programmer who started ArtistShare after he'd heard stories from too many friends about frustrating experiences with record labels. A completely new business model for creative artists, ArtistShare benefits both the artist and the fans by financing new and original artistic projects while building a strong and loyal fan base.

Steve Gordon: Brian, let me start by reading an excerpt from your bio: "Most of my close friends, mostly jazz musicians, were having a hard time with the business. It made me so frustrated to see friends being led down a dead-end street. The frustration was a catalyst for ArtistShare. Being a programmer, I was duly aware of the capabilities of the emerging technologies. Seeing that there would be no feasible solution for protecting digital content from being shared, be it movies, music, text—you name it—the game, it seemed to me, was over. This realization was both disheartening and liberating." Now, there is such a thing as digital rights management, and if you go to iTunes or Rhapsody you'll be able to download music, but only if you pay. Why do you think that DRM is not the answer?

Brian Camelio: There really is no such

Brian Camelio

thing as real protection for music online. I think that there are even legal commercial programs now where you can capture and download the streaming audio coming out of your computer speakers into a digital format. I wrote a simple application in about 30 minutes where anything that I was streaming I could just save it into a WAV file. It's kind of silly, the DRM thing. Really, who are we protecting here?

SG: Well, the issue is: Can the music be protected? There was a 60 Minutes *program last week, and they reported that some movies are available online before they appear in the theater. Same for music—people often get tracks, one way or another, before commercial release, and they become available online before the authorized services can even start to sell them. Of course, once the CDs are released, anybody could and usually does upload them to the P2P networks. So the DRM protection applied by the services may fall short of doing the job.*

BC: Right.

SG: Let's talk about ArtistShare. Among the artists featured in your Web site is Maria Schneider, a prize-winning jazz composer and arranger. She states in the site that she made three discs for a label and sold a respectable 20,000 copies, but she didn't make a dime from it. So she turned to ArtistShare. Can you explain why she didn't make any money?

BC: Well, the way most record deals are structured—I don't know if the public realizes this or not—it's like a bad loan. The record company comes in and says, "Okay, we'll pay for all of the expenses, we'll pay for the record . . . "

SG: Right, production and marketing costs.

BC: Yes, and the way that the contract is usually structured and worded is that the artist has to "recoup" to earn royalties, which means the artist gets nothing until the record company is paid back production and marketing costs. Also, the royalty is subject to all kinds of deductions. So in order to just break even, artists need to sell a huge amount of records. Usually after that there's some fancy accounting that prevents them from getting paid. In Maria's situation it was a little bit different. For her first record I think she paid $20,000 of her own money to make it, and then she licensed and sold it to the record company for $10,000 plus royalties. They sold over 20,000 copies, and I don't think she made another dime off of that, with her contract. So the record companies—it's not that they're evil, although some of them are—it's really the system. With everybody who needs to get paid along the way and the way the royalties are set up, the musician is last in line and usually ends up with nothing.

SG: As a former record company lawyer I'll give a very quick scenario, and then you can tell me how ArtistShare is different. If you go into a record company, say you're a jazz musician, they might give you $50,000 to make the record. You go into the studio and record the album for $40,000. You turn the record over to the label and keep $10,000. But basically, you are $50,000 in debt to the record company! And the royalty is generally 10% to 15% of retail, which generally amounts to less than $1 per unit. So until the label sells 50,000 units, you don't make any recording royalties.

Unless you sell a lot of records—and with pop musicians you're talking about budgets of half a million dollars—and if their royalties are $1, unless you sell a half a million units you're not going to see any royalties. Because the record companies recoup at your royalty rate. If they sell 500,000 units, they may well have money in their pocket because the record wholesales for several dollars, but since they are allocating recoupment at your royalty of $1, until after the 500,000th record has sold, you may still see nothing. So, given that model, how is ArtistShare different?

BC: We're different because our product—or the artist's product—is no longer just a CD. As a matter of fact, that's a very small part of it. The one thing that we can assure the artist is that they're worth more than $1 per CD. The creative experience is really what we're selling. The product is no longer just buying the CD, it is being involved in the experience of the artist's creative process as they're recording the CD, as they're writing the music, as they're giving lectures, as they're teaching lessons. There are a lot of different things involved in making a record.

SG: ArtistShare allows people to invest in the production of the project and also buy particular products. I do want to go into those details, but before we get into the nitty-gritty, can you tell us a little about the musical artists on your program? You have about a dozen now?

BC: Yes. We get new ones every week or so. Maria Schneider, who is a four-time Grammy-nominated composer, was our first artist. Our second artist was Jim Hall, who is a jazz legend among guitar players, and then Trey Anastasio from the band Phish. And there's Rachel Z, who is a prominent jazz pianist and is also in Peter Gabriel's band. There's also Convergence, a jazz-oriented band of amazing musicians. Plus bassist Todd Coolman, an educator; Danilo Perez, an unbelievable piano player who plays with Wayne Shorter and has a great solo career; Bob Brookmeyer, a legendary jazz trombone player…

SG: That's an incredible range of music, especially from Phish to classic jazz. You also have some visual artists?

BC: Yes, we have a photographer named David Korchin who's amazing, and we're working on a site for a fine painter named Joey Kilrain. So we compete for any artist, any type of art. Anything that involves the creative process we're interested in.

SG: Let's use Jim Hall as an example. He's considered to be one of the greatest living jazz guitarists, and he's still very active. In fact, he's making a new record. Has it been completed yet?

BC: Yes, he recorded it in April at the Village Vanguard, and just yesterday we finished mastering it. So it's going to be sent out to all of the people who participated in the project within the next couple of weeks.

SG: Okay, if you click on Mr. Hall's name or his photo in ArtistShare.net, you immediately link to another Web site that says, "This is Jim Hall's official Web site . . . powered by ArtistShare." So you created this new Web site for Mr. Hall?

BC: Exactly. We actually create a working business model for our artists, not just a Web site. We have a complete business plan, a complete business strategy, and a very unique way to develop an audience and bring revenue in for the artist's project. The Web site is part of it.

SG: Did you help produce Mr. Hall's new record? Were you there at the Village Vanguard at the time it was recorded?

BC: Yes, we did the whole thing, and that's what I love to do. I love jazz and I produce a record here and there.

SG: Well, with ArtistShare you not only get a business plan and a full Web site, but you get a producer!

If we go to Mr. Hall's Web site, we have plenty of options. There are interviews with him and other people who participated in the project, a lot of photos, even a couple of guitar lessons. But the first option is the limited-edition CD. It says, "It's part of the ArtistShare experience where we're releasing 5,000 limited-edition CDs of the Village Vanguard recording. The CDs are currently scheduled to ship in early September. Order early to avoid missing out. Participate now." So you click on that, and it gives you even more interesting options. The first one is Player Participant, for $80. "As a Player Participant, you will receive at least two lessons posted online which include instructions on improvisation, exercises, etc.," and then you have the choice of getting more details. There's even an option to be an executive producer for $20,000, and there are more details on what executive producer entails. Has anyone clicked on that one yet?

BC: Sure, a lot of people have *clicked* on it! [Laughs]

SG: Have you had success in getting substantial participation?

BC: Yes. For the projects we have up, we've received a number of fairly high participant-level participants, either from an organization or a company or an individual who is just really interested in the artist.

SG: So this is a good way of financing projects. The last option of the dozen on this particular menu is Active Participant. For $18.95, the Active Participant receives one limited-edition CD, project progress and updates, selected news and streaming audio, plus the reward of being a part of jazz history in the making. I think that's a pretty good deal. If you go into Tower Records you can still buy a CD still for $18.99. You're offering a lot more than that.

BC: And also we're taking the focus off of *just* the CD. The thing that's really interesting about these ArtistShare projects is, especially for Jim's project, if you're a fan of music or art in general, you actually get to see the progress of him writing the music. You may get a taste of him practicing, him talking about how he prepares for the gig, coverage of rehearsal videos, and exclusive streaming interviews with the people involved. So you're getting the total experience. The reason you buy a CD is to listen to these moments of brilliance that happen. All of the forces converge there. And that happens a lot in the process of making the CD, in the process of writing the music, in the process of rehearsing it. The CD is not the only place where this happens. The CD is just a very small snapshot in a timeline of this creative process.

SG: So you're providing an opportunity to create relationships between the artists and the fans.

BC: Absolutely.

SG: You offer some free stuff too, so people should at least check out the Web site because there are pictures and interviews that you can get free. Another nice thing about ArtistShare is, according to the Web site, the artists retain all copyrights in their work, which is very refreshing. Do you actually sign contracts with the artists?

BC: Oh, yes. There is a contract that I sign with the artists, but it really has to do with just making sure that they don't infringe on other people's copyrights by posting stuff they don't own, and just to make sure that they don't screw up by saying that they're going to deliver something and not deliver it.

SG: Is each contract different? With Jim Hall you're actually the producer, so that's something very special.

BC: They're all pretty much the same, but when I work with Jim I don't have a contract. Jazz musicians generally tend to work on a handshake, and that's one of the reasons we get along so well. [Laughs]

SG: As long as the musicians get the money. How do you share income with the artists? Suppose that I did go for the collector's CD with the additional streaming and interviews and so forth. I've paid my $20. How does the money get split up?

BC: I get a 15% cut of the sale, and that is to cover any technical support and software updates to the Web site, and the artist gets 85%.

SG: That's a pretty good deal. The other thing about this is that you're not putting up your own money to create the project, you're offering it to the public to participate. So the artist isn't beholden to or has to repay any particular individual—it's a no-strings-attached sponsorship that doesn't have to be repaid, except with goodwill and the products that you're offering. That's what I want to emphasize—that this is a new way of financing projects for independent artists—music artists and also visual artists. You said you're accepting one or more new artists each week—that's incredible. Considering how much detail and work goes into these projects, how can you possibly find the time?

BC: I've been working on this for four years now, so I've got a good process. We'll get four people coming in a week, and we'll actually sign maybe two people, and over a period of two or three months we will develop the business plan of their Web site. We'll do an analysis of their audience to see which demographics will be good to target immediately and which demographics will be good to target over a period of four or five years. It's really for career artists. We're building a long-term plan for them.

SG: If an artist were interested, how would they go about getting in touch with you?

BC: They can just go to the Web site, ArtistShare.com, or they can e-mail me directly. It's brian@artistshare.com. I'm very accessible, and I'm always in front of my computer.

SG: I can testify to that—you do get back to people. There are a couple of things on the

Web site that I found intriguing, and maybe it will round out the picture of what you're doing to talk about them. One of the items indicates that "ArtistShare will automatically syndicate all artist information to any number of sources, Web sites, PDAs, cell phones, providing up-to-the-minute, multilingual data streaming. Keep the world up-to-date with information on your current projects and activities." How does that work?

BC: That's basically done through our Web services—that's a platform that we built our Web software on. We have feeds for bloggers on there, but we'll also have just a straight XML feed. So if people want to post the artist's information on their own Web sites, it's easy to grab that feed and put it up there.

SG: Suppose we here at MyRealBroadcast wanted to post something; how would we mechanically go about that?

BC: You just contact me, and I'll hook it up for you.

SG: There's another item here: streaming radio. "Create streaming radio and media shows and restrict access to listening/viewing. Perfect for offering downloadable or streaming purchases of live performances, lectures, experiences." A guy like me who lectures about the music business—is that something that interests ArtistShare?

BC: Definitely, yes. Anything where we can convey a person's unique qualities, or anything with their knowledge is perfect ArtistShare material.

SG: There's one more intriguing bit—it says that you can license your work for distribution. How would that work?

BC: Basically, ArtistShare is a catalyst for the artist. I have people coming to me constantly, saying, "Would you offer this to your artists?" I say, "Sure." And I go to the artists and I quickly screen the person coming in, and I put all of the choices on the table. I say, "Well, you can just sell directly to your fans; this is the profit margin, here's the money stream. You can go with this person who's going to distribute all of your records in Japan, and here's the revenue stream for that." It gives them an educated presentation so that they can make a choice. I don't restrict anybody from anything. They can do whatever they want with their content. I just make sure that they're going to make the right choice.

SG: Do you also get requests for the use of music in movies or documentaries or what have you?

BC: Yes, definitely.

SG: What are your plans for the future?

BC: To continue doing what we're doing on a larger scale. I also want to create more avenues for driving new audiences to the existing ArtistShare artists. I'm already working on some deals that I can't really talk about, but the end result will be that ArtistShare artists will have a built-in audience geared towards their specialty and a demographic profile that fits it.

SG: Do you want to incorporate peer-to-peer into your paradigm in any way?

BC: I think that P2P is great—it's possibly one of the most aggressive ways that you can market yourself. I just think that there's not any room for it in my paradigm because it already exists in a really great format. I would say to any artist, "Throw your music up there. Get it out there." Because the product is no longer the end result—the product is the process.

SG: The parody of Bush and Kerry at jibjab.com was accessible for free, and now the creators' Web site is famous—it was incredibly successful as an ad for their work.

One last question: What do you think is the future of the record labels? Do you think that we will still have Warner, Sony BMG, EMI, Universal?

BC: Oh, they're necessary because there's an existing catalog and they're legally bound to protect the copyrights in that catalog.

SG: From a third to over 40% of many record companies' sales are catalog, but do you think that they'll just be dealers in old records? Or do you think that they'll keep on signing, marketing, and publicizing new artists?

BC: I think that they're going to try to keep doing that. But they're going to have to keep cutting out middlemen in order to survive, because the technology came up and caught them by surprise. The brick-and-mortar way of doing business is in decline, and the Internet is on the rise.

SG: And they've fought against it for so long instead of embracing it and finding a new business model. Now they're bleeding money, and the question is, do they have the wherewithal to sign new artists? But I think that the point of ArtistShare is to give artists an alternative to the traditional record-company system.

BC: Yes, definitely, and to make their own choice. Because there are benefits to a record company. They'll give you money up front and they'll claim to promote you, and for some people that's really all they want. People who are not career artists may just say, "You know what? I'd like to just have a hit record and go and retire." You can also buy lottery tickets.

Chapter 19

Webcasting as a Business Model

An Interview with Rags Gupta, Chief Operating Officer of Live365.com

In Chapter 3 we discussed the rules pertaining to webcasting or Internet radio. In this interview with Raghav "Rags" Gupta, Chief Operating Officer of Live365.com, an Internet broadcasting network consisting of thousands of radio stations reaching over 3 million listeners a month, we discuss webcasting from the point of view of a new business model. Live365 represents two business models. The first consists of providing diverse webcast music streams to listener-subscribers, plus the technology and required licenses for those who wish to webcast music. The second business model is for the webcasters: They can use Live365 to promote their music and offer links to sell their music by mail-order and download.

Rags Gupta drives the company's strategy and overall vision. Since joining Live365 in 1999, he has helped the company grow from a service that catered to tech-savvy hobbyists interested in Internet broadcasting into a broadcasting network. Prior to Live365, Gupta was a strategy consultant at Mercer Management, consulting with Fortune 1000 clients in the insurance and publishing industries. Rags also holds a degree from Princeton University, where he majored in Civil Engineering and Operations Research.

Steve Gordon: Rags, what inspired you to get into webcasting?

Rags Gupta: It was frankly kind of dumb luck. I joined the company in mid-1999. At the time—and what inspired the company to get into webcasting—were these new phenomena called MP3s and Winamp and

Rags Gupta

Shoutcast. There were some people who were trying out and putting up Shoutcast severs, and there was a decision to see if there could be some play to be made with the concept of self-publishing on the Internet in terms of audio.

SG: Did you start the company yourself or did you join a company that was already there?

RG: I joined a company that was already there. They were working on a different product before I got there; it was a sort of home-community concept that wasn't getting much traction. This was 1998. In early 1999 they started getting into the webcasting idea. I joined right around when they formally launched the webcasting model at Plug-IN in N.Y. And then the craziness ensued. [Laughs]

SG: Tell us about the business model when they launched this "craziness," and tell us how it evolved into the operation you have today.

RG: There was a 1999 business model that was in place at the time, that is to say not a fully fleshed-out idea. There was a vision of it always being an advertiser-supported site, and we were proceeding on that basis. I think timing and the market scotched that. The company had in some ways a typical dot-com trajectory where you had the birth, which was punctuated by a lot of money being raised for a not fully fleshed-out business model, and then you had the crash of the market, and the dearth of dollars out there. Then the restructuring and cutting-costs period, and really rationalizing the operation and getting a business model in place that would account for the realities of the market. Then the sort of rebirth and the "redemption," if you would [laughs], which is very much what we have gone through. Starting two or three years ago, there was a new management team put in place, which is when I really got involved in the management of the company. We along with a team that was advising us started trying to turn the company around in terms of, one, diversifying the revenue streams including a subscription-based revenue stream, and, two, rationalizing the Internet operation and getting costs under control, etc. We were focusing on a subscription-based business in the last couple of years, and now we starting to look at an advertising model again. The decision to diversify revenue streams really saved the company. We had to make some very tough decisions in terms of charging people money for the services we are providing, and we made some tough choices that were very controversial, or certainly hard decisions to make.

SG: Let's talk about how Live365 really works. I visited the Web site during the last few days, and I started by going to the home page and clicking on "Listen." There I found dozens of different types of music. I clicked on "Goth" under "Alternative," for no particular reason. That took me to more than two dozen "Goth" stations! I clicked on number 17, which was "Cobwebs in the Closet," a catchy title. I downloaded your free player. It took a few seconds— no more than that. A song by a band called the Spectres started to play, and then song by a group called Psycho Charger came on. I noticed I could click on a "buy" button and that would take me to the Amazon Web site, and I could purchase their record without leaving Live365. First, tell us about Cobwebs in the Closet.

RG: Cobwebs in the Closet is one of our broadcasters and also one of our editors' picks—it has already been recognized as a very good station on our network. The person programming it happens to be a big fan of gothic culture and music. And I think what characterizes her—and really the thousands of other DJs and broadcasters in our network—is she is passionate about music. She's so passionate that she's willing to spend money each month to create a channel or station, program the channel, and spend hours of her time to update the station, promote it, interface with listeners, etc. This passion for music—and also talk—is the common denominator across all our different stations.

SG: *If you go to "Broadcast" in the Live365 Web site, you see what creating your own broadcast station is about. It looks like there is a free trial, but the price starts at $9.95 a month to webcast your music through Live365. What are the financial incentives for webcasting on Live365?*

RG: I think this is the best deal going for fledging webcasters out there that want to try it out at relatively little cost. To actually do this on one's own would cost thousands of dollars in terms of royalty fees to three or four licensing agencies, server space, and bandwidth. And the costs only go up if you were to expand your audience. With us, you start at $9.95 a month and everything is covered. The royalties, the streaming, the bandwidth. It's all covered so long as you follow certain rules.

We also pay our broadcasters a bounty for each subscriber to us that they refer. In fact, some people refer so many subscribers that their broadcasting fee is almost nothing, and sometimes we have paid money out.

We are also experimenting with a couple of different potential advertising revenue programs where we share a percentage of advertising back. That's really more for what we call our professional clients who want to have a greater degree of control and flexibility in terms of how they webcast.

SG: *Yes, I did notice a little ad come on—in addition to the banner ads on your site, which are not obtrusive—for the iPod before I heard some music. In certain circumstances, is there a revenue split on that kind of advertising?*

RG: That's the theory. Today, because of the economics, we have two different type of broadcasting tiers. One is the consumer hobbyist tier. The other is the professional tier. For the consumer hobbyist, the arrangement right now is that we pay for everything in terms of royalty and licensing. They pay a small monthly fee to subsidize part of the costs. We control the ad inventory for various reasons, including paying for the required licenses. The professional tier is more for people who want to make it a business. They control their ad inventory, they don't carry our ads, they don't carry our branding. They are using our infrastructure as a very efficient and low-cost way to stream their signal online.

SG: *How would they benefit financially from the arrangement?*

RG: We have clients who are doing their own subscription model. We have some that are doing an ad-supported station. And some are doing the public radio model, which is more of a listener-supported concept. But for a lot of them, it's really the love of the game. Instead of spending money on another type of hobby like painting or gardening, this is their hobby

SG: If I came in as a professional, could I put the Future of the Music Business shows up as a webcast?

RG: Absolutely. In fact, we have similar shows that do just that.

SG: Let's discuss how membership works. If you go to the "Listen" portion of the Web site you can listen to music for free. You can also access up to 5,000 stations. You can also save your favorite stations. All of this for free?

RG: We are always going to have a free option for people who want to listen to free radio that is ad-supported. And there will always be a paid, or premium, option for people who want a better experience or some benefits.

SG: What are the benefits?

RG: Today the benefits of becoming a premium, or "VIP," member is you get thousands of stations that are not available to a free member. You don't get any commercials or pop-up ads. You also get the ability to listen to CD-quality sound for a subset of our stations.

SG: So the CD-quality sound is exclusive to VIP membership?

RG: Exactly. It varies from station to station. It depends on what kind of format they're broadcasting on, but for many of our top stations, you get a "CD decoder" to get it in top quality. The concept is to have this bundle of different benefits so people would sign up for VIP.

SG: Where on the Web site would I click to see these options?

RG: If you go to the "Listen" page, or really any page in the site, you will see an ad or a link to sign up for VIP membership. That will take you to a page where you can learn more about the benefits, and it's a risk-free proposition because you can get a free trial, and you can cancel at any time within that free trial and not be charged.

SG: Which section would I go to to join up as a webcaster?

RG: On our Web site we have a "Broadcast" tab. Click on that and there is information on what it costs and the benefits. Again, you can get a risk-free free trial—that trial is 30 days, which is very generous, and people can play around with it and decide whether they want to do it or not.

SG: Let's talk about licensing. Do you have a statutory license to webcast prerecorded music on Live365? Or do you require your webcasters to secure and pay for that license?

RG: It is a little bit of a can of worms. But just to simplify things: Yes, we are licensed. It is statutory license, but we pay SoundExchange, which is the designated agent to collect on behalf of record companies and the artists.

SG: Technically the license is included in the DMCA—the Digital Millennium Copyright Act. All you have to do is give notice, comply with the rules for webcasting, and pay the mandated fees.

RG: Right—you give notice to the Copyright Office and pay SoundExchange and report to SoundExchange. In a lot of ways SoundExchange is like the IRS—you fill out the form and they collect.

SG: There is one other license, which has to do with the songs. Owners of songs or musical compositions enjoy what is known as a public-performance right. The right of public performance is generally handled by a performing-rights organization, or PRO. In the United States, these PROs are ASCAP, BMI, and SESAC. Do you have public-performance licenses?

RG: We are licensed with all three of those organizations. So we pay them a royalty and we have blanket licenses to stream their repertoire.

SG: And that would cover any webcaster on the site?

RG: It does not cover our professional webcasters. For example, if an FM Clear Channel were to come on our site, or a college radio station, it would not cover them, but we have a very good relationship with all those agencies, and we are able to do pass-along licenses and things like that. I could go on for hours about the different combinations, but the general idea is that we are a one-stop shop that will handle the licensing or arrange for pass-along licenses.

SG: Do you have any competitors, or are you unique in this field?

RG: In this particular field I believe we are fairly unique. There are a lot of Internet radio companies out there, from very large companies that have Internet radio properties such as Yahoo! to small, almost mom-and-pop webcasters that have set up their own stations. To my knowledge there is no one else really doing this concept of self-publishing radio—one-stop shopping.

SG: Let's talk about opportunities for new artists. I saw on your home page a little picture of an artist named Tyler Hilton. I never heard of him—is he with a label?

RG: Yes, he's with Maverick Records.

SG: When you click on his picture you get into his Web site and can even watch something called Tyler TV. And of course there's a connection to his album on Amazon. Is this kind of promotion open to indie artists or artists on indie labels as well?

RG: Absolutely. We work with a lot of indie labels to do a lot of promotions. In fact, we had the manager for Green Day hear a band on our network, and he got in touch with us and signed the band because he was so impressed with it. He heard the band on one of our stations, or it maybe was a promotion—I don't really remember.

We strongly encourage indie artists and labels to get in touch with us. With the variety of content we offer, it is a very compelling thing to have indie labels that focus on a certain kind of music, because chances are we have certain stations that would be thrilled to play that music.

SG: Could an indie label brand their own webcast with the name of their label?

RG: Yes, they can produce their own station. In fact, we have done this with Concord Records, which is one of the greatest jazz labels, based in California. We have various stations that we host for them, but it is their stuff, their repertoire. And we are both very happy with the arrangement.

SG: So Concord can play their music and provide links so people can buy their artists' albums?

RG: Right.

SG: I noticed you have a "Personals" section in the Live365 Web site. What is that about? Is that a dating service?

RG: It *is* a dating services, and it's provided by a third party called Springstreet Network. They provide a personals service for a number of different sites such as the Onion, Chicago Tribune, and Boston.com. It goes with our whole concept of community and connecting people. Broadcasters find listeners, listeners find broadcasters, listeners find listeners, etc.

SG So you can listen to music and get a date at the same time. Do you have any other words for our listeners?

RG: If you don't already listen to Internet radio, I would encourage people to check it out. There is some great stuff on Internet radio—specifically Live365—that you can't find anywhere else. If you really get hooked on it, I would encourage you to set up your own station.

As you know, Steve, the way that we consume music is changing. We are at this historic moment where the music business is going digital, and we are finding with things like iPod, Internet radio streaming, self-publishing your own radio station, that it's going to give to consumers more control over content.

I think that there is some great, interesting, almost revolutionary things going on. And I don't think we are done. There are exciting things down the road that we can look forward to both as listeners and consumers.

Chapter 20

The Future of Peer to Peer

An Interview with Wayne Rosso, President of Mashboxx and Former President of Grokster and Piolet

This interview with Wayne Rosso was recorded in summer 2004 prior to the announcement that certain major labels, including Universal and Sony BMG Music, were in the process of securing deals with authorized P2P services including Shawn Fanning's SNO-CAP and Wayne's new company, Mashboxx. The section in Chapter 9 titled "Will the Labels Embrace P2P?" provides the current status of those deals as of the time this manuscript was submitted for publication. For updates on the labels' overtures to the P2P world, including Mashboxx, see the Web pages updating this book by using the link in the CD-ROM.

Steve Gordon: Wayne, you've had a long history in the music business. Please tell us about it.

Wayne Rosso: I started off in college bringing live concerts to the University of South Carolina back in the late '60s. From there I promoted concerts in Atlanta, Georgia, for a couple of years—it took me about two years to go out of business. And then I migrated to the West Coast, where I held many different jobs, including rack jobber—people don't even know what that is anymore. Back in the old days when we used to sell those 12-inch vinyl things, people would shop for records at their local Kmart or Sears or whatever. They all had record departments, and I would go around and basically stock and maintain all of

Wayne Rosso

these record departments and retail outlets. It was a trenches kind of job. At one point I was even a warehouse worker for the old United Artists Record Distribution—sweeping floors and then pulling record orders.

I worked myself up the chain at United Artist Records at various positions and gravitated to the marketing and PR fields. I went on to form my own PR firm in the late '70s and spent many years in LA. In 1985 I moved to New York City, where business was very good for me. I guess about ten years ago I went into a business called Paradigm Music Entertainment with some music-industry executives that was funded by a Wall Street brokerage firm, and that business was quickly sold to one of the big cable companies. Suddenly I was in the tech business because we had acquired a property called SonicNet that went on to become MTV Interactive. It was very early stages of the Internet, very early! Then of course I worked with Alan McGlade, who was head of The Video Jukebox Network. Now Alan is the CEO of MusicNet. It was off to the races from there . . .

SG: You are also a veteran of the file-sharing movement—you led two of the major P2P services. Can you give us some background the peer-to-peer movement?

WR: In late 1998, a kid named Shawn Fanning came up with Napster—that was the first generation of file-sharing. Napster had 40 to 50 million users, and it was the only game in town, and it was terrific. Now the problem was that their technology was dependent upon central server architecture, which meant that it kept a log of all of the files, of the music that was being traded, amongst all of the different people who were connected to each other—and that was their downfall. Because they had that directory, that index, a judge ruled that they had the wherewithal to filter out copyrighted content. When they tried to install some filtering mechanisms, they were only about 97%–98% effective, and the judge would not let them reopen because it wasn't 100% effective. So Napster spawned a second generation of P2P called Gnutella. Gnutella is an open-source network, that was devised, interestingly enough, by someone who worked for AOL. AOL found out about it and within 24 hours had shut the project down, but in those 24 hours the source code was released on the Internet. So then it was open season. Gnutella is open source. It doesn't require any kind of central library index, and it doesn't keep track of anything. It is what we call totally decentralized. It is really people connecting with each other without having to check in with one central access point. The problem with Gnutella, though, was that it was slow, clunky, and caused a lot of problems. Imagine concentric circles: On an inner circle you'd have a guy with a dial-up modem connections, a whole circle of slow modem connections. Outside of that you would have a lot of guys with broadband cable connections. Outside of that you'd have guys with ISD connections. And outside of that more modem connections. If you were on the inner circle and you were on a dial-up modem and you were trying to download a file from someone at the back who had a high-speed connection, the guy with the dial-up modem would slow everything down. It was real iffy. But since it is an open source, all kinds of developers have been working on it to improve it over the years.

SG: Because now you can download a song in a matter of seconds.

WR: It improved a lot, but it is still not ideal. Nonetheless, Gnutella spawned another source called FastTrack, a closed-source, proprietary technology. Also at that time some developers in Amsterdam came up with a closed proprietary network that was decentralized but also solved all of the problems that Gnutella had. They in turn licensed their content, or their technology, to a company called Streamcast, which is now known as Morpheus. The guys that owned Fastrack also published their own software client called Kazaa. But Kazaa got sued, and they sold to a very mysterious group called the Sharman Network based in an island in the South Pacific with heavy secrecy laws. Then what happened was Morpheus was not getting the updates, the upgrades to their network, and they withheld some royalty payments. So the Sharman people, who now owned the network, and Kazaa basically disconnected Morpheus and all its users from their network and then shifted them to Kazaa, which was a very distant player at the time. And that's how Kazaa started to get very big. Because Morpheus was out of the loop for several weeks to try to get back online. So, for lack of a better phrase, Kazaa basically hijacked the business and became the big player in town.

Then the record industry started a multi-prong terror campaign against file sharers and their users. So they sued Grokster, my former company, and Kazaa for copyright infringement.

SG: You're referring to the MGM vs. Grokster *case.*

WR: Correct! The judge said that the makers of this technology aren't doing any infringing and it can be used for legitimate purposes.

SG: And they couldn't filter out songs under copyright, even if they wanted, because there was no central database.

WR: Correct. The judge said to the record industry, if you want to sue anyone, go after the people that are doing the copying and the users.

SG: In a little bit we'll get into what the record industry is up to. What is the popularity now of peer to peer? How many millions of people use it on a daily basis?

WR: It's hard to say but I would venture that about 150 million people worldwide actively file share.

SG: We know that these services are free—they don't charge the users for the content—so how do they make money?

WR: It's basically an advertising model and a software distribution model. The industry was tagged with distributing something called spyware. That's sort of a misnomer—it's more accurately referred to as adware. It basically feeds up customized advertising or targeted advertising, pop-ups or pop-unders. There are other forms of revenue gathering too, such as distributing other kinds of software, for people who want toolbars or navigation tools or all kinds of Internet utilities.

SG: What are the big players now?

WR: Right now Kazaa is still big, but they have experienced a major drop now that eDonkey is the big mover and shaker. They are neck and neck with Kazaa, and may have pulled ahead a little bit. They are quickly gaining ground. About a year ago it was established that eDonkey was the biggest service in Western Europe, and that started to translate to the U.S. A new file-sharing technology that was not developed for copyright infringement obviously is BitTorrent. BitTorrent has become very popular. Those are the big players now. But right up there is iMesh and LimeWire and another network called Ares, which has been flying under the radar lately. It is an excellent network and they have a lot of traction, and they're growing like a weed. And there are several other smaller ones.

SG: *Have any of these services—including the time you were at Grokster—sought permission from the labels through a blanket license?*

WR: Yes.

SG: *What was the labels' response?*

WR: The answer is yes, yes and get lost.

SG: *If they did want a blanket license, have any of them approached ASCAP, BMI, and SESAC? These organizations offer blanket licenses that allow Internet services as well as broadcasters to transmit songs.*

WR: I don't think anyone has, not to my knowledge. On the other hand, you couldn't find any more organizations that are more forceful to get licenses than ASCAP and BMI. If you open up a hotdog stand, they are going to be knocking on your door to make you buy a license. It works both ways: no one has approached them, and they have approached no one. The only thing I can think of is they think they don't have a case, so they haven't called anybody.

SG: *Let's talk about the labels and their experimentation in the digital music era. They started by creating Pressplay and MusicNet. These services offered music on demand but would not allow people to download. Neither of these services, as you are well aware, were very successful. In fact, Universal and Sony, the founders of Pressplay, sold it to Roxio. Then Steve Jobs came along with iTunes and offered downloads with portability. And he has had some success. What do you think about iTunes?*

WR: I am a recent Mac convert, and I think iTunes is absolutely spectacular. It is elegant, it is simple, it is a beautiful thing.

SG: *You are always assured of getting good quality in terms of the music that you are downloading, not worried about spoofs or incomplete songs or anything like that.*

WR: No question! But let's put it all in perspective. First of all, Apple is not relying on iTunes to make money. In fact, they don't make money on iTunes. They are using iTunes to market the iPod, which they have been highly successful with. And then they further use the iPod to market the iMac and the iBook, so it's the hipbone connected to the thighbone …

SG: *They use iTunes to sell their hardware.*

WR: Yes, iTunes is a loss leader, so to speak, and it is a vehicle. But let's put it even further into perspective and that's the fact that they have sold millions of iPods, but iTunes has only been marginally profitable at best. Furthermore, as of the date of this interview, iTunes just reached the 100,000,000 mark. Well, 100,000,000 in a year and a half. Compare that to 2 billion files traded every month on P2P networks.

SG: Given the incredible success of P2P, have labels tried to integrate this technology in their distribution of music at all?

WR: No, not at all. Unfortunately you'll find that most people at labels just don't understand technology. They frankly have a hard time wrapping their brains around the digital space in any way, shape, or form, as evidenced by their less than rapid employment of the medium. They are notoriously slow in coming to the party and in many ways are still not there. I feel, however, they have convinced everyone else, especially on Capitol Hill, as well as themselves, that P2P means piracy. They drank their own Kool-Aid.

In fact, P2P has nothing to do with piracy. It is no different than coaxial cable that brings cable TV into your home. It is just the digital form of it. I happen to believe that the record companies are starting to realize that they have spent tens, maybe even hundreds of millions of dollars in this campaign to terrorize users and to spoof P2Ps out of business. And they have tried everything in their arsenal—lobbying, courts, everything. And they are not winning the war; they are losing. File-sharing, right now, as we are speaking, is as big, if not bigger than it was a year ago when the record industry started its campaign.

SG: Could the labels integrate their distribution with P2P offered on subscription basis, for instance?

WR: Sure.

SG: How would that work?

WR: It can easily be integrated, but the magic word—subscription—they can't wrap their brains around that. They cannot wrap their brains around a new business model; they are still stuck in a unit-pricing environment, and they have to get out of that.

SG: You can't blame them on one level because they made so much money and have been so successful with the traditional way of distributing records. It's a hard model to leave when it's been so successful.

WR: On the other hand, if they crunch numbers properly they will actually find that they will make more money on a subscription basis.

SG: Well, back in the U.S., we did talk about MGM vs. Grokster *and the fact that the labels lost, but the case is on appeal, oral arguments have been made, and briefs resubmitted. Who do you think will win? [This interview was prior to the appeal to the Ninth Circuit. See Chapter 10.]*

WR: I am sure that the decision will be upheld. To be perfectly honest, I had my doubts in the first go-round—one day I'd be 100% confident and the other day thinking,

Oh, no, we are not going to win. But now, especially after hearing oral arguments, I am convinced that it will be upheld.

SG: As they finish traveling this tortuous legal road, maybe they will look at their alternatives and try to see how else or whether they can work with this new technology. In the meantime, they have been suing some of the kids and the grandmothers with the new raft of lawsuits issued very recently. Do you think that has diminished P2P?

WR: No, not at all. I think they have been focusing on Kazaa. And I don't think the kids are afraid of the lawsuits. It may have had a little bit of an effect, but not really. I think they've figured out how to download anonymously, they've figured out how to do what they want without getting caught. It's not hard. I don't think the lawsuits are a deterrent.

SG: They sued Verizon to try to get the names of the people who were downloading, and Verizon won that case. So they keep on hitting these legal dead ends. The last legal maneuver is called the Induce Act.

WR: Correct!

SG: Which is being sponsored by Orrin Hatch in the Senate. The Induce Act, as I understand it, would make it illegal to "induce" people to infringe copyright, and I understand that recently the Senate put off hearings, which is good for P2Ps, but still the RIAA and Mitch Bainwol are pushing hard for this. Do you think they have a chance at success?

WR: They were trying to push it through without hearings. And our lobby was able to stop it and force hearings. Our lobby along with a coalition of 50 major technology companies including Microsoft and Apple. Everybody started raising hell about this.

SG: They could all get sued, I suppose, since they're all to some degree "inducing" copyright infringement.

WR: Absolutely correct! It would basically turn copyright law on its head.

SG: I see this picture as a battle between huge corporations: on one side, content companies like the big record labels; on the other side, the electronics business and the ISPs who are making a fortune from P2P file-sharing because they do in fact induce it or implement it by selling products that you need to do it. They are making a lot of money and the labels are perhaps losing money. But the consumers, the music lovers, and the kids are caught in-between this turf war between corporations.

Wayne, there is a controversy about whether unauthorized file-sharing diminished record companies' sales. According to the RIAA, sales in year 2000 were around $14.5 billion in the United States alone, and by the end of year 2003, they were down to less than $12 billion. That's more than a 20% loss, and of course they blame file-sharing, although some scholars say that there is no cause and effect. Where do you stand on that issue?

WR: Clearly I am not going to be a Pollyanna and tell you that it hasn't had any effect. I am sure that it has some effect, but I want to go on record saying that people have to learn to pay for the content, the record companies and the artists need to get paid. The question is: How much? That's really the issue.

SG: In the past you said that creators should get paid for content. I am sure that you are going to make many people in record companies who may be listening or reading this a little happier.

WR: I've always said this; it's just that they didn't want to hear it or they ignored it. It's wrong to infringe upon people's copyrights. People should pay, users have to pay. They have to snap out of it and get used to it. Labels serve a purpose, and it does not matter what I may think of them personally. In the meantime, things cannot go on like they are going on. This all-out war is too crazy. I know on our side we have tried, as you brought up earlier, to make peace and work with these record companies many times. Things have gone nowhere. But now I think things have changed. And I can tell you that now the record industry has realized that they have lost the war. That's why they're pushing such ridiculous legislation on Capitol Hill. That's their last stop now. As I like to say, if you don't have the law on your side, it's simple—you just change the law.

SG: If you can . . . But now the record business is pitting itself against new technology that is being supported by even bigger corporations than the big labels—corporate power and money that dwarfs their power and their money.

WR: The Induce Act is now a battle of lobbying. And it's interesting, because even though we in P2P are in the tech industry, these big tech companies would love to leave us out to dry because they blame us for this, but in the meantime they can't fight for technology without us being included in the results, so to speak.

SG: Well, the dirty little secret is that high-speed Internet connections are sold with the idea of getting a lot of free content. And what's the biggest amount of content downloaded on the Internet outside of porn? It's music. So they are making money from peer-to-peer.

WR: Privately these ISPs will tell you that they love peer-to-peer because it helps them sell their service, but publicly they'll sit and complain about it . . . all the bandwidth, blah, blah, blah—it's all baloney. They love it. It's the best thing that ever happened to them.

SG: Suppose the record companies do lose the Grokster *appeal, and they suppose they can't make progress with the Induce Act. And suppose they realize that suing 12-year-olds and grandmothers doesn't work. At that point, maybe, they will seek a different solution. What do you think a solution could be? I'll give you two choices: A voluntary blanket license, or a statutory license under which the legalization of file-sharing would occur in exchange for a tax on computers, ISPs, and the MP3 players that would go to the record companies and the artists. What is your favorite?*

WR: Well, I like them all. [Laughs] But what I think is going to happen—and I think it'll happen very soon, in the next few months—is there will be a big breakthrough. I can't really get in to it, but it's going to involve some voluntary blanket licensing, and in fact, they will not let any kind of statutory licensing come in.

SG: You have been quoted as saying that in a short time something will happen that will change the entire P2P landscape in a new, positive way, and I guess that's what you are referring to.

WR: Yes. As I said, confidentiality agreements forbid me from getting into any kind of detail about this, but I must say that I am convinced that all of the madness is going to come to an end. There is some unilateral executive action being taken that I am convinced will end it all. [See the discussion "Will the Labels Embrace P2P?" in Chapter 9.]

SG: I was just reading Professor Siva Vaidhyanathan's The Anarchist in the Library; *he'll be on the show soon. [This interview is included in the attached CD-ROM.] He wrote in a chapter on peer-to-peer, and I want you to comment on this: "After Napster went quiet, several other peer-to-peer services sprung up. Some, like Kazaa, are run by companies that are likely to be shut down. Others, like Gnutella and FreeNet, are nonproprietary, fully distributed, and seemingly unstoppable." Do you agree?*

WR: Truthfully, yes, I think they are, and I think that there is always going to be people getting content without paying for it. Just like there are hackers, it's always going to happen. Even now if every P2P "would become legitimate" or have authorized content, you can go to the news groups and find anything you want.

SG: They are just too powerful.

WR: Exactly!

SG: In Professor Lawrence Lessig's book, Free Culture, *he provides a little history of the battles between copyrighted content and technology. When conventional radio started becoming popular, for example, the record companies were really afraid that everybody would listen to the radio instead of buying records. They went to Congress and lobbied for an exclusive right for public performance, but Congress did not help them. The radio lobby supported by the broadcast community was too powerful. But in the long run, radio actually ended up helping record companies by promoting sales of records. And in every one of these technology wars—I guess the last biggest one was the Betamax case, where Hollywood felt threatened by video home recording and wanted to outlaw video players because they were also recording devices—the law favored technology. And ultimately in each case the technology helped the copyright owners become even more successful. Home video sales of movies, for example, are now a bigger source of income than theatrical release of movies. So in every one of these legal battles between content and technology, the technologists have won—but ultimately the content owners eventually made more money than before despite their original concerns.*

WR: Absolutely! Unfortunately, they don't learn from their mistakes, and they don't learn from history. It's the dynamic of the business; it's happened, it's historic in the entertainment industry. And by the way, if you refer to the Betamax decision, don't forget that the same thing happened with the audiocassette. About 20 years ago the sky was falling again because supposedly the record industry was going down the toilet because everyone was making copies, recording copies on their little audiocassettes and then using them in their cars.

SG: They were afraid that no one would buy another record. But that never happened. People just bought a lot of the same records they already had in their vinyl collection on cassettes.

WR: Exactly! And what had happened from that point on, if I am not mistaken, with the Audio Home Recording Act, the labels were also able to get a royalty on certain types of copying equipment. This is a system that has worked in Canada and Germany for many years.

SG: Yes, that law imposed a small tax on some forms of digital taping machines and blank tapes on behalf of the copyright owners. Of course in Canada they have been expanding that. For instance, they recently taxed MP3 players, because it has been these machines that have been making money hand over fist while the record companies have been losing it. Canada's solution is to tax the machines that allow the free transfer of music, and the money goes to the artists and record companies. I think short-term profits may be the problem here. Major record companies are looking to the next quarter, they are looking for the next blockbuster hit to bring in the money to make their corporate bosses happy. And if they think they are going to lose a couple million sales on the next Eminem record, their short-term goals interfere with their long-term interests.

WR: I think that is the mentality. When you look at it, of the currently five major record companies, soon to be four, there is only one true, pure public play, and that's EMI. That's the only one with true shareholder pressure. Yet the gestalt extends to the entire industry. Something interesting came out of a Bear Sterns Conference I attended last week. A message that I took away is that the indie labels are the mavericks of the world now—they are the ones who are really the genesis of the record business—and now the indies are the ones who are major entrepreneurs. The indies are doing it right, yet they don't have the money, while the majors are screwing it up, but they've got all of the money.

SG: If there is a lot less short-term money, do you think that the multinationals that own four of the five majors—soon to be four with BMG and Sony about to merge—might back away from the business and let the indies have it again? After all, Time Warner already sold off Warner Records to a group of private investors.

WR: No. You've got to realize it's still a very profitable business. You keep forgetting that they've been losing revenues, but they haven't lost money—there is a big difference. What's happened is that peer-to-peer has helped lower prices and end the waste in spending that the record industry grew up on.

SG: The price of the CD has come down to compete.

WR: Not enough—but it has come down. It's forced these guys to lower their prices in the war for the consumer. The other day Mr. Roger Faxon, the CFO of EMI, was saying how they are working hard to change the behavior of the consumer. They've spent hundreds of millions of dollars trying to do this. Why wouldn't it be easier and cheaper to adapt to the habits of the consumers?

SG: That's where your solution comes in again—that's why we are going to have you back on our show—but I do want to offer our listeners a chance to hear your prediction for the future of the business; particularly, what advice would you have to new artists that are trying to get into the business and entrepreneurs trying to set up a business in the music industry?

WR: It's tough out there. It's really, really difficult. The first thing that I'd say to anybody who wants to get into the music industry is: Don't—it's very difficult if you are a little guy. But the good news is that the Internet and peer-to-peer especially—and this is the scary thing for record labels—helps to level the playing field a little bit.

SG: If you put an MP3 on your Web site, you've got a worldwide audience.

WR: Absolutely. However, what kids, artists—especially emerging artists—bands and entrepreneurs have to learn is that you've got to perform live. You've got to go back to the original vehicle, and that is where it's at. The Internet doesn't mean crap. A lot of guys get lazy; they think that there is a silver bullet—they get excited about having videos on MTV—Oh boy, I have a video on MTV and I don't have to tour and I'm fine and I'm a star, and guess what: Those guys never had a hit again, and they lost all of their money and right now they're selling ice cream cones at Ben and Jerry's. The same thing applies to the Internet. It is not a silver bullet, it is a tool. It all boils down to getting out and busting your ass on the road.

Chapter 21

The Digital Runway: The Convergence of Music & Fashion (Will Fashion Labels Become Record Labels?)

Music and fashion have never been so intimately connected. Recording artists such as Gwen Stefani are using their fame to sell apparel and handbags. Some have even initiated their own fashion lines, for instance Sean "Puffy" Combs and his "Sean John" fashion line. His motto is "It's not just a label, it's a lifestyle." In the first section of this Chapter I argue that it is largely technology that is responsible for this increasing convergence between music and fashion. It was television, specifically music-video services such as MTV, that brought together the performer's style and fashion into the same place where pop rock and hip-hop music were presented to a mass audience.

What about the future? Is further convergence between music and fashion possible? Yes. The second section of this chapter points out that again, it is technology, this time the Internet, that will drive an even deeper convergence between music and fashion. If Web sites such as CD Baby (for independent music) and iTunes (for the major labels and established artists) become the new music stores, why can't cutting-edge fashion labels whose Web sites reach a worldwide audience and whose customers crave new music as well as new fashion, produce and create their own music and sell directly to their customers? Well, this is already happening!

Convergence of Music and Fashion, Part I. I went to the library to do some research for this chapter. I thought I would find a huge amount of material. In fact, I found almost nothing on the history of music and fashion. What I did find were books and articles on how music has influenced fashion in the last several generations. For instance, the book by Tommy Hilfiger with Anthony DeCurtis, *ROCKstyle*, goes back in time as far as Motown and Elvis. Another example is *Rock/Fashion* by Joshua Sims, which goes back only as far as rock 'n' roll.

It appears that in regard to the influence of music on fashion that the real action has taken place only recently. Perhaps it is only in recent times that music has grown in influence in our culture to the extent that it has started to provide us with a new way of identifying ourselves as well as merely entertaining us.

Let me give you some examples: James Henke, the vice president of the Rock and Roll Hall of Fame, wrote in the introduction to Hilfiger's book, "It was Elvis who defined the extremes of rock style. Back in the mid '50s he laid out the blueprint for the rock 'n' roller as REBEL—the black pants, the jacket, the hair, the snarl."

Henke continues: "It's not an exaggeration to say that Elvis and the Beatles were cultural phenomena that literally changed the world. They redefined the images of what was culturally 'sexy,' 'hip,' or 'cool.' Dressing like your rock idol meant you were, or aspired to be, kindred spirits with that artist's musical and 'Spiritual' Message." In other words, those icons gave people something to be!

We could go back a little further—dressing like Miles Davis was being cool without being a member of the establishment. Miles showed us we could wear a suit without being a suit! The same could be said for Chuck Berry. Of course, Mick Jagger gave us a number of styles and identities to choose from.

The point is that these artists not only gave us music to identify who we are, they gave us a look and a style as well.

I wondered what all these characters had in common and why they had more influence

Elvis Presley

on style and fashion than any of the musicians before them. For instance, Mozart, Beethoven, and Bach basically dressed like the people who listened to their music. Why have contemporary artists had more of an impact on fashion and style? The answer, it seems to me, is two letters: TV. It was television that gave music special power by making the music accessible to millions of people around the world and made the music visual.

Think of it: Before television and music videos, singers, and musicians were mainly heard and not seen. You could listen to them on the radio, but it was necessary to leave your house, travel to a club or a theater, and pay a ticket or a cover to see an artist in order to absorb his fashion style. It was the coalescence of the music, rock 'n' roll and television that allowed the distinctive sound and *look* of such fashion icons as the Beatles and Elvis to be seen by people around the world.

And I think it was television that encouraged these artists to push the envelope in terms of visual style: For instance Mr. James Brown looked the part of the Godfather of Soul. And the Doors looked the part of hippie rebels.

Of course, the apotheosis of the coalescence of music, fashion, and celebrity came about later with the advent of MTV. Like or not, MTV helped create some of the best celebrities of our times. And of course each of these artists had their own special identity, style, and look, for instance, the "Material Girl" (Madonna) and the "King of Pop" (Michael Jackson.) The result of this coalescence of celebrity, music, and fashion: Sean John. I believe Mr. Combs gets it exactly right by saying, "It's not just a label, it's a lifestyle."

He's selling an identity through music and fashion. And he's selling music and fashion through creating his identity, which he calls his "lifestyle." In fact, he's selling the American dream—the guy who has it all and did it his own way. And now you can dress like him as well as identify with his music. The same goes for Eve with her Fetish line and Gwen Stefani with her recently launched apparel line, L.A.M.B. We've all heard about these endorsement deals. But what drives them is that you can now identify with your favorite performer by dressing like your favorite performer, instead of just listening to his or her music.

But what is the future of the convergence of music and fashion? Will it grow even more and take different forms? Will fashion sites that sell a celebrity's clothes start to sell their music as well?

Convergence of Music and Fashion, Part II. Diesel, the Italian-based retail clothing chain and fashion label, is a fashion brand that is engaging in the music business in an original and significant manner. Diesel has launched its own music label, Diesel-U-Music. According to www.diesel-u-music.com, which is linked to the general Diesel site: "Diesel-U-Music represents a challenge to voice the most talented new artists' creativity."

Diesel-U-Music sponsored an international competition of baby bands, DJs, and producers. The label solicited over 6,000 demos and fully mixed recordings through their Web site and Diesel.com. Both Web sites are elegant and easy to use, and both enjoy a large and worldwide audience.

Next, Diesel took the best of the submissions and pressed four different CDs. These CDs are now available for purchase through the Diesel-U-Music Web site and Diesel's retail stores. Each of the four CDs represent different musical styles: rock, urban, electro, and dance music, mixed by the internationally recognized DJ Claudio Coccoluto. Each CD contains the best selections of the contest winners. In all, the CDs embody 48 tracks representing new sounds from the U.K., U.S.A, Italy, the Benelux countries, and Switzerland. Diesel also collaborated with Stefano Cecchi Records, which sells the CDs by mail order on their site.

Diesel is acknowledging the convergence of music and fashion by giving their customers what they want—new fashions and new music. They are harnessing the power of the Internet to sell music directly to their customers. The traffic on Diesel's sites is huge because the demographics of their customer base represent kids who are not only fashion savvy but Internet savvy as well. Why not use the traffic on their sites to sell their customers what they crave—new music as well as new fashions?

Acknowledgments

To Katie Monaghan, for encouraging me to write this book.

I would like to acknowledge my interns Kyra Wiedenkeller, Alyona Mindlin, Reuben Atlas, and Nils Shillito, who helped me with everything from research to transcribing the interviews. And thanks Nils with helping on all those PowerPoint presentations for my live seminars.

I would like to express my appreciation to *Entertainment Law and Finance*. I have been writing articles for this publication for many years as well as serving on its Board of Editors. Chapter 3 on Webcasting and Chapter 6 on Music Licensing are largely based on articles that I wrote for *ELF* and updated for this book. I have also reprinted with *ELF*'s kind permission the section on Tips for Music Licensing in Chapter. 6. I especially want to thank Stan Soocher, who has been my editor at *ELF* for all these years, for his brilliant editing of all those articles we published in *ELF*.

Thank you to those who helped me with their expertise, insights and encouragement, including Rob Auritt, Esq., Moses Avalon, Jan Bridge, Powell Burns, John Colletta, Esq., Eric de Fontenay, Professor Peter Fader, Zouheir Faraj, Steve Friedman, Ricky Gordon (a.k.a. "Dirty Red"), Charlie Grappone, Professor Justin Hughes, Eric Kline, Ira Landes, David Levine, Marty Majeske, Esq., Steve Masur, Esq., Greg McBowman, Scott Meldrum, Jeffrey D. Neuberger, Esq., John Paige, Esq., Vincent Peppe, Esq., Rascal (the Artist), Paul Resnikoff, Wayne Rosso, Charles Sanders, Esq., John Simson, Esq., Ed Steinberg, Ariel Taitz, Esq., Peter Thall, Esq., Fred von Lohmann, Esq.

For helping me do research for Chapter 13, thanks to James E. Moeller, Hugh Dornbush, Gilad Majerowicz, Esq., Alphonzo Terrell, and NYU Law students Mario Mendolaro and Mason Weisz.

Special thanks to Dan Coleman, the producer of my Internet radio show on the future of the music business at MyRealBroadcast.com. Many of the interviews in this book were originally produced for that series. Dan is also the producer of the CD-ROM accompanying this book. Dan, you are talented and tireless.

Finally I would like to acknowledge some old bosses: my Entertainment Law professor at NYU, Mel Simensky, who hired me for my first entertainment law job. Thanks Mel. To Alan Arrow, one of the smartest music lawyers there ever was. And to Jerry Durkin, who hired me for Sony Music, where I worked for ten years. Thanks Jerry; it was a terrific ride. To John Koshel, who sadly is no longer with us, my boss at SESAC. John was a great teacher. Finally, to my latest mentor and great friend, Eric Kulberg of Universal Media.

Author's Note

I hope you will use the link in the CD-ROM accompanying this book to keep up with the most recent developments in the music business. You can also listen to new interviews with industry leaders, artists, and journalists by tuning into my radio series, The Future of the Music Business, at MyRealBroadcast.com.

Photo Credits

Page 147: Robert Goldberg
Page 179: XM Satellite Radio
Page 183: Pat Johnson
Page 193: Hosea Johnson
Page 197: Sheila Newbery
Page 213: Sarah St. Clair Renard
Page 234: David Korchin
Page 258: Photofest

About the Author and Editors

Author: A New York City–based entertainment attorney and consultant, Steve Gordon represents producers, labels, artists, and entrepreneurs in the production of music-based video, television, and film projects. He is also an instructor at the City University of New York Graduate Center, where he teaches courses on the future of the entertainment industry, and at the Fashion Institute of Technology, where he teaches a class on music and fashion. Gordon was formally the director of Business Affairs at Sony Music (TV/video) and is a graduate of the New York University School of Law. You can listen to his music-business radio show at MyRealBroadcast.com and read his blog at DigitalMusicNews.com. For published articles, upcoming speaking engagements, and contact information, see SteveGordonLaw.com.

Editor: Robert W. Clarida, Esq., Cowan, Liebowitz & Latman P.C. Chair, Copyright and Literary Property Committee, Association of the Bar of the City of New York. Chair, Copyright Committee, American Intellectual Property Law Association. Adjunct Faculty, Columbia University School of Law. Editor, *Journal of the Copyright Society of the USA*. Ph.D. in music composition; Former Assistant Professor of Music at Dartmouth College.

Technical Advisor: Ralph De Palma, Esq., of Counsel, Pryor, Cashman, Sherman & Flynn LLC.

Index

WHEN IT COMES TO MUSIC, WE WROTE THE BOOK.

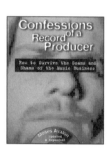